Virtual Social Identity
and
Consumer Behavior

Virtual Social Identity
and
Consumer Behavior

Natalie T. Wood and Michael R. Solomon, editors

Society for Consumer Psychology

M.E.Sharpe
Armonk, New York
London, England

Library of Congress Cataloging-in-Publication Data

Virtual social identity and consumer behavior / edited by Natalie T. Wood and
Michael R. Solomon.
    p. cm.
Includes bibliographical references and index.
ISBN 978-0-7656-2395-9 (cloth : alk. paper)—ISBN 978-0-7656-2396-6 (pbk. : alk. paper)
1. Group identity. 2. Consumer behavior. 3. Virtual reality. I. Wood, Natalie T., 1970–
II. Solomon, Michael R.

HM753.V57 2009
306.3—dc22   2008053550

Printed in the United States of America

The paper used in this publication meets the minimum requirements of
American National Standard for Information Sciences
Permanence of Paper for Printed Library Materials,
ANSI Z 39.48-1984.

∞

MV (c)   10   9   8   7   6   5   4   3   2   1
MV (p)   10   9   8   7   6   5   4   3   2   1

Contents

Introduction:
Virtual Social Identity

Welcome to the Metaverse

MICHAEL R. SOLOMON AND NATALIE T. WOOD

In his 1992 science fiction novel *Snow Crash,* the author Neal Stephenson first developed the construct of the Metaverse. This seminal book depicts a future where individuals inhabit two parallel realities; their everyday physical existence and their avatar existence in a 3D computer-mediated environment. The complicated marriage of everyday mundane life with a fantasy world in which an inhabitant assumes other identities opened the door to thoughts of digital social experimentation—and presented a pathway to self-aggrandizement for those whose "real world" lives are less than ideal: the book's protagonist is a humble pizza delivery boy in the real world, but a sword-wielding warrior in the Metaverse.

Since the release of *Snow Crash* almost twenty years ago, technology now allows Stephenson's vision to become a reality. Over the last few years a flood of virtual worlds have come online. From *Second Life* to *The World of Warcraft,* There.com to MTV's *Virtual Pimp My Ride,* millions of consumers live a parallel life in a digital reality. A *virtual world* is an online representation of real-world people, products, and brands in a computer-mediated environment (CME). To many mainstream consumers and advertisers, this is largely an unknown or underground phenomenon—but it has real marketing consequences (Wood and Solomon, forthcoming). We are pleased to present selected papers in this volume from the first academic conference to specifically address these issues: the 2008 Advertising and Consumer Psychology Conference sponsored by the Society for Consumer Psychology (www.sju.edu/academics/centers/ccr/vsocialidentity. html) in Philadelphia.

Why the focus on this topic? In mid-2007, Charles River Ventures proclaimed that the virtual goods market was worth approximately $1.5 billion and growing rapidly. With more than 150 of these immersive 3D environments now live or currently in development, the number of consumers who come into contact with virtual goods as they navigate these worlds is projected to rise rapidly ("150+ Youth-Oriented" 2008). Indeed, according to one estimate, by the year 2012, 53 percent of kids and 80 percent of active Internet users will be members of at least one virtual world ("Kids" 2007; "Virtual Greats Enters" 2008).

Clearly, virtual environments will fuel new consumer trends over the next decade. McKinsey predicts that "Virtual worlds such as *Second Life* will become an indispensable business tool and vital to the strategy of any company intent on reaching out to the video-game generation" (Richards 2008). The *Harvard Business Review* predicts that within the next five years virtual environments are likely to emerge as *the* dominant Internet interface. In addition to corporate websites, companies will operate virtual stores where customers can browse and interact with assistants (Sarvary 2008). To date, numerous companies including IBM, GE, and Toyota have created CMEs for internal and external applications. Eventually, these CME forums may rival traditional marketer-sponsored e-commerce sites in terms of their influence on consumer decision making and product adoption.

However, due to the newness of the medium, advertisers still struggle to figure out the best way to talk to consumers in these environments—or to decide if they should enter them at all. Ironically, this challenge is compounded by the unparalleled latitude both advertisers and consumers possess in these environments to assume virtually (pun intended) any physical form they wish. How will our understanding of source effects apply to advertising contexts where a company spokesperson's *avatar* (or digital representation) is a fiery dragon, a sultry siren, or both at once? How does that company relate to a consumer whose avatar resembles George Bush, a furry creature, or a superhero? Welcome to the wild and woolly world of advertising in virtual worlds.

The last few years have been a bit of a Gold Rush for the brand-new virtual worlds industry as marketers eagerly competed to be "the first" in to stake a claim in a CME. Unfortunately many of these efforts failed to live up to expectations and we have been subjected to a slew of negative press. Virtual worlds are a fad, many naysayers claim. Gartner estimates that upward of 90 percent of virtual worlds that businesses launch will fail; most within the first 18 months. Yet, the same analysts also predict that 70 percent of organizations will establish their own private virtual worlds by 2012 (Cavall 2008). Despite such prominent failures as American Apparel and Starwood Hotels, there are many examples of success, including campaigns by Cosmo Girl and Toyota Scion in There.com and Nike in *Second Life*.

When executed properly, we firmly believe that virtual environments offer a higher level of immersion, interactivity, and engagement than many other web-based technologies. The promise is real, but it's no longer sufficient just to plant a virtual stick in the ground. Advertisers need to think carefully about how to calibrate their strategic objectives with the unique characteristics of these environments.

This book focuses exclusively on one key aspect of CMEs: the unprecedented ability they offer to visitors to craft one or many social identities at will. We address some of the fascinating consequences and ramifications of *virtual social identity*. A sampling of the intriguing issues that await resolution includes the following items.

WHO IS "THERE" IN A VIRTUAL WORLD?

In the real world, an advertiser can usually identify the recipient of a persuasive communication.[1] But in virtual worlds individuals are free to experiment with different identities; and it is not at all uncommon for veteran residents to have more than one avatar. For example, some people have one avatar that they use for work-related activities and another they inhabit to cruise nightclubs. They can alter their appearance, age, gender, or even choose to take on a nonhuman form. They may experiment with personas that are far from their real self, so it can be problematic to infer the true identity of an avatar using traditional visual cues. We may think that we are speaking to a 35-year-old male engineer from Manchester, UK, when in reality we are conversing with a 52-year-old female hair stylist from Manitoba. Advertisers are often left to ponder a Zen-like question: "To whom do we market—the avatar or the 'real' person?"

As in the real world, the answer most likely depends in part upon each resident's level of involvement with the virtual environment. Individuals who fully immerse themselves in CMEs experience a greater sense of *social presence* than do individuals who visit as casual tourists (Blascovich et al. 2002; Schroeder 2002; Slater et al. 2000; Short, Williams, and Christie 1976). Clearly, as more people take these experiences seriously the experiential dynamics will evolve as increasing numbers of us experience a *flow state* that transforms the online experience from passive browsing to agentic, first-person immersion (Csikszentmihalyi 1991).

WHAT ARE THE PUBLIC POLICY IMPLICATIONS FOR VIRTUALITY?

Like it or not, our society is morphing into a digital platform. More than 16 million people worldwide belong to the virtual world of *Second Life,* more than 10 million play the online game *World of Warcraft,* and 44 percent of Koreans belong to *CyWorld.* Add to that the millions more who play *The Sims Online* or who visit other computer-mediated environments such as There.com, *Entropia Universe,* MTV's *Virtual Laguna Beach,* and so on and you're looking at a lot of serious role playing.

The evolution of virtual society is even more telling when we look at the proliferation of youth-oriented sites such as *Webkinz, Whyville,* and *Habbo Hotel* (Wood, Chaplin, and Solomon 2008). Researchers estimate that the audience of teens in virtual worlds will more than double, to 20 million members, within the next three years (Olsen 2007).

Identity exploration is an essential developmental task for adolescents (Erikson 1963; Harter 1999; Marcia 1993). Traditionally, it was family and friends who served as a reference for identity exploration. Today, the Internet affords adolescents many new and exciting opportunities to experiment with their identities (Katz and Rice 2002; Rheingold 1993; Smith and Kollock 1999; Stern 2004; Subrahmanyam, Smahel, and Greenfield 2006; Turkle 1995). Virtual worlds are poised to become the next great laboratory for identity exploration.

But, this is a sword that cuts both ways; the expanded potential to experiment with a range of identities (e.g., gender) coupled with the inevitable presence of predators who prey on vulnerable targets creates a huge set of issues and concerns. We understand very little about how the identities we choose in CMEs relate to our real life (RL) identities. Already we know that when people take on avatar forms, they tend to interact with other avatars much as their RL selves interact with other RL people. For example, just as in RL, males in *Second Life* leave more space between themselves and other males than they do with versus females, and they are less likely to maintain eye contact than are females. And when avatars get very close to one another, they tend to look away from each other—the norms of RL do creep into the virtual world (Svensson 2007). We've only scratched the surface to understand how socialization processes will change as a result.

An April 2008 study of kid-oriented virtual worlds reported that the average visitor logged 78 minutes per month, while many users literally spend hours per day in these environments (A. Bryant, personal communication, June 5, 2008). This level of interaction is bound to influence identity formation; just as in the early days of TV, we know nothing about the impact this will have—but we can be sure it will be significant.

HOW SHOULD ADVERTISERS EMPLOY AVATARS AS SPOKESPERSONS?

Researchers agree that interacting with avatars may deliver positive benefits to online shoppers (Wood, Solomon, and Englis 2005, 2008; Holzwarth, Janiszewski, and Neumann 2006; Keeling et al. 2004; Keeling, McGoldrick, and Beatty 2006); that the "right" avatar can help to build trust in the e-tailer (McGoldrick, Keeling, and Beatty 2008); and this in turn leads to greater levels of satisfaction, confidence, and intention to purchase as well as a more positive evaluation of the site's information and entertainment value (Wood, Solomon, and Englis, 2008; Holzwarth, Janiszewski, and Neumann 2006). But this facilitation is selective; just as is the case with spokespeople in other advertising contexts, an inappropriate avatar can alienate customers (Keeling et al. 2004; McBreen et al. 2000).

The selection of an appropriate source is central to the marketing communication process, but the choice is a complex one. Advertisers face the challenge to select a source that is not only credible and attractive, but also someone with whom the target audience can identify. Ironically, marketers easily spend huge sums of money and time to carefully select spokespeople for their real-life campaigns, but there's no evidence that they think much about this crucial issue when they create an avatar to represent them in a virtual world. Some specific choices include:

- Should the avatar appear realistic or more like an animated cartoon character?
- Should the avatar resemble a human form or something else?
- Should the avatar mirror the user's own appearance, should it depict another real/typical person, or should it take the form of an idealized image or a fantasy figure?
- Should the avatar resemble a stereotypical male or female image or be more androgynous?

SHOULD THE SAME AVATAR REPRESENT THE BRAND UNIFORMLY TO ALL IN-WORLD VIEWERS?

Ads transmitted on broadcast media present the same image to an entire audience. In contrast, an online advertiser can modify direct or interactive messages for different purchasing contexts or even individual users. Virtual worlds have the potential to take message customization even farther because (at least in theory) they actually allow the *recipient* to design the source. Wood, Solomon, and Englis (2005, p. 148) pose the question, "Is it possible to have a match-up between source and the *consumer* that will yield similar or even better results than a match-up between the source and the product?" Their research revealed that in online shopping scenarios people do not always respond in a similar fashion to the same avatar. So, what if we instead match the communication source to each user's preferences?

As with other types of consumer-generated media, one of the downsides of handing the asylum over to the inmates (i.e., giving consumers control over a brand's imagery) is that the sources consumers choose may not be consistent with the brand personality a sponsor hopes to communicate. What if the user decides that a message source for (say) a financial services ad should take the form of a fire-breathing gremlin wielding a bayonet? What if the female avatar who urges you to try a new fragrance looks like a cross between Carmen Electra and Paris Hilton? How do these images impact consumers' perceptions of the brand's personality that companies spend millions of dollars to create?

HOW DOES VIRTUAL SOCIAL IDENTITY INFLUENCE GROUP DYNAMICS—AND VICE VERSA?

Many virtual world relationships and interactions mimic those we find in the physical world. Avatars form friendships with other avatars, they discuss real-life problems, they argue, they go on virtual dates; some even get married (and divorced), purchase virtual real estate, and mourn the deaths of other players without ever meeting in the flesh. These parallels make it reasonable to assume that not unlike what we experience in the real world, the dynamics of social influence that are so well documented in physical contexts—especially those related to conformity and social contagion—transfer to virtual group relationships as well.

Furthermore, just as in the real world, the ability to interact with others may lead to an increase in risk-taking behavior in virtual worlds. Individuals may feel more confident to try out new experiences, engage with different products, and experiment more freely when they are in others' company. These effects may also extend to in-world purchasing. For instance, the retailer Lands' End introduced a "Shop with a Friend" feature that enables people in different geographic locations to shop together online (Leavitt 2004). This innovative (but woefully understudied) application highlights the potential of immersive technology to impact both the type and volume of purchases.

TAKING IT FROM HERE

This volume does not purport to answer (or even address) all of the questions we pose above, but we do get off to a healthy start. We divide the dozen of papers in this book into four sections: The Virtual Experience, Consumer Behavior in Virtual Worlds, Youth Consumers, and Person Perceptions in Virtual Worlds:

1. In Part I—The Virtual Experience—Kozinets and Kedzior explore auto-netnography as a research methodology for virtual worlds. El Kamel then presents an analysis of the metaverse from a postmodern experiential consumption perspective.
2. In Part II—Consumer Behavior in Virtual Worlds—Hinsch and Bloch discuss consumers' motivations to join virtual worlds and the implications for marketers and consumer behaviorists. Brown and Tuten examine in-world communication and product recommendations as they explore whether in-world product guidance is more impactful to consumers relative to other venues as well as whether residents trust the advice they receive. Next, Keeling, Keeling, de Angeli, and McGoldrick offer a theoretical model to explain how and why specific aspects of avatar interactions relate to behavioral intentions. Crete, St-Onge, Merle, Arsenault, and Nantel examine the influence of personalized avatars on perceptions, attitudes, and intentions. And through a netnographic inquiry on the Chinese online gaming community, Wang, Zhao, and Bamossy examine how CME activity takes on aspects of sacred consumption.
3. In the part on Avatar Creation and Appearance, Bryant and Akerman investigate the social-psychological development of kids and teens and how this impacts their interactions with and affinity for different types of avatars. Then,

Kim and Sundar examine the effects of avatar presence and customization on users' attitudes toward social networking sites and advertising.

4. In the final section—Person Perceptions in Virtual Worlds—Appiah and Elias report the findings of a study in which they paired intelligent animated agents with human voices that are either congruent or incongruent with the ethnicity of the agent. Lutchyn, Duff, Faber, Cho, and Huh take a similar approach when they examine the effect of interracial morphing on attitudes toward the spokesperson and the advertisement. Finally, Bublitz, Claybaugh, and Peracchio discuss the formation of thin-slice judgments of avatars and their impact on online marketing.

According to Gartner, by 2015 more money will be spent on sales and marketing online than offline (Broitman and Tatar 2008). Given the predicted growth rates of virtual worlds it is reasonable to assume that a significant portion of future advertising expenditures will be directed to these environments. To ensure that these financial resources are invested wisely and yield positive results, advertisers need to understand and appreciate the characteristics of this brave new world. We are just beginning to comprehend its ramifications and we must remember that Rome wasn't built in a day, not even a virtual one.

NOTE

1. We add the caveat that there is always some uncertainty about a receiver's identity, even in direct marketing or online campaigns, when we make a leap of faith to assume that the person at the computer is actually the person the advertiser intends to target.

REFERENCES

"150+ Youth-Oriented Virtual Worlds Now Live or Developing." 2008. *Virtual Worlds Management Report,* August 22. Available at www.virtualworldsmanagement.com (accessed August 24, 2008).

Blascovich, J., J. Loomis, A.C. Beall, K.R. Swinth, C. Hoyt, and J.N. Bailenson. 2002. "Immersive Virtual Environment Technology as a Methodological Tool for Social Psychology." *Psychological Inquiry* 1 (3): 103–124.

Broitman, A., and J. Tatar. 2008. "How to Reach Real People in a Virtual World." iMedia Connection, May 30. Available at www.imediaconnection.com/content/19487.asp (accessed July 7, 2008).

Cavall, E. 2008. "90 Percent of Business-Launched Virtual Worlds Fail." Wired.com. Available at www.wired.com (accessed May 19, 2008).

Csikszentmihalyi, M. 1991. *Flow: The Psychology of Optimal Experience.* New York: Harper and Row.

Erikson, Erik. 1963. *Childhood and Society.* New York: Norton.

Harter, Susan. 1999. *The Construction of the Self: A Developmental Perspective.* New York: Guilford Press.

Holzwarth, M., C. Janiszewski, and M. Neumann. 2006. "The Influence of Avatars on Online Consumer Shopping Behavior." *Journal of Marketing* 70 (4): 19–36.

Katz, James E., and Ronald E. Rice. 2002. *Social Consequences of Internet Use: Access, Involvement, and Interaction.* Cambridge, MA: MIT Press.

Keeling, K., S. Beatty, P.J. McGoldrick, and L. Macaulay. 2004. "Face Value? Customer Views of Appropriate Formats for ECAs in Online Retailing." *Hawaii International Conference on System Sciences,* 1–10.

Keeling, K., P.J. McGoldrick, and S. Beatty. 2006. "Virtual Onscreen Assistants: A Viable Strategy to Support Online Customer Relationship Building?" In *Advances in Consumer Research,* vol. 34, ed. Gavan J. Fitszimons and Vicki G. Morwitz, 138–144. Duluth, MN: Association for Consumer Research.

"Kids, Teens and Virtual Worlds." 2007. eMarketer, September 25. Available at www. emarketer.com (accessed October 23, 2007).

Leavitt, N. 2004. "Online Clothes Lines." iMedia Connection, August 3. Available at www. imediaconnection.com (accessed August 14, 2008).

Marcia, J.E. 1993. *Ego Identity: A Handbook for Psychosocial Research.* New York: Springer.

McBreen, H., P. Shade, M. Jack, and P. Wyard. 2000. "Experimental Assessment of the Effectiveness of Synthetic Personae for Multi-Modal e-Retail Applications." *Proceedings of the Fourth International Conference on Autonomous Agents* (Agents-2000), 39–45.

McGoldrick, P.J., K.A. Keeling, and S.F. Beatty. 2008. "A Typology of Roles for Avatars in Online Retailing." *Journal of Marketing Management* 24 (3–4): 433–461.

Olsen, S. 2007. "What Kids Learn in Virtual Worlds." CNET, November 15. Available at http://sympatico-msn-ca.com.com/What-kids-learn-in-virtual-worlds/2009–1043_3–6218763.html (accessed November 15, 2007).

Rheingold, Howard. 1993. *The Virtual Community: Homesteading on the Electronic Frontier.* Reading, MA: Addison-Wesley.

Richards, J. 2008. "McKinsey: Ignore Second Life at Your Peril." Times Online, April 23. Available at http://technology.timesonline.co.uk (accessed April 23, 2008).

Sarvary, M. 2008. "Breakthrough Ideas for 2008." *Harvard Business Review* (February): 17–45.

Schroeder, R. 2002. "Social Interaction in Virtual Environments: Key Issues, Common Themes, and a Framework for Research." In *The Social Life of Avatars: Presence and Interaction in Shared Virtual Environments,* ed. R. Schroeder, 1–18. London: Springer.

Short, J., E. Williams, and B. Christie. 1976. *The Social Psychology of Telecommunications.* London: Wiley.

Slater, M., A. Sadagic, M. Usoh, and R. Schroeder. 2000. "Small Group Behavior in a Virtual and Real Environment: A Comparative Study." *Presence: Teleoperators and Virtual Environments* 9 (1): 37–51.

Smith, Marc A., and Peter Kollock. 1999. *Communities in Cyberspace.* London: Routledge.

Stern, Susannah R. 2004. "Expressions of Identity Online: Prominent Features and Gender Differences in Adolescents' World Wide Web Home Pages." *Journal of Broadcasting and Electronic Media* 48: 218–243.

Subrahmanyam, Kaveri, David Smahel, and Patricia Greenfield. 2006. "Connecting Developmental Constructions to the Internet: Identity Presentation and Sexual Exploration in Online Teen Chatrooms." *Developmental Psychology* 42 (3): 395–406.

Svensson, Peter. 2007. "Study: Virtual Men Are Standoffish Too." *USA Today* (February 21). Available at http://www.usatoday.com/tech/news/2007–02–21-virtual-men_x.htm (accessed February16, 2009).

Turkle, Sherry. 1995. *Life on the Screen: Identity in the Age of the Internet.* New York: Simon & Schuster.

"Virtual Greats Enters $1.5 Billion Virtual Goods Market." 2008. Business Wire, June 9. Available at www.businesswire.com (accessed June 9, 2008).

Wood, Natalie T., Lan Chaplin, and Michael Solomon. 2008. "Virtual Playgrounds." Paper presented in Summer American Marketing Association Special Session on Adolescents Stepping Out with Online Technology, San Diego, California.

Wood, Natalie T., and Michael R. Solomon. Forthcoming. "Adonis or Atrocious: Spokesavatars and Source Effects in Immersive Digital Environments." In *Handbook of Research on Digital Media and Advertising: User Generated Content Consumption,* ed. Matthew S. Eastin, Terry Daugherty, and Neal M. Burns. Hershey, PA: IGI Global.

Wood, N.T., M.R. Solomon, and B.G. Englis. 2005. "Personalisation of Online Avatars: Is the Messenger as Important as the Message?" *International Journal of Internet Marketing and Advertising* 2 (1/2): 143–161.

———. (2008). "Personalization of the Web Interface: The Impact of Web Avatars on Users' Response to E-Commerce Sites." *Journal of Website Promotion* 2 (1/2): 53–69.

PART I

THE VIRTUAL EXPERIENCE

CHAPTER 1

I, Avatar

Auto-Netnographic Research in Virtual Worlds

ROBERT V. KOZINETS AND RICHARD KEDZIOR

A recent article in that paragon of buttoned-down professional journals, the *Harvard Business Review,* contained the following description in its opening: "Birdsong and a gentle breeze enliven the scene at dawn, and as you walk by a house later in the day you may hear music emanating from an open window" (Hemp 2006, p. 1). Birdsong and emanating music? Hemp's poetic prose is put to good use describing the embodied experience of being in *Second Life,* a virtual world where, as he aptly puts it, "You're not you."

As Hemp's article, and a raft of cover stories in top business magazines like *BusinessWeek* attest, the growing popularity of virtual worlds has attracted tremendous media and marketing attention from industry, marketers, and marketing and consumer researchers lately. Hemp (2006) adroitly recognized that consumption and marketing turned, in the virtual world experience, to a large extent on how marketers would now relate to the consumers' avatar, or avatars.

The emphasis on the avatar, and the re-embodiment of the consumer into new and perhaps multiple online "bodies," is enough to make many marketers' and marketing researchers' heads spin. "Consumption" and even "marketing" changes in these contexts because of the re-embodied (rather than disembodied) nature of the virtual world experience.

Addressing the need for new and rigorous research methodologies suitable for virtual worlds, this chapter briefly overviews the cornerstones of the netnographic method before extending and developing them into this pervasive and important new context. Although netnography has many elements and facets (see, e.g., Kozinets 2002, 2006, 2007), this chapter will focus on and extend one element identified in Kozinets (2006). In that methodological chapter, Kozinets examined variations in the application of netnographic technique and speculated about the notion of "auto-netnographies," where individuals use in-depth field noting and observations to "reflect on their own online experiences and then use these field notes and observations to provide insights into online consumer practices and meanings" (p. 133).

We extend this line of speculation by further advocating for and developing auto-netnography as a technique ideally suited to some of the contingencies of netnography conducted within virtual worlds. By adopting an auto-netnographic approach, we present various sites of avatars' identity work in a virtual world. The presentation follows a trajectory of our virtual social enculturation, from creating a vivid existence and embodying ourselves in avatars, to fully participating in a social life of a virtual world.

Our chapter proceeds by first providing an overview and examination of some of the most important elements of cultural research in virtual worlds. It then introduces and explains auto-ethnography, outlining some of the strengths and limitations of the method, and then adapting these elements to the conduct of netnography. Along the way, the chapter explores some of the issues specific to virtual worlds. These issues include such unprecedented elements as the exploration of and situation within an entirely new sense of world, the researcher's embodiment (i.e., recreating a body and establishing a sense of social presence), and the researcher and residents' more general plural existence (i.e., possibility of being represented by more than one avatar). We provide a number of examples drawn from our own research and that of others. The result is an outline of auto-netnography for avatar-driven inquiries in three-dimensional virtual environments. In the chapter's conclusion, we describe and briefly demonstrate some of the burgeoning opportunities for auto-netnographic research in online virtual worlds.

VIRTUAL WORLDS AND CULTURAL INQUIRY

Virtual worlds, the topic of this volume, are persistent, three-dimensional, networked computer represented spaces consisting of digital code and represented to people through a human-computer interface, most usually a keyboard for human input and a screen for computer output. In virtual worlds, people appear to have different bodies and to experience their lives through animated representations called avatars. The worlds are persistent, meaning that, unlike standalone or console-driven video games, the worlds continue on even after the player has exited them. In virtual worlds such as *Second Life, Entropia Universe, The World of Warcraft, Lineage, The Sims Online,* or *Star Wars Galaxies,* human-controlled avatars engage in a variety of social practices, some dictated by game-like rules, others purely explorational and relational. Oftentimes, avatars communicate in a chat-like manner, using voice or text-based instant messengers for private discussions. Aesthetically, virtual worlds can "feel" like an animated computer game. Indeed, all virtual worlds developed from "massively multiplayer online role-playing games" (abbreviated at MMORPG and pronounced "more pig"). However, some of the more heralded recent virtual worlds like *Second Life* and *Entropia Universe* differ from games because they lack rules, character maintenance requirements, and explicit goals.

We identify three key characteristics of virtual worlds, and relate these to the conduct of cultural research. The first unique characteristic of virtual worlds is the notion of *re-worlding* and the related idea of *plastic worldrules*. This element is ontological in a new sense. Whereas ontology refers more generally to the nature of reality, previously considered mainly from a philosophical point of view, this element refers to the experiential dimensions of virtual worlds in which (1) an apparently new world is experienced—which we term re-worlding, and (2) that this world has malleable rules—which we term plastic worldrules. So, as an example of the latter, people can fly in many virtual worlds, or experience places where gravity is radically altered.

The second key characteristic to consider is the notion of re-embodiment, in which the consumer or researcher (or consumer researcher) is both required and able to choose a new bodily form to represent him or herself in the virtual world. This element has been much considered and written about in popular and even many academic accounts of virtual world experiences (e.g., Taylor 2002; Cooper, Dibbell, and Spaight 2007). However, we consider that this crucial facet has been mentioned frequently but not accommodated or even acknowledged methodologically.

The third characteristic, related to the prior one but also quite distinct from it, is the notion of multiperspectivality, or multiple perspectives. In this contingency, consumers have the option of occupying not only one new world, but many. A consumer can, for instance, occupy virtual worlds in many of the same games simultaneously, having different avatars operating in open windows on *Second Life, Project Entropia,* and the *Habbo Hotel.* The consumer also has the option of occupying more than one body at a time, duplicating bodies, or programming autonomous bodies to acts as its virtual agents. Each of these elements lends a literally multiphrenic nature to the usually individualized point of view, a tangible sense of the multiple personalities explored by many postmodern writers, from Gergen (1991) to Firat and Venkatesh (1995).

Each of these three elements—re-worlding, re-embodiment, and multiperspectivality—entails perspective changes as well as alterations in learning. In many cases, these changes are personal transformations of the relationships between the individual and their own perceptions of reality, of body, of self, of world. They familiarize the consumer with elements of the new virtual world (such as its rules, representations, and persona) and defamiliarize elements of physical reality (partly by making explicit its previously naturalized rules and representations). Because of this, at least some of the important effects of virtual worlding (as a verb) take place on an interior dimension of perspectival change and experience. Thus we suggest here that these particular elements may not be as tractable to researchers employing traditional methods of data gathering.

Let us very briefly consider three different methods for gaining insight into virtual worlds—surveys, experiments, and observational techniques—and consider how they would handle these unique contingencies. First, consider the survey. Although survey-bots are one answer to researching in virtual worlds, the notions of re-worlding and re-embodiment lead us to wonder about certain areas of this research enterprise. Do the rules about questionnaire answering in the "real world" of everyday life also translate to these new virtual world contexts, where motivations for answering might be different, and the idea of answering "in character" or out of character might become relevant? Indeed, the very notion of multiperpectivality draws us to wonder who or what exactly we may be surveying.

Experimental testing labs that bring in avatars as subjects and expose them to particular stimuli might conceivably tell us some interesting things about in-world consumption patterns and responses. However, we would need to ensure that the rules of the experiment were aligned with the rules of the virtual world. We would also need to ensure that the identity fluxes of multiperspectivality were attuned to the particular subjects we were hoping to test (i.e., that gender, age, and even human/bot differences were somehow either irrelevant or built into the test itself).

Observational recordings of avatar behavior are possible; in fact, they are practically built into the nature of these environments. Data recording and storage all but guarantee that the owners of virtual worlds are awash in data that portray avatar activity at aggregate levels. Massive modeling of this data can be extremely interesting, producing a cloud of avatar activity that can be mined for insights into traffic motion, popular locations, and popular activities in the same way that satellite telemetry and best-seller lists can. But like surveys and experiments, this aggregate level of analysis must of necessity leave open critical questions of meaning that matter on the level of language, culture, and basic human understanding. In fact, these key areas, where self and community interact with various types of material and nonmaterial "consumption," are largely impervious to the modes of study in our usual methodological toolkit. They need some other approach.

This intriguing naturalistic blind spot has been noted and explored more generally by many in the field of consumer research (e.g., Belk 1987; McCracken 1997; Sherry 1991; Sunderland and Denny 2007). The simple truth is that, even after over quarter of a century of lamentation, we still actually know very little about the best way to approach and talk to consumers while they are busy living their lives. This is true whether we are talking about consumers shopping in malls, cooking in their kitchens, or relating to one another in online environments. We have only recently begun to consider how online lives link to the actual real world or "RL" (Real Life) of consumers. We have but scratched the surface of considering how to test our given knowledge about communities, cultures, and selves among the e-tribes of virtual worlds, or to consider what lessons these explorations might hold for our greater understanding of all naturalistically situated consumption. In the next section, we begin to explore the relationship between an online offshoot of the naturalistic, anthropological approach of ethnographic research and our central topic of research in virtual worlds.

FROM ETHNOGRAPHY TO NETNOGRAPHY
TO AUTO-NETNOGRAPHY

There is little doubt that a role for almost every marketing and consumer research method exists to be played out in cyberspace generally and in virtual worlds more specifically. These roles would be driven by various research questions. A question about what percentage of avatars are female in appearance could be handled by observational or survey research. Questions about the opinions expressed by avatars could be settled by in-world questionnaires and surveys. Virtual world context studies of identity, community, culture, and consumption will require adaptations of anthropological methods. Anthropological methods have a history in marketing and consumer research that stretches back over half a century, to Sidney Levy's pioneering work (Levy 1959). Based on the notion of participant-observation of in situ consumption, marketing anthropologists have been conducting fieldwork in people's homes, retail stores, and other natural settings in order to grain insights into the actual everyday meanings, rituals, and acts of consumers (Sunderland and Denny 2007). In recent times, these anthropological techniques have been found useful in understanding consumers' online experiences and the ways that these occurrences play a part in their lives. In particular, netnography (see Kozinets 1998, 2002)—the rigorous and systematic adaptation of an anthropological approach specifically altered to the contingencies of online behavior and interaction—has an especially important role to play in this quest for understanding.

In this chapter we begin the development of an adaptation of netnography especially suited to the identity work in virtual worlds that involves the avatar experience. Our argument for this adaptation is that one of the three characteristics of the virtual world parallels the cultural difference and alterity already experienced by ethnographers. Just as ethnographers must adapt to a new cultural world and set of rules, so must a consumer of a virtual world adapt to an entirely new sense of a world and its rules. Re-embodiment is quite different from anything experienced by traditional anthropologists, although it is perhaps akin to learning about new garb, adornment, and modes of presentation of the self. The idea of having multiple perspectives and multiple bodies also seems quite unique. Each of these elements, however, requires a particular kind of learning in order to feel natural to the consumer. And because virtual worlds tend to be social worlds where people use the computer interface to interact with other living, breathing human beings (distanced in space, sometimes even in time), and not to interact with a computer system (as opposed to, say, a traditional free-standing videogame), there is an enculturation that occurs, a social learning and cultural induction into a particular community whose immersive nature is extremely familiar to the anthropologists and sociologists who deploy ethnography. This is because the experience and much of the appeal of virtual worlds lies in the way that they transform the relationship between individuals and their own perceptions of reality, of their own bodies, of the aspects of their identities, of the world itself. We believe that these elements of virtual worlds are generative and worthwhile areas of investigation for scholars. Further, we hold that these elements are cloistered into areas of personal experience that can be very difficult if not impossible for other methodologies to reveal. It is for this reason—the intensely personal nature of the avatar experience—that we suggest considering and exploring the potential for an online application of auto-ethnography.

Auto-ethnography, at its core, is an element of all rigorous ethnography. To put it simply, it is the deliberate study and representation of cultural knowledge by one or more members of the culture under examination. Auto-ethnography has existed since modern anthropology emerged and has gained increasing attention over the last twenty years (Buzard 2003). David Hayano's (1979) work brought the term to the fore in contemporary anthropology, and he has used it in a manner than emphasizes the autobiographical, personal, reflective aspects of ethnographic writing. As Wall (2006) notes, auto-ethnography is grounded in anthropology's "crisis of representation" response to postmodern perspectives, and is linked to the growing debate about reflexivity and voice in social research. The intent of auto-ethnography is, therefore, to directly acknowledge the unbreakable link between the personal and the cultural—and even exploit it for the sake of research. Within this reflexive and deliberate acknowledgment is considerable room for experimentation, introspection, and nontraditional forms of inquiry and expression (for examples in our field, see Brown 2006; Gould 1991; Hirschman 1991; Holbrook 2005). Auto-ethnography since Hayano has therefore entailed a personalized writing style linked to autobiography where a reflexive drawing upon the author's direct experience is carefully utilized to extend wider understanding about a societal phenomenon.

We now develop ethnography into the practice of netnography in order to produce auto-netnography. Auto-netnography is an approach to netnography that highlights the role of the netnographer's own own online experiences. It captures and documents these experiences through the careful personal observation of online participation, autobiographical attention to the interrelation of various experienced "worlds"—both online and off/real—reflexive field noting, self- and first-person image and other data captures, and first-person narratives that make their way into the final representation carried in the netnographic text. The purpose of auto-netnography is to provide added personal participation to the study of online cultural and communal phenomena in order to comprehend their nuances from a necessarily and suitably engaged position, and to faithfully represent this engagement in order to provide enhanced understanding of the cultural nature of online experience.

Auto-netnography can certainly exist necessarily as a freestanding technique in which the author writes about his/her cultural experiences in online communities, paying particular attention to the interior impacts of the experience. However, we would recommend that it be incorporated as one important element of the ethnographic voice, as part of an overall multimodal netnographic (or even ethnographic) research exploration (see Kozinets 1998). This would entail joining auto-ethnography with detailed observational data collection, with interviews, and with other types of netnographic and ethnographic participation.

Auto-netnography seems well suited to help gain understanding of the three particular elements of virtual world experience: re-worlding and plastic worldrules, re-embodiment, and multiperspectivality. In execution, auto-netnography can also help to enhance research challenges to understandings particular to our knowledge of virtual worlds in three ways. First, because virtual worlds are diverse, complex social environments, auto-netnography permits a longitudinal exploration of the process of virtual enculturation. This occurs from a "deep N of 1" context that can often offer more profound insights than observation of other avatars and elicitation of their retrospective self-reports (see Foley 2002).

Second, because avatar-driven identity projects and the identity formations of virtual worlds are so vital to many of their theoretical implications, auto-netnography allows a more authoritative authorial voice to emerge, one that speaks not only as a cultural member and a holder of particular avatar identity or identities, but as a researcher with skills, a particular social situation, and multiple agendas who can present and then represent the avatar experience in all of its "real" virtual world complexity (see Buzard 2003; Dupuis 1999). The result can be critical and analytical in a way that other techniques cannot (Anderson 2006).

Finally, from a temporal and practice-related perspective, the auto-netnographic method allows an uninterrupted participant-observation of an alternative life, permitting a naturalistic unfolding of the flow and flux of cultural and communal play, persons, and places. In the final section of this chapter, we provide an evocative set of illustrations drawn from our own and others' writing within virtual worlds to illustrate the utility of auto-netnographic research and writing within this unique new context.

AUTO-NETNOGRAPHY IN VIRTUAL WORLDS

> Concerns about the situatedness of the knower, the context of discovery, and the relation of the knower to the subjects of her inquiry are demons at the door of positivist science. The production of [what has been considered] "legitimate" knowledge begins by slamming the door shut. (McCorkel and Myers 2003, p. 200)

In this chapter, we move beyond post-positivist considerations of social situation and epistemology to argue that auto-netnography provides the depth of observation required in order to capture some of the unique contingencies of the virtual world phenomenon. As Ellis (1991, p. 30) has noted, auto-ethnography changes the focus of research attention, moving it from "use of self-observation as part of the situation studied to self-introspection or self-ethnography as a legitimate focus of study in and of itself." Denzin and Lincoln (1994) note that new epistemologies such as auto-ethnography help to mitigate some of the risks inherent in the research representation of others (such as assuming that we "know" what an avatar is doing or trying to represent), allow for the production of new knowledge by a unique and uniquely situated researcher (the "deep N of 1"), and offer small-scale knowledge that can inform specific problems and specific situations (such as those in particular virtual worlds).

In order to illustrate these crucial points, we will draw both upon others' first-person narratives of being-an-avatar in a virtual world, as well as writings from our own fieldwork conducted (independently of one another) over the past twenty months in the popular virtual world *Second Life*. We find the situation facing researchers of avatars in virtual worlds to be analogous in many ways to that facing psychotherapists interested in theories of identity and self. Because autobiographical or other "single-case" research focuses on intrasubject variation, there is relevance to such a comparison. The study of intrasubject variation is relevant to psychotherapy process research, and the term *process* implies a type of temporal unfolding that is also familiar to the nature of adaptation and adjustment to being an avatar in a virtual world (Hilliard 1993).

The following quote from an adept's detailed book about his experiences in the world of *Second Life* illustrates the important internal shift that occurs when a person enters a virtual world and must adapt to the in-world role of being represented as and through an avatar.

> I remember logging into Second Life initially as a tourist or explorer. Carmen and I had become close friends over the previous ten years . . . and it was she who invited me to this odd place. . . . Initially, like the vast majority of the people who enter these systems, my image of myself was most important to me. My dumb little default avatar—the Ken-looking brunette fellow—had nothing at all to do with me, or who I thought of myself being. Because I am a portrait artist, I made my avatar as I make the figures in my paintings: I stretched the body tall, gave him big hands and skinny arms, and evaporated anything that wasn't necessary so that he ended up bony, pale, and graceful. . . . And I named him Pighed, more out of habit than anything. . . . It was while I was working on [programming] my shoes, just a few hours after I'd logged into Second Life, that a message appeared on my screen. It was from Carmen, the same Carmen I had met on The WELL in 1993 and who had invited me to try Second Life. . . . The screen lit up and I saw what appeared to be a glade . . . I also heard a man's laugh, and then the snap of a whip, and I turned to the right and there was my friend, Carmen—or rather, her avatar—on her knees in front of another avatar dressed up like Conan the Barbarian. . . . Whatever they were up to, it appeared to be a kind of personal and very private ritual. I was confused. (Meadows 2008, pp. 29–32)

In this one rich paragraph, the author describes some of his intentions and his motivations. In order for us to make sense of his initial experiences as an avatar, Meadows has actually had to provide considerable information about his prior online experiences (meeting Carmen on *The WELL,* joining past online communities that had to do with pigs, being a portrait artist, his actual physical appearance, his spiritual orientation to images of tall, thin people) and, in fact, his everyday life. This autobiographical social contextualizing becomes crucial data that help us to understand the choices and experiences the author makes. Further, his first-person perspective is critical to taking us in an evocative way into this strange new world of choices, and to also experiencing alongside him the sense of awkward embarrassment as he is bidden to witness a sexual ritual involving his friend Carmen. We further experience his confusion as he must learn the new social rules of this other culture, and his explanations and perspective leave little doubt in the reader's mind that the experience of entering this virtual world is a highly cultured affair. Things and actions have particular and new meanings—and he (and we) has not yet mastered the cultural code of the place.

Consider again some of the similarities between this type of self-related avatar study and the self-related aspects of psychotherapy research. Kiesler (1980) and Greenberg (1986), among others, have argued that global psychotherapeutic interventions must be studied as a series of smaller interrelated changes. This shifts the focus from a particular outcome to the process of change (Hilliard 1993). Greenberg (p. 4) offered the following broad description of this approach:

> In studying the process of change, both beginning points and end-points are taken into account, as well as the form of the function between these points. With processes of change as the focus of the investigation, the emphasis is not on studying what is going on in therapy (process research) nor only on the comparison of two measurement points before and after therapy (efficacy research) but rather on identifying, describing, explaining, and predicting the effects of the processes that bring about therapeutic change over the entire course of therapy.

We find the situation with the study of the avatar generally analogous. The emphasis in the study of the virtual world need not be exclusively on the global change of a person identifying with their avatar and using it as an object of self-expression or self-expansion, or a comparison of the person before and after they became adapted to experiences within a virtual world, but rather could be about the identification, description, and explanation of the processes that bring about these identifications across the entire course of virtual world experience. The processes of learning, adaptation, identity exploration, and enculturation are important changes in perception and sociality that occur as a person interacts through an avatar with a virtual world. In the following three sections, we outline some of the particular types of adaptations required for in-world situated research into avatars and illustrate them with particular examples from our own and others' research and experiences. Our guidelines are the three particular elements of virtual world experience: re-worlding, re-embodiment, and multiperspectivality.

RE-WORLDING

Re-worlding has consequences for how consumers and researchers interpret reality in virtual worlds. Solidified matters of physical "reality" (to respect Nabokov's perspicacious suggestion) that we usually do not have influence over in our daily offline lives can become transmuted into matters of choice in a virtual world. These choices and changes, however, have special meanings not easily captured through outward observation.

Virtual worlds offer also another form of re-worlding such as the ability to affect the forces of nature and to choose the position of the virtual sun or the simulated weather conditions at any particular point in time. These god-like powers have a strongly evocative character and allow for a shaping of the ambience of virtual surroundings. The ability to remodel the virtual environment extends the identity project far beyond the body, bearing witness to the skills and sense of aesthetics of virtual creators. Therefore, places in virtual worlds can also be considered to be vivid markers of virtual identity.

Most virtual worlds are modeled as utopian spaces, where there is no disease, aging, or permanent death. Abilities are enhanced in many of these worlds. A commonplace ability, for instance, is the ability to fly. Another common ability is teleportation. Limiting physical rules no longer hold. The place is decidedly magical, in that with an "incantation" of code, almost anything can be materialized, dematerialized, or transformed.

This is not to say that virtual worlds are all lands of eternal bliss. Indeed, the wonders of instant transport and freedom from consequences can lead to expressive acts that have decidedly psychopathic taints. Witness, via an auto-netnographic account, "griefing."

> I was reclining on the couch in my living room contemplating my next build when the front door opened and in walked an avatar dressed in a gray ninja outfit, wielding a sword. The avatar's first name was MrGrieferBanMe. . . . After assessing the situation, Mr. Griefer drew his weapon and proceeded to slash away at me as I relaxed on the couch. (White 2008, p. 358)

Individuals who find enjoyment in negatively affecting the experience of other people in virtual worlds are known as "griefers." Even though no one gets physically hurt during acts of griefing, virtual scenes of blood and violence or displays of offensive materials seem to affect inhabitants of virtual worlds in a similar manner to acts of crime offline. Many of these acts of re-worlding can also concern reinterpretation of societal norms and values. So, for example, there are many different types of viral world, and domains within virtual worlds. Many are based upon science fiction or fantasy novels or scenarios. Others allow particular kinds of social (particularly sexual and expressive) freedoms. Many of these social freedoms become expressed in the interface of becoming a new body in a new world, as the next section of our chapter demonstrates.

RE-EMBODIMENT

The avatar bodies consumers and researchers create and use in virtual worlds are inseparable from the performance of self and are crucial to engagement in in-world social life. They are the facilitators of interaction and the locus for virtual identity. Therefore, re-embodiment is usually characterized as a high-involvement and time-consuming enterprise. Consider this example from Kedzior's field notes:

> I was excited and overwhelmed by the number of choices that I had to make. The whole experience resembled a make-over reality show. And even though I was aware that it is only my avatar that's getting a treat, for some reason it felt it was all about me. Knowing that I can modify my looks endlessly left me experimenting with every single option. It took me probably ten minutes only to decide on the shape of my nose. After forty minutes of modeling my new body I was exhausted. (Kedzior unpublished notes)

Essential to conducting cultural research in a virtual world is the realization that avatar bodies affect the way researchers are perceived. Much will depend on the specific cultural world in question. It seems quite universal that engagement with life in a virtual world is usually reflected in the amount of work invested in creating and personalizing the avatar. For example, in order to create distinct identities of their avatars in *Second Life,* consumers have to invest in well-scripted clothes that imitate the movement patterns of the real fabric on the body and custom-made animations that allow the expression of a whole variety of emotions. Otherwise it is very difficult to function (or research) a world in which one is perceived as an outsider.

It has to be pointed out, however, that the process of re-embodiment often transcends a plain choice of an avatar body and constitutes a broader theme of identity work performed by creating an avatar profile and choosing a name. Again, from the Kedzior's field notes:

> Suddenly, I realized that picking a last name [for an avatar in *Second Life*] is like entering a new family, becoming a part of a clan that I was yet to meet. And what's more important than a nice sounding name? . . . You know I believe in numerology and that letters and numbers have their own vibrations. Before I selected my name, I consulted my charts and based on that came up with a first name that would be both unique and lucky.

As our bodies are the instruments through which we experience the world, and the ability to malleably change our body allows us to redefine our social existence. This makes elements such as aging and disability a choice in a virtual social life. Here is another example from the second Kedzior's *Second Life* field notes: "I saw an avatar riding a wheelchair. Unfortunately, I didn't manage to talk to him and ask why he chose to appear disabled. I was confused. In a world where one doesn't need to walk because you can fly and teleport yourself someone wanted to be disabled." The intentional appearance of being disabled causes us pause, and makes us wonder about what this avatar is intended to represent.

The malleability of a virtual body also affects the meaning we attribute to the practice of virtual sex and intimate relationships. As the following example illustrates, the fluidity of identities creates paradoxical situations that are rather difficult to imagine in offline reality.

> So there's this man who's male in real life but a woman in Second Life (even though in real life he's into women), and then there's this other man who's also heterosexual in real life whose avatar in Second Life was male for a while, but then decided to be a woman instead, and guess what: These two straight guys met in Second Life and fell in love, and so now they're married there. So, you know, just another avatar-based romance. (Au 2008, p. 80)

And, indeed, as with dream interpretation, the degrees of freedom of the transformation open up an internal mirror through which we can gaze and interpret with self-realization. As Stein (2006), wrote in an auto-netnographic account of *Second Life* in *Time* magazine:

> But Second Life is different enough (flying! teleporting! cloning!) that it functions as a therapist's couch on which you learn about yourself by safely exploring your darkest desires. Mine, I was shocked to find, do not involve sex. In fact, in my ultimate fantasy life, I do not have a penis. And since genitalia do not come without charge in Second Life, I could free myself from the gnawing distraction of a sex drive. Which meant that for the first time, I would be able to focus all my energy on a quest for power. I planned to put the Reuters guy out of business, own some kind of island where drone armies did my bidding and force people to follow laws based on my insane whims. Unfortunately, the other thing I learned about myself on Second Life, after spending half an hour learning how to walk, was that I'm too lazy to do any of those things. Or even draw my hair and eyebrows right.

MULTIPERSPECTIVALITY

In the realm of virtual worlds, some consumers maintain the consistent perspective that comes from the use of a single avatar, whereas others tend to have multiple characters. These can be multiple characters within one virtual world, or even common characters that stretch across multiple different environments. Multi-perspectivality refers to the ways in which consumers use and maintain more than one avatar body's perspective, and the ways in which they adapt to and use these multiple perspectives.

> Since I'm leading a double life (or a Second Life if you prefer) I thought I'd create one [blog] for Jojamela Soon, because she, like many folks living a Second Life, is a figment of imagination, an alternate personality, separate from Real Life with thoughts and experiences felt but not quite real. I need a way to separate the real from the fantasy because if I posted my SL experiences on my real blog I might come across as a bit strange or maybe even a little insane. Jojamela Soon allows me to be someone else for just a little while. Much of my personality comes through her, but I'm really trying to keep her personality different, maybe work on her shyness and get her out of her shell (Jojamela Soon blog, February 12, 2007)

This example illustrates the subtleties of interconnectedness between online and offline personas and the influence the two have on each other. Inhabiting and researching spaces where people are not necessarily limited to only one body is an obvious challenge for our research, one partially met by a researcher's autobiographical experiences captured in careful field notes. As the example also indicates, the avatar can also express as a separate persona whose identity project is pursued in the virtual world. Therefore, an auto-netnographer could certainly write an auto-netnography from the perspective of an online avatar, or even multiple avatars, in order to learn from and express this modality of virtual world experience.

The possibility of occupying many different virtual spaces means that the people who inhabit them perform several, often complicated, configurations of identity (Taylor 1999; Turkle 1995). Apart from representing an obvious challenge to researchers, this contingency represents an enhanced opportunity of experiencing and learning from a variety of perspectives about virtual—and perhaps even general psychological—existence.

> I was intrigued by his gender swapping and asked him why he did it. Instead of answering, he suggested I should do it too and see for myself what it feels like to change the gender. When I agreed he gave me something that was called a Marilyn box and instructed how to step-by-step transform myself into a woman. Dressing up and changing appearance was still a task, so I needed help. After the transformation was complete, my avatar was a sexually provocative woman. . . . The moment we teleported there, male avatars approached us and started chatting. It was much easier to make a contact as a woman but I didn't feel quite comfortable appearing as a female because it felt like I am trying to deceive all these guys. (Field notes)

Gender swapping in virtual worlds is an expression of multiperspectivality and can be seen as a risk-free opportunity to learn about the otherwise inaccessible world of members of the opposite sex. As illustrated by the example, it can also be a source of researcher's self-reflection on the consequences of having gender in the social, virtual world.

IN-WORLD AND INCONCLUSIVE

Even though virtual worlds are composed of computer code, manifested through hardware, and able to produce reams of quantitative data about consumer actions, they remain cultural spaces through which an embodied avatar moves and interacts with other embodied avatars. These spaces possess their own complex, unique, and dynamic sets of rituals, rules, symbol-systems, and meanings. Therefore, researchers in this environment experience a range of unique new methodological considerations.

Through the process of studying the cultural aspects of virtual worlds, researchers become re-embodied and immersed. As ethnographers in a new culture, they adopt a dual role. On the one hand, they become as native members in the social world under study learning "emic" terms. On the other hand, they must act as researchers of that new world, translating their findings into the "etic" theoretical terms and literatures of their own scientific field.

Although research methods such as surveys, experiments, and observational techniques can be adapted to the study of many of the important dimensions of new online phenomena, they are not fit to explore the personal dimensions of virtual worlds' cultural consumption experience. In this chapter we outlined and discussed a new research approach—auto-netnography—and offered a brief sketch that begins to demonstrate its potential to empower researchers for an in-depth understanding of the deeply personal experiences encountered when researching the culture of virtual worlds through the active engagement of an avatar.

The early explorations of text-based virtual spaces on the Internet (e.g., Turkle 1995; Markham 1998) illuminated the social and cultural character of many early online interactions. These early works took a postmodern view of technology. They suggested that, because technology provides an open-ended way to represent oneself through text, it encourages people to experiment with their identities in a fluid way. A parallel stream of research (e.g., Jenkins 1995; Kozinets 1997) studied the culturally constitutive character of the Internet and addressed the cultural dynamics of virtual communities centered on mass media fan cultures and subcultures of consumption. This growing interest in conducting a systematic investigation of the cultures that arose out of textual virtual spaces gave rise to the early, systematic practice of netnography (Kozinets 1998, 2002).

Building on previous auto-ethnographic research (Hayano 1979; Gould 1991; Ronai and Ellis 1989), we demonstrate in this chapter how acknowledging the researcher's own authorial voice can be a source of knowledge about the virtual experience in general and life-as-an-avatar in particular. The mating of the reflexive, autobiographical mode of auto-ethnography and the online participant-observational approach of netnography spawns auto-netnography.

A recent shift in online communication from text-based environments to animated, graphic virtual worlds expands the boundaries of virtual identity projects and in many ways enriches the cultural element of online interactions. It has generated new waves of research interest (e.g., Castronova 2005; Meadows 2008) that exposes the nuances, dynamism, and complexity of virtual spaces and indicates new challenges for researchers. By identifying three unique contingencies of virtual world that are relevant for cultural inquiries—which we have termed re-worlding, re-embodiment, and multiperspectivality—we hope to contribute to our growing understanding of these domains.

Using the three contingencies as a backdrop for our presentation, we have illustrated how auto-netnographic data can uncover multiple layers of consciousness, connecting the personal to the cultural in the pursuit of virtual identity. Auto-netnography, as discussed here, can be seen as a part of an overall multimodal netnographic research with capacity to complement other approaches during the exploration of complex cultural phenomena online. We also seek to contribute to and expand the netnographic toolkit as we continue to press forward in exploring, interpreting, and playing The Game of Life and Culture online and, particularly in this chapter, in virtual worlds.

REFERENCES

Anderson, L. 2006. "Analytic Autoethnography." *Journal of Contemporary Ethnography* 35 (4): 373–395.

Au, Wagner James. 2008. *The Making of Second Life: Notes from the New World.* New York: HarperCollins.

Belk, Russell W. 1987. "A Modest Proposal for Creating Verisimilitude in Consumer Information Processing Models and Some Suggestions for Establishing a Discipline to Study Consumer Behavior." In *Philosophical and Radical Thought in Marketing,* ed. A. Fuat Firat, Nikhilesh Dholakia, and Richard P. Bagozzi, 361–372. Lexington, MA: Lexington Press.

Brown, Stephen. 2006. "Autobiography." In *Handbook of Qualitative Research Methods in Marketing,* ed. Russell W. Belk, 440–452. Cheltenham, UK, and Northampton, MA: Edward Elgar.

Buzard, J. 2003. "On Auto-Ethnographic Authority." *The Yale Journal of Criticism.* Available online at https://muse.jhu.edu/demo/yale_journal_of_criticism/v016/16.1buzard.html.

Castronova, Edward. 2005. *Synthetic Worlds: The Business and Culture of Online Games.* Chicago: University of Chicago Press.

Cooper, Robbie, Julian Dibbell, and Tracy Spaight. 2007. *Alter Ego: Avatars and Their Creators.* London: Chris Boot Ltd.

Denzin, Norman K., and Yvonna S. Lincoln, eds. 1994. *Handbook of Qualitative Research.* Thousand Oaks, CA: Sage.

Dupuis, S.L. 1999. "Naked Truths: Towards a Reflexive Methodology in Leisure Research." *Leisure Sciences* 21 (January): 43–64.

Ellis, Carolyn. 1991. "Sociological Introspection and Emotional Experience." *Symbolic Interaction* 14: 23–50.

Firat, Fuat, and Alladi Venkatesh. 1995. "Liberatory Postmodernism and the Reenchantment of Consumption." *Journal of Consumer Research* 22: 239–267.

Foley, D.E. 2002. "Critical Ethnography: The Reflexive Turn." *International Journal of Qualitative Studies in Education* 15 (July): 469–490.

Gergen, Kenneth. 1991. *The Saturated Self: Dilemmas of Identity in Contemporary Life.* New York: Basic Books.

Gould, Stephen Jay. 1991. "The Self-Manipulation of My Pervasive, Vital Energy Through Product Use: An Introspective-Praxis Approach." *Journal of Consumer Research* 18 (September): 194–207.

Greenberg, Leslie S. 1986. "Change Process Research." *Journal of Consulting and Clinical Psychology* 54: 4–9.

Hayano, D. 1979. "Auto-ethnography: Paradigms, Problems and Prospects." *Human Organization* 38: 99–104.

Hemp, Paul. 2006. "Avatar-Based Marketing." *Harvard Business Review* 84 (6): 48–57.

Hilliard, Russell B. 1993. "Single-Case Methodology in Psychotherapy Process and Outcome Research." *Journal of Consulting and Clinical Psychology* 61 (June): 373–380.

Hirschman, Elizabeth C. 1991. "Secular Morality and the Dark Side of Consumer Behavior: Or How Semiotics Saved My Life." In *Advances in Consumer Research,* vol. 18, ed. Rebecca H. Holman and Michael R. Solomon, 1–6. Provo, UT: Association for Consumer Research.

Holbrook, Morris B. 2005. "Customer Value and Autoethnography: Subjective Personal Introspection and the Meanings of a Photograph Collection." *Journal of Business Research* 58 (1): 45–61.

Jenkins, Henry. 1995. " 'Do You Enjoy Making the Rest of Us Feel Stupid?': alt. tv.twinpeaks, the Trickster Author, and Viewer Mastery." In *Full of Secrets: Critical Approaches to Twin Peaks,* ed. David Lavery. Detroit: Wayne State University Press

Jojamela Soon. 2007. February 12. Available at http://jojamelasoon.blogspot.com/.

Kiesler, Donald J. 1980. "Psychotherapy Process Research: Viability and Directions in the 1980s." In *Psychotherapy; Research and Training,* ed. W. DeMoor and H.R. Wijngaarden, 71–76. Amsterdam: Elsevier/North Holland Biomedical Press.

Kozinets, Robert V. 1997. "'I Want to Believe': A Netnography of the X-philes' Subculture of Consumption." In *Advances in Consumer Research,* vol. 24, ed. M. Brucks and D.J. MacInnis, 470–475. Provo, UT: Association for Consumer Research.

———. 1998. "On Netnography: Initial Reflections on Consumer Research Investigations of Cyberculture." In *Advances in Consumer Research,* vol. 25, ed. Joseph Alba and Wesley Hutchinson, 366–371. Provo, UT: Association for Consumer Research.

———. 2002. "The Field Behind the Screen: Using Netnography for Marketing Research in Online Communities." *Journal of Marketing Research,* 39 (February): 61–72.

———. 2006. "Netnography 2.0." In *Handbook of Qualitative Research Methods in Marketing,* ed. Russell W. Belk, 129–142. Cheltenham, UK, and Northampton, MA: Edward Elgar.

———. 2007. "Advancing Netnography." *Association for Consumer Research Pre-Conference on Online Consumers.* Memphis, Tennessee, October 25.

Levy, Sidney J. 1959. "Symbols for Sale." *Harvard Business Review* 37 (July–August): 117–124.

Markham, Annette N. 1998. *Life Online: Researching Real Experience in Virtual Space.* Wallnut Creek, CA: AltaMira Press.

McCorkel, Jill, and Kristen Myers. 2003. "What Difference Does Difference Make? Position and Privilege in the Field." *Qualitative Sociology* 26 (2): 199–231.

McCracken, Grant. 1997. *Plenitude.* Toronto, ON: Periph. Fluide.

Meadows, Mark Stephen. 2008. *I, Avatar: The Culture and Consequences of Having a Second Life.* Berkeley, CA: New Riders.

Ronai, Rambo Carol, and Carolyn Ellis. 1989. "Turn-ons For Money: Interactional Strategies of the Table Dancer." *Journal of Contemporary Ethnography* 18 (3): 271–298.

Sherry, John F. Jr. 1991. "Postmodern Alternatives: The Interpretive Turn in Consumer Research." In *Handbook of Consumer Theory and Research,* ed. Thomas S. Robertson and Harald H. Kassarjian, 548–591. Englewood Cliffs, NJ: Prentice Hall.

Stein, Joel. 2006. "My So-Called Second Life." *Time,* December 16. Available at www .time.com/time/magazine/article/0,9171,1570708,00.html.

Sunderland, Patricia L., and Rita M. Denny. 2007. *Doing Anthropology in Consumer Research.* Walnut Creek, CA: Left Coast Press.

Taylor, Tina Lynn. 1999. "Life in Virtual Worlds." *American Behavioral Scientist* 43 (3): 436–449.

———. 2002. "Living Digitally: Embodiment in Virtual Worlds." In *The Social Life of Avatars: Presence and Interaction in Shared Virtual Environments,* ed. R. Schroeder, 40–62. London: Springer-Verlag.

Turkle, Sherry. 1995. *Life on the Screen: Identity in the Age of the Internet.* New York: Simon & Schuster.

Wall, Sarah. 2006. "An Autoethnography on Learning About Autoethnography." *International Journal of Qualitative Methods* 5 (June): 1–12.

White, Brian A. 2008. *Second Life: A Guide to Your Virtual Life.* Indianapolis: QUE.

CHAPTER 2

For a Better Exploration of Metaverses as Consumer Experiences

LEILA EL KAMEL

METAVERSES, GROWING CONSUMPTION, AND LACK OF ACADEMIC RESEARCH

The democratization of access to the electronic network is a fact that has been widely covered by an abundant scientific and public literature and no longer needs to be demonstrated. Researchers and scientists in various disciplines cannot remain indifferent to the economic, political, social, and technological implications of the Internet for everyday life. By revolutionizing spatio-temporal references, the Internet transformed the way people perceive reality, the way they live, individually and collectively, as well as their way of entertainment. Following from the evolution of video games and network games, current metaverses (massively multiplayer online games [MMOGs] and synthetic worlds) allow thousands of residents around the world to meet in the same environment. The growth of metaverses can be explained by the immersive and rewarding experience that edition companies offer to players and residents[1] to play and interact.

In metaverses, the consumer chooses a character (an avatar) that serves as a virtual identity. It has been suggested that anonymity, the inherent freedom of choice in creating a virtual identity, and the ease with which residents create their avatars and objects constitute the most important aspects of the metaverse experience for them. These experiences generate billions of dollars to the companies that create editions of metaverses and to residents (Castronova 2005). The phenomenon has been so widespread that researchers in social and human sciences have begun to have a particular interest in the study of its different aspects. However, despite the fact that metaverses possess the characteristics of experiential consumption, little work in consumer psychology and behavior has focused on their elucidation. This chapter aims to provide an insight into metaverses from a psychological consumption perspective. It begins with the presentation of a conceptual map including all major contributions focused on metaverses, especially MUDs (multi-user domains) and MMOGs. It then presents an analysis of the metaverses phenomenon as postmodern experiential consumption. Finally, it suggests the exploration of the notion of avatar from a psychological perspective in order to reach a better understanding of metaverses as a platform for online experiential consumption.

CONCEPTUAL MAP OF A MULTIDISCIPLINARY RESEARCH OBJECT

Metaverses are online persistent worlds where thousands of residents or players meet to entertain. Currently, two types of metaverses can be grouped in this category: MMOGs and synthetic worlds. The former are the massively multiplayer online games in which players connect to play in a universe often inspired from science fiction or medieval fantasy, such as *The World of Warcraft*. The games' ultimate objective is for players to improve their performance level by accumulating experience points. The latter are persistent universes where residents live an experience of creation and imagination without seeking to achieve a given level of performance. For a lot of residents, it is not a game at all but a life experience. The most famous example of these metaverses is *Second Life*.

Metaverses are the playful practice of a new age that appeared with the enlargement of bandwidth, the amelioration of the interface, and the capacity of hardware and software programming and real-time simulation of phenomena. Unlike their precursors—video games, network games, and multi-user domains—metaverses allow several thousand players around the world to meet in persistent worlds through avatars. Metaverses are not time-limited and continue to function even when residents or players are disconnected. Navigating for hours and hours, residents or players create parallel worlds to their real world. In doing so, they have freedom to choose one or more individual and collective identities, involving consumption choices. A metaverse is characterized by a universe and characters who act individually or in groups and who experience the universe according to practices established by residents or players themselves.

Given the recent nature of the phenomenon and the lack of academic works on metaverses, a literature review focused on MMOGs and their predecessors (video games, network games, and MUDs) was conducted. Combining technical and social aspects, video games, network games, MUDs and MMOGs have been studied principally in the fields of information, communication, social psychology, and sociology. In this work, existing studies are highlighted by the major conclusions they have reached. The literature in this area is still scarce and many of the contributions are found in conference proceedings, articles, books, and doctoral theses. The multidisciplinary nature of existing works certainly involves rich and interesting contributions, but it also requires some vigilance regarding the apprehension of different concepts.

Apart from technical considerations, existing studies reviewed in this work show that the main aspects covered are: economy, demography, motivation, experience, identity, sociality, and subversion area. These studies did not address these issues in a mutually exclusive way, but each focused on one or two of the relevant features.

Economic Issues

The enthusiasm for online games reflects the existence of three different economic systems: (a) the direct revenue generated from the sale of the game by publishers, (b) the parallel economy taking place within metaverses themselves, and (c) the trade of virtual goods in real life.

Apart from an Internet subscription, residents or players in MMOGs must buy a powerful hardware platform and a license for the game. To these expenditures must be added money spent on services and derived products marketed by publishers and other businesses in the chain of production, and the marketing of these consumptions. Furthermore, there is a virtual parallel economy that takes place within metaverses. In most persistent worlds, life in the metaverse is inspired by the social and economic system of real life. An avatar created by a resident or a player can have a status, a function, and a remuneration.

From an economic point of view, Castronova (2004) considers that, whether virtual or not, players are running a real economy. Enthusiasm for online games took an unexpected turn among publishers. Players have started to sell objects and avatars created within games because they want to have a return on invested hours of play. The importance given to the successful and valuable items in the persistent worlds has led to the creation of a secondary market for virtual goods. Time spent playing becomes a remunerable activity (Largier 2003). Castronova (2005) considers that eBay has witnessed an annual volume of transactions amounting to more than $30 million for the exchange of goods emanating from virtual worlds. However, there is still a gray area concerning the private or public character of creations made in virtual worlds. Are they the property of residents or publishers?

According to Eriksson and Gill (2005), there is no consensus on the issue yet, as players treat objects and avatars as virtual private property. In summary, the main findings of works dealing with economic considerations in online games, particularly in metaverses, attest that they are currently growing increasingly and are part of a growth industry. Part of this economy is real, taking place in real life, and the other is virtual, taking place inside the synthetic world. Nevertheless, as shown below, the boundary between the real and virtual economies as yet remains unclear.

Demographic Issues

Several researchers have studied the demographic profiles of people who participate in multiplayer online games. Through the study of demographic factors, these works seek to understand the complexity of the online gaming phenomenon by studying behaviors of players according to their demographic profiles. The main demographic variables considered are: gender, age, and country of origin.

Gender

Studies on online games and video games seem to be unanimous concerning the male character of gaming. Indeed, studies following online players show a wide disparity between men and women with regard to use rate. Men account for over 80 percent of total worldwide subscriptions. However, the IGDA (International Game Developers Association) concluded that in 2004, women spent more time every week in online games than men. Furthermore, contrary to the idea that men are more versed in fighting games and strategy, Carr (2005) shows that women have a preference for fighting games, racing, and action and adventure games. They have a particular preference for games where they can exert control. However, a study by Jenson and Castell (2005) suggested that women prefer playing with men rather than with other women. Moreover, they especially appreciate the freedom and the independence of the adventure.

Because of the anonymity provided by Internet technology and the absence of the physical body, the gender of players is not important within the context of the game. In metaverses, it is the gender of the avatar that matters most. The players or the residents choose the gender of their avatars in compliance, or not, with their gender in real life. Paradoxically, research conducted by Yee (2001) on the game *Everquest* shows that more than 47 percent of male players play with female avatars against only 23 percent of women playing with male avatars. The reasons why players carry out this permutation are diverse: the role-play, the improvement of visual appearance, the gaining of some advantages in the game, and the exploration of the opposite gender. The most recent versions of metaverses provide the opportunity for residents to have a neutral gender.

Age

Yee (2006) considers that the idea that online games are exclusively intended for a tiny proportion of teenagers does not encourage academic research in this field. The results of his studies on players of multiplayer online games do not support these conclusions since the average age of players is 26.57. Players' age ranges between 11 and 68 years.

Country of Origin

Unlike video games, metaverses are distinguished by their ability to gather thousands of residents or players in the same environment, which means that these persistent worlds are inhabited by avatars managed by players from different countries with various cultures and ethnicities. Allocation of players or residents between servers is done primarily along geographic and linguistic specificities. Despite the importance of cultural aspects for the design of metaverses, very few studies have been undertaken to explore the cultural differences among players or residents. Haize and Pican (2003) attempted to catalog the differences between players in network games according to their country of origin. Results have enabled them to identify differences among American, Japanese, British, and French players.

Motivational Issues

By entering virtual worlds, residents are mainly looking for fun. However, the nature of this experience seems to be complex. This complexity has encouraged researchers to study what makes these persistent environments so attractive to residents and players. Several researchers have therefore focused on the study of players' motivations for spending so many hours in front of their computers. Some have led to a typology of motivational player profiles. The best known and oldest is that of Richard Bartle, built from observations in MUDs. The majority of studies in this direction remain purely empirical without a theoretically robust framework (Bartle 1996; Yee 2002a; Taylor 2003a; Lucas and Sherry 2004; Seay et al. 2004; Alix 2005; Iversen 2005; Kellar, Watters, and Duffy 2005). Several motivations can drive players or residents to go into virtual worlds: immersion, leadership, relationships, and achievement. In MMOGs in particular, researchers seem to agree that there are two main motivations and two dominant player profiles: *role-players* and *power gamers* (Taylor 2003a; Jaulin 2002). *Role players* are driven by satisfaction from the interpretation and play of avatars while *power gamers* are driven by pleasure from the accumulation of experience points.

Experiential Issues

Once players or residents join the virtual world, the experience is the result of interaction between avatars. Main works studying the different aspects of the experience in online games have focused on: narratology versus ludology; immersion; and the concept of player-actor.

According to Trappey et al. (2005), the determinants of the experience of online games are factors of the game play such as: image (graphic arts, display of roles), scenario, game mode (diversity, novelty), quality of voice and sound, and controllability; and factors of the player: emotional reactions (accomplishment, tension, and excitement, expression of feelings), interaction with others, learning capacities, cost, and challenge. In the same vein, two theoretical frameworks exist in the literature on the design and development of online games: the narratology and ludology frameworks (Arsenault 2005; Brand and Knight 2005; Heliö 2005; Løvlie 2005; Mateas and Stern 2005; Salazar 2005; Smith 2005; Warnes 2005). The former focuses on the symbolic and cultural content contained in games. The experience is very dependent on the ability of symbolic reproduction and semiotic narratives. The latter puts aside the content to focus on rules, the game itself, and its particular design perspective, topography, adaptability, safeguarding, and determinism.

Several researchers in the game design field have focused on the study of immersion as an important component of the experience in online games (Bartle 2004; Ermi and Mäyrä 2005; Esposito 2005; Gomes 2005). Each virtual world has its own immersive capacity. Some are more immersive than others. Ermi and Mäyrä (2005) were able to distinguish three types of immersion: immersion linked to senses, to challenges, and to imagination. The results were used to generate their model of immersion in the online gaming experience.

Tavares, Gil, and Roque (2005) have paid special attention to the notion of player-actor as an important facet of the particularity of experience in virtual worlds. Involvement of players in the design of online games comes as part of an emancipator movement. This emancipation takes place at several levels: the creation of one's own avatar, objects, and environments; and the test and evaluation of beta versions of games before launching in the market.

Identity Issues

Once in the metaverse, residents or players must choose an avatar. They must choose its class, gender, race, appearance, and skills, and they must write its history. This is the most important act for players and residents because the identity they have chosen will affect their image and guide their destiny in the virtual world. Players and residents are evolving in the virtual world through a graphic, intangible, scalable, and chosen virtual identity. The avatar is a vehicle allowing players to communicate what they want others to think of them and what they think of themselves. Lankoski (2005) considers the avatar to be the most important aspect in online games. Online games are therefore excellent spaces to experience another self.

According to Turkle (1995), the game becomes a space to reflect on some aspects of identity with greater mastery and control. In the same vein, Young (2005) considers that players are often embodied in a better body and do what they are not able to do in real life. In addition, the majority of players evolve three to four characters simultaneously (Seay et al. 2004). According to Whang and Kim (2005), the aspects that players consider important in their choice of avatar are: its impact in the game, its competence, its name, and its visual appearance.

The impact of the character in the game seems to be the most important criterion. Once players integrate the social space of the virtual world, their avatars are redefined in terms of shared standards that are built by players or residents themselves. Expectations and player personalities also have an influence on the role of their chosen avatars. The avatar goes through three phases: design of basic elements, remodeling according to the group, and individualizing depending on the personality of its player.

Social Issues

In the beginning, online games were regarded as a contributor to player loneliness and isolation. Soon, researchers in the social sciences discovered that online games are ideal environments for creating and expanding networks. However, online gaming sociality is completely different from sociality in video games and traditional games. This difference comes mainly from the absence of the physical body in online games. Several researchers believe that online games, especially persistent environments, generate social relations. Yee (2006) believes that there are unique and specific characteristics to multiplayer online games that facilitate social relationships.

In addition to the emotional investment that players put in these environments, they embody a certain preset compatibility with one another through their field of work or by their passion for role playing. In the same vein, Ducheneaut and Moore (2004) believe that the organizational structure of life in persistent worlds makes sociality inescapable. Several aspects of the world are set up to facilitate interaction among players or residents, including text, social gestures, and so on. Also, some places are meant to be visited as a group. Shulga (2003) calls these places the *inevitable sociality zones*. However, it is important to avoid falling into the trap of considering persistent environments as sociality generators or isolation generators. We should not forget that motivations of individual players or residents can be different.

The relational side is a motivational factor and not the only aspect sought by players or residents. Since a synthesis of works dealing with motivation shows that some players play to interact with others and participate in the creation of a common history, others are looking rather at the quality of the environment and the accumulation of experience points (Taylor 2003a). Shulga (2003) distinguishes two levels of sociality: sociality among avatars and sociality among players. In the former, players evolve their characters as social beings. The majority of virtual worlds are based on the construction of a history and a collective story, allow the coexistence of multiple virtual avatars in the same environment, and have means of text and graphic communication. These environments give players or residents the opportunity to forge links between characters such as friendship, love or marriage, and so on.

The sociality among avatars falls into two categories: an intimate level between two avatars, as in the case of marriage (Yee 2002b), and a collective or communal level as in the case of guilds (Berry and Brougère 2002). These links can also be lasting or ephemeral. Players or residents meet and bond online through their characters, but some of them are trying to know the real identity of other players and connect for this purpose either electronically or through face-to-face meetings. New relationships are thus created by disincarnating the player of his character (Craipeau 2002). Several researchers have reflected deeply on these interactions and formulated conceptual frameworks and categories or clusters of relations relying on different criteria. For example, for Pargman and Eriksson (2005), there are private, micro-public, meso-public, and macro-public levels. Myers (2005) highlights three levels: the guild, the super group, and the supra group.

Subversive Issues

Several subversive behaviors related to persistent worlds have attracted the attention of researchers and have left the door open to the public press to discredit the entire industry. Yet, academic researchers seem to be divided on the subversive nature of these behaviors, including addiction, violence, and confusion of virtuality with reality.

Addiction

Given the amount of time players or residents spend in virtual worlds, they were considered to have developed a kind of dependence on these environments. Indeed, Yee (2006) has shown that players spend more than an average of 22 hours a week in these spaces. However, Yee (2002a) believed that criticisms of this sort have their origins in an urban legend about the suicide of a player in the context of *Dungeons & Dragons*. An addiction is a recurring unhealthy behavior that the individual cannot stop. In the absence of the substance causing this behavior, the individual feels anger, anxiety, irritability, and frustration. For Yee (2002a), this is not the case for online players. In other words, the number of hours that the player devotes to games does not indicate addiction. In the same vein, Roustan (2002) considers that the cellist who devotes his entire life to his passion will never be considered dependent on the instrument.

Violence

Violence is a subversive aspect that virtual worlds have inherited from video games. Whether it is due to video games or virtual worlds, the fascination with violence is a concept that is related to the society and not to media supports. Lin and Sun (2005) view violence and death as an integral part of our society. They are reproduced in all fictional forms—painting, films, stories, and plays. However, it is common that some players show aggressive and psychologically or physically violent behavior, for example, white-eyed players, whose ultimate goal is to disrupt other players (Lin and Sun 2005). The white-eyed players are players who rebel against game rules. They break the laws (codes and rules of conduct) of their game worlds and violate the norms and etiquettes of their communities. These behaviors are normally challenged and condemned by members of the player community.

Confusion of the Virtual and the Real

Players escape reality and its problems through immersion in the virtual world, and researchers are divided on the implications. Indeed, Yee (2002c) believes that online games can provide a safe space for young people to experiment with different identities and personalities without risking serious repercussions. The virtual world can provide the necessary support for players in a safe space. Beyond safety, some players consider having a role of responsibility in the game that helps them be more self-confident in real life. In the same vein, Jaulin (2002) believes that online games encourage players to communicate and to adapt to new situations. As well, adolescents can test, through their avatars, different personalities and build their identities on a virtual mode without real significant effect because in virtual worlds the failure is accepted. Also, a survey allowed Seys (2002) to highlight the benefits of online games in the treatment of certain mental disorders, such as personality disorders and problems with intimacy.

Existing works on video games, network games, MUDs, and MMOGs were carried out in various disciplines according to different perspectives and frameworks. The contributions take the form of a patchwork whose individual pieces could not be used for the development of a common framework to help consumer researchers understand and explore metaverses as online experiential consumption.

METAVERSES AS POSTMODERN CONSUMPTION

Game editors are making significant efforts to strengthen sociality among residents and especially to expand opportunities for residents to customize the virtual universe. In doing this, publishers motivate residents to deal with aspects of their identities and the metaverse in which they are evolving. Metaverses seem to offer a hedonistic experience for their residents that enable them to live a thrill. This is a new kind of consumption that fits with the importance of ludic aspects in contemporary consumption. Indeed, existing studies reveal that metaverses are a growing phenomenon. This growth is reflected in part by an increasing number of residents and players. Indeed, as of 2007 there were more than 14 million players of MMOGs excluding the 15 million visitors to the synthetic world *Second Life*.

The craze for metaverses can be explained by the uniqueness of the experience in which consumers live and participate. The peculiarity of the experience of metaverses lies in the multiplicity of their spaces. Given the uncertain boundary between reality and virtuality in a metaverse, it is difficult to place exactly the experience's space: Is it the Web site, the universe of the metaverse, the physical space the resident inhabits, or the online forum? In metaverses, forums are available to residents or players to share their experiences and construct collectively the meaning of these experiences. Residents share their views on stories and characters. The area of consumption that is the site of the metaverse becomes a place for discussion and debate.

The characteristics of this experience show that metaverses closely match the current dominant concepts in the discipline of consumer behavior. Metaverses are mainly based on dramatization of the world through the design and spectacularization of the universe. Marketers, writers, graphic artists, anthropologists, and sociologists are involved in the creation of this new kind of experiential consumption in order to make it as attractive and as immersive as possible. In what follows, conditions of the postmodern consumption identified by Firat and Venkatesh (1995) are used as a conceptual framework to examine this new phenomenon of metaverses as postmodern experiential consumption.

Hyperreality

According to postmodernism, *reality is constructed rather than given.* Thus, in metaverses, universes are none other than simulations of imaginary worlds. Some are a pastiche or imitation of the real world; others are invented worlds and are the fruit of the imagination of editors and residents or players. Immersing themselves in the virtual world, residents live a kind of *blurring of the distinction between real and nonreal.* Residents seem to be driven by this re-enchantment of their everyday lives. Unlike transient experiences, metaverses are persistent, allowing residents to live a sufficiently intense experience that they want to extend and to repeat. In addition, given the latitude available to residents to create their avatars, their objects, and their environment based on their imagination, the structure of *signifier is signified* is replaced by the notion of *endless signifiers.* Residents create their own avatars and objects that can be meaningful only for themselves. Meanings and significance are thus in constant flux.

Fragmentation

In metaverses, a resident is a human subject who has *a divided self.* Metaverses are places where residents can choose identities that are different from their identities in real life. They can also choose many avatars. They are free from seeking or conforming to one sense or experience of being, and free to act through chosen identities. They are experimenting in chosen "schizophrenia" for a purely hedonistic purpose. So, metaverses are universes where *terms such as "authentic self" and "centered connections" are questionable.* In addition, with the anonymity allowed by metaverses, residents are not required to join or *to commit to any central theme.*

Reversal of Production and Consumption

The abandonment of the notion that production creates value while consumption destroys it is not only present in metaverses but is also the success factor of this experiential consumption. Residents are active producers of the consumption experience. Indeed, the enthusiasm for metaverses could be attributed to the possibility of creation and bricolage offered to residents to design their own characters, objects, histories, and environments. Consumers are also involved in evaluating and improving the products they consume. For example, some residents are selected to verify and test out beta versions before the final launch on the market. Web sites designed by players in order to discuss and debate technical problems also reflect a desire for a co-production by consumers. Residents are engaged in a double evaluation: they evaluate resident and administrator behaviors and criticize the errors and inconsistencies of metaverses.

Decentered Subject

Unlike in the real world, in virtual worlds humans are subjects that are built and subjects that build their selves. Given the evolutionary dynamic of the definition of self and the existence of multiple selves that can be contradictory for one subject, we as humans assist in a destabilization of the traditional notion of self. For example, in metaverses there is a questioning of the notion of gender. Indeed, a resident can choose an avatar with a gender that is similar or different from his real gender (Taylor 2003b). One can also choose an avatar without obvious gender since one can be an animal, an imaginary being like an elf or dragon, or even an object like a flying piano or a ball. "You can be male, you can be female, you can be neither by creating or choosing an avatar that's gender-neutral . . ." Rymaszewski et al. (2007). We can say that from a postmodern point of view, there is a rejection of modernist subject as a male subject in metaverses.

Juxtaposition of Opposites

The postmodern consumption thought considers that consumption experiences are not meant to reconcile differences and paradoxes but allow them to exist freely. In the same vein, metaverses are places where millions of residents coming from different countries, religions, and cultures, belonging to different social layers and having different intellectual levels, meet. It is a form of tolerance for juxtaposition of anything with anything else. In other worlds, instead of seeing consumers belonging to one group consuming the same thing, fragmentation becomes the basis of consumption.

Figure 2.1 **Dynamics of the Animation of Synthetic Identity in Metaverses**

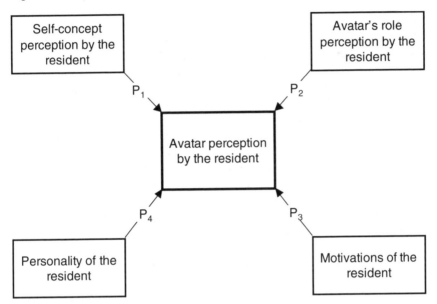

Despite the phenomenal growth of this industry and the craze for this contemporary experiential consumption, metaverses have not yet received attention from researchers in consumer psychology and behavior. Few researchers in the marketing field have considered the richness of the metaverse experience as a new phenomenon to explore.

THE STUDY OF AVATARS TO EXPLORE EXPERIENTIAL CONSUMPTION IN THE METAVERSE

As we see above, the subject remains at the heart of postmodern thinking. We can consider that the exploration of the avatar will be a good way to reach a better understanding of metaverses as experiential consumption. Indeed, identity considerations have taken an important place in existing works on virtual environments. Their contributions are significant but do not provide explanations about how consumers choose avatars and the way players or residents evolve them in the persistent world. Relying on the contributions of existing works and using robust theories in psychology and social psychology such as self-concept theory, role theory, motivation theory, and personality theory, this program of research will permit reaching a better understanding of the identity considerations in virtual worlds and the dynamics of the animation of these synthetic identities. The conceptual framework is summarized in Figure 2.1.

Avatar as a Manifestation of Self-Concept

The self-concept is not an objective view of what we are but a reflection of ourselves as we perceive ourselves. Metaverses allow consumers to be free from premises, real bodies, and real statutes. Disincarnated from their real selves, players and residents choose fantasized synthetic selves. Theses identities are reflexive and are redesigned in terms of interaction with others. However, no research has explained what kind of fantasized self-individual consumers want to express through their choices.

For Malhotra (1988), the self-concept is a multidimensional construct with three components: the ideal self (*the person as I would ideally like to be*), the real self (*the person that I believe I am actually*), and the social self (*the person as I believe others see me*). Each of these components has been studied differently depending on the approaches adopted by researchers and scholars. In this research program we consider these three components in order to explore the avatar as a manifestation of the self-concept of player or resident in metaverses. Thus we try to study the animation of the avatar fantasized by the consumer and its degree of congruence with the ideal, real, or social self-concept.

Moreover, several researchers in the consumer behavior field have considered that consumers choose their consumption in congruence with their ideal, real, or social self-concept (Belch 1977; Ekinci and Riley 2003; Graeff 1996; Grubb and Hupp 1968; Hamm and Cundiff 1969; Zinkhan and Hong 1995; Kleine, Kleine, and Allen 1995; Landon 1974; Richins 1994; Ross 1971; Sirgy 1985; Zouaghi and Darpy 2003). We can view the avatar as a virtual identity that players or residents choose to communicate an ideal, real, or social self-concept in the metaverse. This analysis leads us to formulate the first research proposition:

P$_1$: In metaverses, the avatar is a form of expression of the self-concept that the consumer chooses in congruence with his or her ideal, real, and/or social self.

Avatar as an Attributed Role

In his book *Mind, Self and Society,* Mead (1963) considers the self as the role that everyone has to play in a social situation. A rich understanding of the intervention of the self-concept of consumers in the way in which they led their avatar in metaverses also requires consideration of the role that the consumers choose to play in this parallel life experience. Furthermore, it would be simplistic not to appeal to the theory of the role for understanding the dynamics of the animation of the avatar by the consumer in role-playing spaces such as metaverses. Indeed, Castronova (2005) believes that the popularity of synthetic worlds comes mainly from role-play. Therefore, role theory will serve as a second conceptual pillar in this research in order to understand the way consumers choose and animate their avatars in metaverses.

The three founders of role theory are Mead, Moreno, and Linton. This concept has been very popular, but the notion of the role has evolved gradually in several social sciences. Therefore, some developments have taken place while others have been ignored or violated. Thus, Biddle (1986) traces the existence of five different perspectives of role theory: functional (Linton 1936), interactionist (Mead 1934), structural (Burt 1982; Mandel 1983; White et al. 1976), organizational (Gross et al. 1958; Khan et al. 1964), and cognitive (Moreno 1934). However, it should be noted that there is no general theory of role. The interactionist approach will be considered as a theoretical foundation for the second research proposition. Turkle (1995) and Boudreau (2005) show that an avatar is an expression of a reflexive and a scalable self. This malleability and reflexivity presents a second common point with the interactionist notion of role. Metaverses are favorable to constructing a fluid self and residents continuously remodel their avatars in response to interactions with others. In the same vein, interactionist role theorists consider the enactment of role as a reflexive and evolutionary process (Sarbin and Allen 1968). By choosing an avatar, the consumer takes a role in the metaverse; exploring how the consumer perceives the role he was assigned in the metaverse could enrich our understanding of his choices related to avatars.

P$_2$: In metaverses, the avatar is a reflection of the role that the consumer chooses to enact in the virtual world.

Avatar as a Reflection of Motivations

The concept of motivation lies at the heart of the study of consumer psychology and behavior. Existing works on this concept are very rich but disparate. Some consider motivations, others needs, desires, reasons, or values. Despite the lack of consensus on this concept, some researchers like Fennel (1975), Sheth (1976), and Hanna (1980) have attempted to draw up specific types of motivations in the consumer field. In virtual environments, several researchers were interested in studying the motivations of the players. As shown below, a review of existing works examining online games shows that the motivations of play (relationship, immersion, exploration, leadership, accomplishment, etc.) have been the subject of much research in a variety of disciplines; for example Bartle (1996), Yee (2002a), Taylor (2003a), Lucas and Sherry (2004), Seay et al. (2004), Alix (2005), Iversen (2005), and Kellar, Watters, and Duffy (2005). The common objective of these works was to develop a typology of motivational profiles. For the consumer field, these profiles are major contributions in terms of segmentation criteria.

This research aims at a deeper understanding of consumer avatar choice according to the consumer's motivations. Thus, in seeking to build relationships, to immerse in the virtual world, to manipulate others, to accomplish or to exercise leadership, consumers choose avatars that are best suited to meet their motivations. The third research proposition will be to discover the extent to which the avatar chosen by the consumer in metaverses is a reflection of his motivations.

P$_3$: In metaverses, the avatar chosen by the consumer is a reflection of his or her motivations.

Avatar as a Reflection of Personality

In psychology, there are several studies and theories of personality. Ryckman (2004) has identified five perspectives: psychoanalytic (Freud, Jung, Adler, Horney, Erikson, Kohut), traits (Allport, Castell, Eysenck), cognitive (Kelly), humanist and existential (Maslow, Rogers, May), and social and behaviorist (Skinner, Rotter, Bandura). In addition, relying on the link that may exist between the behavior of the individual and his or her personality, several researchers in consumption have appealed to some of the above-mentioned theories to understand consumer behavior (Horney 1945; Goldsmith and Hofacker 1991; Richins and Dawson 1992; Shimp and Sharma 1987; Rokeach 1960).

In the field of online games, Yee (1999) is the only author who sought to establish a link between the personality of the player and his or her motivations in MMORPGs (massively multiplayer online role-playing games), setting up the personality profiles of players. His model groups the personality traits into five dimensions: extraversion, agreeableness, consciousness, emotional stability, and openness. We can consider the notion of personality to enrich our understanding of the avatar choice process in metaverses. In other words, as open-minded, kind, or dominant, the consumer would choose an avatar that is consistent with his or her personality. The fourth research proposition is therefore to consider the extent to which the consumer's choice of identity in the metaverse is a reflection of his personality.

P$_4$: In metaverses, the avatar chosen by the consumer would be a reflection of his or her personality traits.

Methodological Approaches

Empirical studies with metaverses must be conducted in order to validate the consistency of these propositions. For this purpose, the synthetic world *Second Life* can be considered as a relevant platform. Created in 2003 by Linden Lab in San Francisco, *Second Life* is a metaphysical world where consumers choose an avatar to lead a life in a parallel persistent world. According to the *Second Life* website, the synthetic world currently has over 15 million visitors around the globe with an average session of 30,000 residents. It derives its popularity from the freedom offered to consumers in terms of creation of avatars and objects.

Its second advantage over other simple MMOGs lies in the fact that the access to this synthetic world is free. However, in order to create, consumers must buy or win Lindens (*Second Life* currency). In addition to entertainment, the world becomes a true synthetic market where all creations can be sold, bought, leased, and traded. The number of subscribers has grown so phenomenally that companies like Telus, IBM, Toyota, American Apparel, Wells Fargo Bank, BBC, Harvard, and College Lassalle use it to publicize their products and services, or provide a meeting and entertainment place for their staff. For this research program, *Second Life* presents two particularities.

The Avatar

Unlike other MMOGs, where the consumer is limited by a variety of characteristics (race, class, and profession) predefined by the edition company, the choice of the avatar in *Second Life* is absolutely free. This freedom does not limit consumers to select predefined aspects with existing symbolic meaning that can influence the choice itself. In addition, in the majority of MMOGs, the theme of the game determines the nature of the experience. Thus, in the game *The World of Warcraft,* avatars are all creations inspired by the medieval fantasy, like elves and gnomes. In contrast, in the game *The Sims,* avatars are only humans. *Second Life* provides the opportunity for consumers to freely choose the nature of their avatars, which can be human, fantastic, or a combination of the two. In addition, the *Second Life* avatar can be changed at any time without difficulty. It therefore can be seen as the fruit of the consumer's pure imagination.

The Community

With more than 15 million visitors, *Second Life* is among the most famous and popular metaverses. The size of the community is important in terms of empirical investigative work. When the community is large, it is easier to reach consumers and collect data. The importance of community size also reflects the frequency of exchanges between residents and the richness and relevance of the data available. Concerning the methodology, given the dynamic, reflexive, and evolving nature of the concept of an avatar and the psychological factors considered (self-concept, role concept, motivation, and personality), it would be more appropriate to consider a qualitative and longitudinal method. The *netnography* will be a relevant approach. In netnography for Kozinets (1997, 1998, 1999, 2001, 2002) and *virtual ethnography* for Hine (2000) and Williams (2007), the participant observation of online communities has emerged as an adaptation of traditional ethnography to the context of Internet and virtual worlds. In addition to observation and immersion in the game, the observation of blogs on *Second Life* will be an additional source of data. Online focus groups also can serve as a complementary method (Stewart and Williams 2005).

CONCLUSION

Given the lack of academic research and studies dealing with metaverses, the research program laid out here can constitute a starting point to explore this new consumption phenomenon. The research propositions defined for this program were founded particularly on the contributions of existing works dealing with online and video games. This research program gathers in one single integrative framework four psychological elements participating in the resident's choice of an avatar and refers to robust theories in social psychology to study an increasingly important phenomenon of consumption. Also, in an industry characterized by fierce competition, a better understanding of metaverses as sites of experiential consumption would allow edition companies a deeper understanding of market needs. Publishers and those choosing to integrate synthetic worlds by placing their products and brands in the metaverses must be equipped to offer consumers an experience of extreme immersion. For this, they need a useful framework to illuminate their decisions in the light of targeted psychological segments. This research program is merely one simple step toward the exploration of metaverses as consumer experiences. Further work must be carried out according to different perspectives in order to study this new type of consumption.

NOTE

1. "Players" for MMOGs and "residents" for synthetic worlds.

REFERENCES

Alix, Avery. 2005. "Beyond P-1: Who Plays Online?" In *Changing Views: Worlds in Play.* Proceedings of the Digital Games Research Association 2005 meeting, Vancouver, June 16–20.

Arsenault, Dominic. 2005. "Abstract of Dynamic Range: When Game Design and Narratives Unite." In *Changing Views: Worlds in Play.* Proceedings of the Digital Games Research Association 2005 meeting, Vancouver, June 16–20.

Bartle, Richard. 1996. "Hearts, Clubs, Diamonds, Spades: Players Who Suit MUDs." *Journal of Online Environments* 1(1).

———. 2004. *Designing Virtual Worlds.* Indianapolis: New Riders.

Belch, George E. 1977. "Beliefs Systems and Differential Role of the Self Concept." *Advances in Consumer Research* 5: 320–323.

Berry, Vincent, and Gilles Brougère. 2002. "Jeu et communautés virtuelles sur Internet." Actes des journées d'étude: Internet, jeu et socialisation. Paris: 5–6 (December).

Biddle, Bruce J. 1986. "Recent Development in Role Theory." *Annual Reviews of Sociology* 12: 67–92.

Boudreau, Kelly. 2005. "Role Theory: The Line Between Roles as Design and Socialization in Everquest." In *Changing Views: Worlds in Play.* Proceedings of the Digital Games Research Association 2005 meeting, Vancouver, June 16–20.

Brand, Jeffrey E., and Scott J. Knight. 2005. "The Narrative and Ludic Nexus in Computer Games: Diverse Worlds Ii." In *Changing Views: Worlds in Play.* Proceedings of the Digital Games Research Association 2005 meeting, Vancouver, June 16–20.

Burt, Ronald. S. 1982. *Toward a Structural Theory of Action: Network Models of Social Structure, Perception, and Action.* New York: Academic.

Carr, Diane. 2005. "Contexts, Pleasures and Preferences: Girls Playing Computer Games." In *Changing Views: Worlds in Play.* Proceedings of the Digital Games Research Association 2005 meeting, Vancouver, June 16–20.

Castronova, Edward. 2004. "The Price of Bodies: A Hedonic Pricing Model of Avatar Attributes in a Synthetic World." *Kyklos* 57 (2):173–196.

———. 2005. *Synthetic Worlds: The Business and Culture of Online Games.* Chicago: University of Chicago Press.

Craipeau, Sylvie. 2002 "Internet vers une rationalisation des jeux et de la sociabilité." Actes des journées d'étude: Internet, jeu et socialisation. Paris: 5–6 (December).

Ducheneaut, Nicolas, and Robert Moore. 2004. "The Social Side of Gaming: A Study of Interaction Patterns in a Massively Multiplayer Online Game." Conference on Computer Supported Cooperative Work, Workshop on Representation of Digital Identities, Chicago: 6–10 (November).

Ekinci, Y., and M. Riley. 2003. "An Investigation of Self-Concept: Actual and Ideal Self-Congruence Compared in the Context of Service Evaluation." *Journal of Retailing and Consumer Services* 10 (4): 201–214.

Eriksson, Anders, and Kalle Grill. 2005. "Who Owns My Avatar? Rights in Virtual Property." In *Changing Views: Worlds in Play.* Proceedings of the Digital Games Research Association 2005 meeting, Vancouver, June 16–20.

Ermi, Laura, and Frans Mäyrä. 2005. "Fundamental Components of the Gameplay Experience: Analysing Immersion." In *Changing Views: Worlds in Play.* Proceedings of the Digital Games Research Association 2005 meeting, Vancouver, June 16–20.

Esposito, Nicolas. 2005. "Immersion in Game Atmospheres for the Video Game Heritage Preservation." In *Changing Views: Worlds in Play.* Proceedings of the Digital Games Research Association 2005 meeting, Vancouver, June 16–20.

Fennel, G. 1975. "Motivation Research Revisited." *Journal of Advertising Research* 15: 23–28.

Firat, Fuat A., and Alladi Venkatesh. 1995. "Liberatory Postmodernism and the Reenchantment of Consumption." *Journal of Consumer Research* 22: 239–267.

Goldsmith, Ronald E., and Charles F. Hofacker. 1991. "Measuring Consumer Innovativeness." *Journal of the Academy of Marketing Science* 19 (3): 209–221.

Gomes, Renata. 2005. "The Design of Narrative as an Immersive Simulation." In *Changing Views: Worlds in Play.* Proceedings of the Digital Games Research Association 2005 meeting, Vancouver, June 16–20.

Graeff, Timothy R. 1996. "Using Promotional Messages to Manage the Effects of Brand and Self-Image on Brand Evaluations." *Journal of Consumer Marketing* 13 (3): 4–18.

Gross, Neal., Ward S. Mason, and Alexander. W. McEachem. 1958. *Explorations in Role Analysis: Studies in the School Superintendency Role.* New York: Wiley.

Grubb, Edward L., and Gregg Hupp. 1968. "Perception of Self, Generalized Stereotypes, and Brand Selection." *Journal of Marketing Research* 5 (1): 58–63.

Haize, Jean François, and Nathalie Pican. 2003. "Le réseau comme terrain de jeux." In *Les jeux en ligne,* ed. Nicolas Auray and Sylvie Craipeau. Paris: Lavoisier.

Hamm, B. Curtis, and Edward Cundiff. 1969. "Self-Actualisation and Product Perception." *Journal of Marketing Research* 6 (4): 470–472.

Hanna, G.L. 1980. "A Typology of Consumer Needs." *Research in Marketing* 3: 83–104.

Heliö, Satu. 2005. "Simulating the Storytelling Qualities of Life: Telling Stories with the Sims." In *Changing Views: Worlds in Play.* Proceedings of the Digital Games Research Association 2005 meeting, Vancouver, June 16–20.

Hine, Christine M. 2000. *Virtual Ethnography.* London: Sage.

Horney, Karen. 1945. *Our Inner Conflicts.* New York: Northon.

Iversen, Sara Mosberg. 2005. "Challenge Balance and Diversity: Playing the Sims and the Sims 2." In *Changing Views: Worlds in Play.* Proceedings of the Digital Games Research Association 2005 meeting, Vancouver, June 16–20.

Jaulin, Régis. 2002. "Anarchie en ligne." Actes des journées d'étude: Internet, jeu et socialisation. Paris: 5–6 (December).

Jenson, Jennifer, and Suzanne Castell. 2005. "Her Own Boss: Gender and the Pursuit of Incompetent Play." In *Changing Views: Worlds in Play.* Proceedings of the Digital Games Research Association 2005 meeting, Vancouver, June 16–20.

Kahn, Robert. L., Wolfe, D. M., Quinn, R. P., Shock, J., Rosenthal, R. A. 1964. *Organizational Stress: Studies in Role Conflict and Ambiguity.* New York: Wiley.

Kellar, Melanie, Carolyn Watters, and Jack Duffy. 2005. "Motivational Factors in Game Play in Two User Groups." In *Changing Views: Worlds in Play.* Proceedings of the Digital Games Research Association 2005 meeting, Vancouver, June 16–20.

Kleine, Susan Schultz, Robert E. Kleine III, and Chris T. Allen. 1995. "How Is a Possession 'Me' or 'Not Me'? Characterizing Types and an Antecedent of Material Possession Attachment." *Journal of Consumer Research* 22 (3): 327–343.

Kozinets, Robert V. 1997. "'I Want To Believe': A Netnography of The X-Philes' Subculture of Consumption." *Advances in Consumer Research* 24 (1): 470–475.

———. 1998. "On Netnography: Initial Reflections on Consumer Research Investigations of Cyberculture." *Advances in Consumer Research* 25: 366–371.

———. 1999. "E-tribalized Marketing? The Strategic Implications of Virtual Communities of Consumption." *European Management Journal* 17 (3): 252–264.

———. 2001. "Utopian Enterprise: Articulating the Meanings of Star Trek's Culture of Consumption." *Journal of Consumer Research* 28 (1): 67–88.

———. 2002. "The Field Behind the Screen: Using Netnography for Marketing Research in Online Communities." *Journal of Marketing Research* 39 (1): 61–72.

Landon, Laird E. 1974. "Self Concept, Ideal Self Concept, and Consumer Purchase Intentions." *Journal of Consumer Research* 1 (2): 44–51.

Lankoski, Petri. 2005. "Building and Reconstructing Character. A Case Study of Silent Hill 3." In *Changing Views: Worlds in Play.* Proceedings of the Digital Games Research Association 2005 meeting, Vancouver, June 16–20.

Largier, Alexandre. 2003. "La guilde dorée. Une organisation de jueurs en ligne." In *Les jeux en ligne,* ed. Nicolas Auray and Sylvie Craipeau. Paris: Lavoisier.

Lin, Holin, and Chuen-Tsai Sun. 2005. "The 'White-Eyed' Player Culture: Grief Play and Construction of Deviance in MMORPGs." In *Changing Views: Worlds in Play.* Proceedings of the Digital Games Research Association 2005 meeting, Vancouver, June 16–20.

Linton, Ralph. 1936. *The Study of Man.* New York: Appleton Century.

Løvlie, Anders Sundnes. 2005. "End of Story? Quest, Narrative and Enactment in Computer Games." In *Changing Views: Worlds in Play.* Proceedings of the Digital Games Research Association 2005 meeting, Vancouver, June 16–20.

Lucas, Kristen, and John L. Sherry. 2004. "Sex Differences in Video Game Play: A Communication-based Explanation." *Communication Research* 31 (5): 499–523.

Malhotra, Naresh K. 1988. "Self Concept and Product Choice an Integrated Perspective." *Journal of Economic Psychology* 9: 1–28.

Mandel, Michael. J. 1983. "Local roles and social networks." *American Sociology Review* 48: 376–86.

Mateas, Michael, and Andrew Stern. 2005. "Build It to Understand It: Ludology Meets Narratology in Game Design Space." In *Changing Views: Worlds in Play.* Proceedings of the Digital Games Research Association 2005 meeting, Vancouver, June 16–20.

Mead, George. H. 1934. *Mind, Self and Society.* Chicago: University. Chicago Press.
———. 1963. *L'esprit, le soi et la société.* Paris: Presses Universitaires de France.
Moreno, Jacob L. 1934. *Who Shall Survive?* Washington, DC: Nervous and Mental Disease Publishing Company.
Myers, David. 2005. "Hide: The Aesthetics of Group and Solo Play." In *Changing Views: Worlds in Play.* Proceedings of the Digital Games Research Association 2005 meeting, Vancouver, June 16–20.
Pargman, Daniel, and Andreas Eriksson. 2005. "Law, Order and Conflicts of Interest in Massively Multiplayer Online Games." In *Changing Views: Worlds in Play.* Proceedings of the Digital Games Research Association 2005 meeting, Vancouver, June 16–20.
Richins, Marsha L. 1994. "Valuing Things: The Public and Private Meanings of Possessions." *Journal of Consumer Research* 21 (3): 504–521.
Richins, Marsha, and Scott Dawson. 1992. "A Consumer Values Orientation for Materialism and Its Measurement: Scale Development and Validation." *Journal of Consumer Research* 12: 265–280.
Rokeach, Milton. 1960. *The Open and Closed Mind.* New York: Basic Books.
Ross, Ivan. 1971. "Self-Concept and Brand Preference." *Journal of Business* 44 (1): 38–50.
Roustan, Mélanie. 2002. "La pratique du jeu vidéo-anthropologie d'une technique du corps comme technique de soi." Actes des journées d'étude: Internet, jeu et socialisation. Paris: 5–6 (December).
Ryckman, Richard M. 2004. *Theories of Personality.* 8th ed. Belmont, CA: Thomson/ Wadsworth.
Rymaszewski, M., W.J. Au, C. Ondrejka, and R. Patel. 2007. *Second Life: The Official Guide.* Hoboken, NJ: Wiley.
Salazar, Javier. 2005. "On the Ontology of MMORPG Beings: A Theoretical Model for Research." In *Changing Views: Worlds in Play.* Proceedings of the Digital Games Research Association 2005 meeting, Vancouver, June 16–20.
Sarbin, Theodore R., and Vernon L. Allen. 1968. "Role Theory." In *The Handbook of Social Psychology,* ed. Lindzey Gardner and Elliot Aronson. 2d ed. Reading, MA: Addison-Wesley.
Seay, Fleming, William Jerome, Kevin Sang Lee, and Robert Kraut. 2004. "Project Massive: A Study of Online Gaming Communities." Conference on Human Factors in Computing Systems, Vienna: 24–29 (April).
Seys, Bertrand. 2002. "Place et rôle des usages des tic dans la souffrance psychologique." Actes des journées d'étude: Internet, jeu et socialisation. Paris: 5–6 (December).
Sheth, J.N. 1976. "A Psychological Model of Travel Mode Selection." *Advances in Consumer Research* 3 (1): 425–430.
Shimp, Terence, and Subhash Sharma. 1987. "Consumer Ethnocentrism: Construction and Validation of the Cetscale." *Journal of Marketing Research* 24: 280–289.
Shulga, Tatiana. 2003. "Présence médiatisée et construction de l'espace d'interaction: Comparaison entre jeux de rôles classiques et MMORPG." In *Les jeux en ligne,* ed. Nicolas Auray and Sylvie Craipeau. Paris: Lavoisier.
Sirgy, Joseph M. 1985. "Using Self-Congruity and Ideal Congruity to Predict Purchase Motivation." *Journal of Business Research* 13: 195–206.
Smith, Jonas Heide. 2005. "The Problem of Other Players: In-Game Cooperation as Collective Action." In *Changing Views: Worlds in Play.* Proceedings of the Digital Games Research Association 2005 meeting, Vancouver, June 16–20.
Stewart, Kate, and Matthew Williams. 2005. "Researching Online Populations: The Use of Online Focus Groups for Social Research." *Qualitative Research* 5 (4): 395–416.

Tavares, José Pedro, Rui Gil, and Licinio Roque. 2005. "Player as Author: Conjecturing Online Game Creation Modalities and Infrastructure." In *Changing Views: Worlds in Play.* Proceedings of the Digital Games Research Association 2005 meeting, Vancouver, June 16–20.

Taylor, T.L. 2003a. "Power Gamers Just Want to Have Fun? Instrumental Play in a MMOG." Level Up Games Conference Proceedings, Utrecht.

———. 2003b. "Multiple Pleasures: Women and Online Gaming," *Convergence* 9 (1): 21–46.

Trappey, Charles, Claire Chang, Teng-Tai Hsiao, Tien-Chun Chang, Ming-Hung Che, and Wei-Jie Chiu. 2005. "Consumer Driven Computer Game Design." In *Changing Views: Worlds in Play.* Proceedings of the Digital Games Research Association 2005 meeting, Vancouver, June 16–20.

Turkle, Sherry. 1995. *Life on the Screen: Identity in the Age of the Internet.* New York: Simon & Schuster.

Warnes, Christopher. 2005. "Baldur's Gate and History: Race and Alignment in Digital Role Playing Games." In *Changing Views: Worlds in Play.* Proceedings of the Digital Games Research Association 2005 meeting, Vancouver, June 16–20.

Whang, Leo Sang-Min, and Jee Yeon Kim. 2005. "The Comparison of Online Game Experiences by Players in Games of Lineage and Everquest: Role Play vs. Consumption." In *Changing Views: Worlds in Play.* Proceedings of the Digital Games Research Association 2005 meeting, Vancouver, June 16–20.

White, Harrison. C., Scott A. Boorman, and Ronald L. Brieger. 1976. "Social structure from multiple networks: I. Blockmodels of roles and positions." *American Journal of Sociology* 81:730–80.

Williams, Matthew. 2007. "Avatar Watching: Participant Observation in Graphical Online Environments." *Qualitative Research* 7 (1): 5–24.

Yee, Nick. 1999. "Through the Looking Glass: An Exploration of the Interplay Between Player and Character Selves in Role Playing Games." Available at www.nickyee.com/rpg/quesres.html.

———. 2001. "The Norrathian Scrolls: A Study of Everquest." Available at www.nickyee.com/eqt/home.html.

———. 2002a. "Facets: 5 Motivation Factors for Why People Play MMORPGs." Available at www.nickyee.com/facets/home.html.

———. 2002b. "Befriending Ogres and Wood-Elves: Understanding Relationship Formation in MMORPGs." Available at www.nickyee.com/hub/relationships/home.html.

———. 2002c. "Mosaic: Stories of Digital Lives and Identities." Available at www.nickyee.com/mosaic/home.html.

———. 2006. "The Psychology of Massively Multi-User Online Role-Playing Games: Motivations, Emotional Investment, Relationships and Problematic Usage." In *Avatars at Work and Play: Collaboration and Interaction in Shared Virtual Environments,* ed. R. Schroeder and A.-S. Axelsson. Dordrecht: Springer.

Young, Brian-Mitchell. 2005. "Gaming Mind, Gaming Body: The Mind/Body Split For a New Era." In *Changing Views: Worlds in Play.* Proceedings of the Digital Games Research Association 2005 meeting, Vancouver, June 16–20.

Zinkhan, George M., and Jae W. Hong. 1995. "Self-Concept and Advertising Effectiveness: The Influence of Congruency, Conspicuousness, and Response Mode." *Psychology and Marketing* 12 (1): 53–77.

Zouaghi, Sondes, and Denis Darpy. 2003. "Du soi au groupe: naissance du concept du nous et exploration d'une échelle de mesure du nous idéal." *Recherche et applications en marketing* 18 (4): 3–22.

PART II

CONSUMER BEHAVIOR IN VIRTUAL WORLDS

CHAPTER 3

Interaction Seeking in *Second Life* and Implications for Consumer Behavior

CHRISTIAN HINSCH AND PETER H. BLOCH

Psychologists have long argued that humans have a basic urge to interact with each other. For example, Maslow (1948), McClelland (1982), Baumeister and Leary (1995), and Deci and Ryan (2000) all place belongingness and social contact as preeminent individual needs in their theories of motivation. In modern industrialized nations, it is increasingly difficult to satisfy this basic need, and despite relentless population growth and rampant urbanization, many people today feel a genuine sense of isolation. We are less likely to know our neighbors than in past generations and the religious and social organizations that once dominated society now play a much smaller role. Labor force mobility has increased the distance between family members while our automotive/commuter culture has further magnified feelings of isolation. Many of us back out of our driveways, close the garage door, and drive to work without any social interaction. Retail outlets have also become less useful as sources of social connections as they increasingly employ self-service concepts and Internet retailing (Weitz 2006). The increasing degree of isolation that people face in our society has created a demand for products that facilitate social interaction to replace what has been lost as society has evolved (O'Guinn and Muñiz 2005).

Given these societal changes, it is not surprising that marketers have stepped forward with products designed to meet the increasing demand for social interaction. In particular, Internet services have become a primary new venue for social connections with innovations such as blogs, listservs, dating sites, networked multiplayer video games, and social networking sites. This chapter will focus on one of these Internet services, a phenomenon called *Second Life,* and attempt to explain why people are turning to *Second Life* in a search for social interaction. We will discuss the nature of *Second Life* and position it in the context of other

Figure 3.1 **The World of *Second Life* as an Opportunity for Analysis**

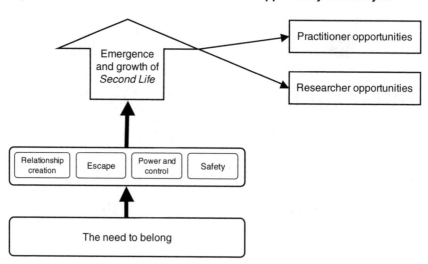

socially focused Internet options, and we will explore some of the factors that are drawing users to the *Second Life* medium. Finally, this chapter will address the implications that *Second Life* holds for marketing practitioners as well as consumer behavior researchers. *Second Life* allows marketers to create product-focused experiences and promotional placements within a thriving virtual marketplace. The virtual world of *Second Life* also offers researchers the opportunity to study the "want" element of consumption isolated from the "need" element based in practical constraints, societal norms, and felt responsibilities. Because *Second Life* management has not erected barriers to in-world research, the medium is wide open for future development and testing by both academics and practitioners (Hemp 2006). See Figure 3.1 for a visual representation of the framework for this chapter.

THE WORLD OF *SECOND LIFE*

Second Life is a prime example of virtual world or a computer-simulated environment. In *Second Life,* users operate in a simulated world via graphical representations of humans called avatars. The term *avatar* is derived from a Sanskrit word used to describe the presence of a god on earth (Holzwarth, Janiszewski, and Neumann 2006). In many religions, it is believed that a human does not have the ability to perceive a god directly and survive. When a human interacts with a god it is not with the god itself, but rather with a likeness that is representative of the actual god. The avatar in a virtual world follows a similar model. The individuals are not interacting in a physical space, but their agents (avatars) interact in the virtual world. The theory of social response states that people will treat computers as social actors even when they know that they are dealing with machines that do not have feelings or human motivations (Moon 2000). Recent advances in virtual world technology can blur the line between human and nonhuman interaction (Nowak and Biocca 2003). As people respond socially to machine-generated actions in the cyberspace, the blurring of the line between the real and virtual worlds may explain how virtual worlds have become viable markets for social interaction.

The virtual world phenomenon is independent of the geographical arrangement of its residents. According to the *Second Life* website, the highest percentage of residents comes from the United States, but this figure is only 27 percent. The only requirements for participation in the virtual world seem to be a computer with the requisite hardware, a broadband connection, and a reasonable grasp of the English language. Unlike video gamer demographics, *Second Life* is more gender equal, with females comprising 42 percent of the residents (Seryte and Storgaard 2007).

Second Life **as a Cultural Phenomenon**

The growing impact of *Second Life* is evidenced by its visibility in diverse aspects of society. Colleges are offering seminars in *Second Life* while politicians are holding press conferences in the virtual setting (Rubin 2007). Companies like KPMG and Kelly Services are using the virtual world to recruit real-world employees, and others like CNN, Nike, Anheuser-Busch, Levi Strauss, McDonalds, and Coke all have some level of marketing presence in the virtual world (Rubin 2007; Hemp 2006). In one week, *Second Life* made appearances on two primetime television shows. It was the focus of an episode of "CSI: New York," a highly rated CBS prime-time drama, in which a detective chased a real-life killer through the virtual world. Later that week, *Second Life* was the focus of a comedy bit on NBC's hit comedy "The Office."

Second Life is not a video game because it lacks the need to act, and it is more than a social networking site because it is not based on any particular reality. As the name implies, *Second Life* offers individuals an alternative to existing solely in the real world. The *Second Life* world allows residents to build an alternate identity and lifestyle while exploring a complex and engaging environment. Most importantly, it allows participants to socialize with other residents. Several aspects of the more traditional social networking sites, such as a "friend" function and group membership, can be found on the *Second Life* platform. Business has been booming in the *Second Life* world as both the number of users and the amount of time spent "in world" have been growing quickly (see Figures 3.2 and 3.3). In April of 2008, the virtual world of *Second Life* boasted over 13 million users and the site hosts between 25,000 and 50,000 users online at any one time.

Castronova (2001) states that virtual worlds have three defining features:

Figure 3.2 *Second Life* **User Hours**

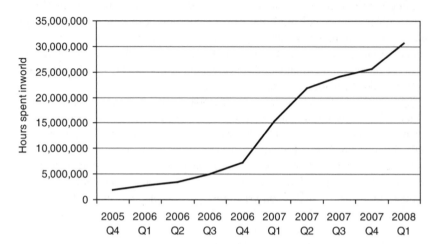

interactivity, physicality, and persistence. Interactivity refers to the ability of an individual to access the world remotely and for the individual's actions to impact the actions of other individuals within the world. Physicality refers to the virtual world's representation of the physical laws of the real world (time, matter, gravity). While most physical laws exist in the virtual world, *Second Life* takes some allowances, as residents are able to fly and even teleport from place to place. The final component of persistence means that the virtual world continues to operate without regard to the presence of any given user. In addition, persistence facilitates exchange in the virtual world. That is, virtual versions of material goods can be owned and transferred from one participant to another.

Second Life users have considerable freedom in the design and creation of their personal avatar. A user may attempt to create a close representation of him- or herself in terms of appearance and demographic characteristics, or he/she may create an avatar that is quite different from the real-world self. Given its name, it is not surprising that a primary appeal of this virtual world is the opportunity to design an avatar based on an idealized or fantasy persona of the user. An avatar can be more beautiful, more powerful, younger, or of a different race or gender than the actual user. The avatar need not represent its creator's actual self. The preponderance of supermodel physiques in the virtual world can be seen as evidence that many avatars are built around the ideal self of the avatar's creator (Sirgy 1982). Recent research shows that individuals adjust their attitudes and behaviors based on the physical characteristics of their avatars (Yee and Bailenson 2007).

Figure 3.3 ***Second Life* Users by Quarter**

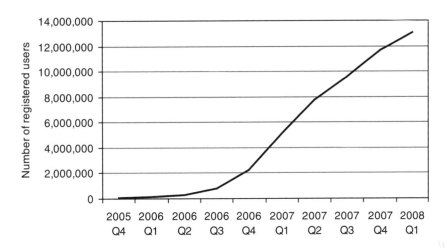

Second Life and Related Media

Second Life has several key differences from other online venues for social inter-action. Although video games have increasingly added multiplayer, interactive content, *Second Life* is far from a traditional video game. Games like *World of Warcraft* and *Everquest* use virtual worlds to create venues for social interaction. However, socializing in these worlds is secondary to in-game activities like slaying beasts or virtual combat. In these virtual worlds, the focus is on the game with a potential for social interaction, whereas *Second Life* is socially focused with some potential for gaming elements. There are gaming elements in some areas of *Second Life,* but the vast majority of the world is not devoted to gaming. A player in other virtual worlds must enter the game and usually show a certain level of game-related skill before he can use the game to socialize.

Social networking sites (SNS) such as MySpace and Facebook are also growing in significance, but are distinct from a world such as *Second Life* (Enders et al. 2008). The purpose of traditional social networking sites is to create and maintain relationships in the real world, and online interactions associated with these sites typically revolve around real-life interaction (Ellison, Steinfield, and Lampe 2007). In other words, these sites use technology for the creation and preservation of social capital by facilitating relationships among people (Coleman 1988). There are at least two forms of social capital, bridging and bonding (Putnam 2000). Bridging social capital is focused on broadening the self and including individuals who would be otherwise unrelated (Putnam 2000), and can be defined as loose connections between those who may provide useful information or new perspectives but stops short of offering active emotional support (Ellison, Steinfield, and Lampe 2007). Both SNS and *Second Life* can be seen as tools that enable users to create and maintain this loose form of social capital. The *Second Life* medium combines the role-playing and fantasy focus from MMORPGs (massively multiplayer online role-playing games) with the social focus that drives traditional social networking sites.

Why Inhabit *Second Life*?

People may turn to this form of online interaction in an effort to reduce the dissatisfaction associated with not meeting real-world interaction goals. As noted in the introduction to this chapter, it can be quite difficult to achieve one's desired level of social interaction in today's culture, and dissatisfaction with one's real-world interaction levels may be quite prevalent (Baumeister and Leary 1995). Turning to a virtual world for interaction could become an effective substitute and a way to satisfy ones goals in a different context. Interaction goals that are modified to include virtual social interaction provide individuals with a greater potential to successfully achieve their desired level of interaction.

An alternative explanation comes from social response theory and the increases in "presence" felt by residents of virtual communities. Earlier, we noted that social response theory predicts that humans may treat nonhuman actors as humans with respect to social situations. The term "presence" refers to the sense that an inhabitant feels that she is "there" or the degree to which she is immersed in the virtual world (Nowak and Biocca 2003). The goal of many virtual worlds has been to create an environment that is as realistic as possible and to offer an alternative to the "real world." For some, the avatars as agent concept and the degree of presence offered by new technologies may make the virtual world a viable substitute for real-world interaction. These individuals no longer make a distinction between a real-world interaction and an interaction in the virtual world. In a survey with almost 7,000 respondents, Yee (2006) found that players of *Everquest,* an MMORPG, were primarily motivated to play by the relationships formed in the game. Two other studies also found that social aspects constituted the predominate driving factor in the games that they studied (Kim et al. 2002; Vorderer, Hartmann, and Klimmt 2003). This view is consistent with the world of *Second Life,* where serious, long-term relationships are often formed (Hemp 2006). Marriages and adoptions are not uncommon in the virtual world, and many have led to real-world encounters. One study notes that after the closing of a virtual world, users mourned the loss of the world and the relationships that had been a significant part of their lives (Castronova 2001). Users see other players as residents of a shared space, and technology trends suggest that social interaction in online environments will only grow in importance (Castronova 2004; Hemp 2006). "A competition has arisen between Earth and the virtual worlds, and for many, Earth is the lesser option"(Castronova 2001 p. 9).

In the next section, we will outline four key drivers that are enticing individuals to seek interaction, belongingness, and social capital in the virtual world of *Second Life*.

WHY ENTER *SECOND LIFE*?

Ease of Relationship Creation

A new player exposed to *Second Life* for the first time may find that the most interesting part of the experience is that you don't need to do anything. There are no monsters to evade and there is no time urgency. If a new player considered *Second Life* to be a video game, s/he may be disappointed because the experience does not have a traditional driving force of beating the game. The initial impression after arriving in the virtual world is, "I am here, now what do I do?" The *Second Life* experience is so different from traditional games that it quickly becomes clear that social interaction is motivating people to inhabit this world.

Initial contact with another resident is quite simple, with no need for travel or appointments. However, such contacts still involve the uncertainty of a real-life meeting. A resident can simply move to within earshot of a player and say or text "Hello." If the other resident wishes to converse, s/he will respond, otherwise the communication attempt will simply be ignored. Rejection does still occur, but the intensity of the felt rejection is buffered by the mediation of the avatar as well as the mediation of the computer. The virtual world exists to facilitate social interaction, and social self-efficacy issues can be left in the real world. The virtual world of *Second Life* acts as an aggregator, bringing people together for the purpose of social interaction. The virtual world provides a location that is accessible from almost anywhere, and the opportunities for socializing are virtually limitless with tens of thousands of residents online at any one time.

Second Life acts as a ready marketplace for buyers and sellers of social capital. This market is particularly attractive to individuals who do not have convenient or inexpensive access to traditional forms of social capital generation. When a resident feels the need for a dose of interaction, s/he simply logs on and either initiates contact or explores the world and waits for someone else to initiate contact. When the need for interaction is satiated, the user simply logs off or moves on to explore other aspects of the virtual world. Both parties benefit from the transaction. The main function of the virtual world is to bring buyers and sellers (often identical) of social capital together. The unique properties of the virtual environment make interaction in the virtual world comparatively inexpensive, painless, and simple.

Escape

For centuries, people have used fiction, fantasy, and stories to escape from the unpleasant or mundane aspects of everyday life (Hemp 2006; Seryte and Storgaard 2007). The fast-paced nature of current age has created higher demands for escape, and technology has evolved to meet this demand (Mathwick and Rigdon 2004). As an individual becomes more involved in an escapist activity, s/he is often increasingly isolated from traditional sources of social capital generation such as a geographic community or other forms of group membership. This is not necessarily the case with virtual worlds. Involvement in virtual communities will likely increase the potential for social capital production while providing element of fantasy and escape.

Players can escape their problems through virtual worlds because others can only connect with them through their own virtual world avatar (Castronova 2004). Because there is no real-world interaction that is not authorized by the user, the virtual world allows for "audience segregation" between the two worlds (Goffman 1959, p. 49). A *Second Life* resident has the freedom to customize the self presented to the virtual world as well as his environment. A resident of this virtual world simply constructs an avatar with features that are desirable to the self and the larger community. This avatar can be entirely different from the user's real persona, allowing strong elements of fantasy and escape. In traditional social networking sites, users typically present a self that is an extension of a user's real-world life, and online interactions do not necessarily remove people from their offline world. Users of traditional SNSs that embellish or fabricate self-related information may feel disingenuous, and such deceptions are likely to be discovered as the user's network grows. In contrast, *Second Life* users are expected to be masquerading as something that is often quite different from their real-world persona. Thus, the potential for escape is much greater in *Second Life* than in other social networking sites.

A concept that is tightly woven into the fabric of escape is role playing. From the dawn of society, individual decisions and circumstances have forced people into roles that they may not wish to play and away from roles that they find desirable. Most people simply accept their lot and live their lives without focusing on achieving these lost desires. *Second Life* allows users to take on the role of their choice and escape from the enforced real-world situation. A resident of *Second Life* is free from the role requirements that include the very specific role-forbidden and role-required behaviors that combine to form a significant force in real life (Grayson 1999).

Goffman (1959) argued that life is essentially a performance designed to control our impressions on others. A great deal of effort usually goes into the self presented to other members of society. The true self is rarely expressed, as virtually all people have aspects of their personal or professional lives that are not congruent with their role performance. Self-expression is often a casualty of growing status and responsibility as a person is required to mold his/her image to real-world expectations. "All the world is not a stage, but the crucial ways in which it isn't are not easy to specify" (Goffman 1959, p. 72).

Virtual worlds present an outlet that is uniquely tailored to people who are not satisfied with the hand that life has dealt them. Within *Second Life*, the disabled individual can be without infirmity, the unattractive can have movie star beauty, and the underappreciated worker can have a glamorous profession. In terms of social identity theory, a user can tailor a new virtual image to that of any in-group, thus increasing opportunities for the creation of social capital (Brown 2000). A user can create an avatar with knowledge gained from real-life experience. Past decisions that are viewed negatively do not need to be repeated in *Second Life*. This is a new creation, a fresh start that is not dependent on the real world.

A large draw of role playing is the fact that people don't like the rules that society forces them to follow. Rules that are incongruent with a player's beliefs and desires are de-motivating to the point that a person may attempt to sabotage a situation or a particular authority if they disagree with rules that are imposed (Rhee and Sigler 2005). Some scholars believe that following rules can be intrinsically motivating, and that it can lead to a state of interaction competency that is rewarding to an individual (Grayson 1999). Cognitive dissonance theory suggests that rules are only motivating if they are congruent with a person's internal desires and needs (Aronson 1992). *Second Life* allows players to choose their role and thereby choose the set of rules that they will follow. Each avatar develops this social role based on his/her abilities and needs (Castronova 2001). The ability to play the role of one's choosing may reduce the cognitive dissonance that the resident feels in his/her real-life role (Aronson 1992). The role chosen by a *Second Life* user may be more in line with the resident's true goals and desires, resulting in a more pleasurable virtual world experience.

The users of *Second Life* and traditional SNSs may be seeking the same loose forms of social capital, but users are addressing two different audiences. Social self-efficacy issues and a lack of social interaction in real life may drive users to seek social capital in the virtual world of *Second Life*. Traditional social networking sites will be used to enhance the social experience of users who already have a social base that they would like to grow or maintain. Communication and interaction are the focal aspects of involvement in virtual worlds and residents build social capital through these activities. Many players choose to do this through *Second Life* roles that are different, even antithetical, to the roles with which they are yoked in real life.

Power and Control

Leisure researchers commonly point to desires for mastery and control as motivators of recreational choices (Beard and Ragheb 1983). The virtual world of *Second Life* delivers on this benefit by allowing residents to obtain levels of power and control that are unavailable in the real world. Outside of *Second Life*, nearly everyone is accountable to someone or something. In contrast, no driving-force element of *Second Life* is required, allowing feelings of power and control rarely available elsewhere. You live out the life that you choose to live and the attraction is obvious.

As noted above, a participant first has the opportunity to create and enhance an avatar in whatever image is desired. The player can decide exactly where the avatar goes and what it does. The avatar allows the player to project a type of self that may be repressed in the real world because it is incongruent with real-world responsibilities and expectations. The creator can fully control the avatar: its actions, exploration decisions, venturesomeness, demographic profile, consumption decisions, and appearance. This sense of freedom offers significant benefits to users and is a major draw of *Second Life* (Deci and Ryan 2000; Hagerty 1997; McClelland 1982).

Consumer reasoning is a major field of study in the realm of consumer behavior. Simonson and Nowlis (2000, p. 49) proposed that "when consumers expect to explain decisions they are about to make, the focus of the decision shifts from the choice of good options to the choice of good reasons." Real-world consumers anticipate the need to justify their consumption decisions, and this affects the types of goods and services that they consume. *Second Life* users are not accountable to these real-world authorities when in the game, and this gives these users the freedom to consume products that they truly desire. Social interaction and social capital production may not be cognitively viewed as a productive use of time. Participation in a virtual world may provide individuals with the power to fulfill affective desires such as social capital production and group membership.

Power is manifest in the equality that the setting bestows on all avatars at conception. An avatar comes into *Second Life* with nothing and, with perseverance and hard work, it can achieve extremely high levels of attractiveness and success. This is the American Dream operating in cyberspace. As in real-world society, people are not equal in *Second Life* for very long. The desires for power and achievement motivate some users to acquire resources in off-market locations. For example, one can purchase *Second Life* currency—Linden dollars—on eBay for use in enhancing one's avatar. Residents who are able to invest a great deal of time and/or money in their avatars are significantly more well off than the occasional player (Castronova 2001). All players are born as no one, but all have the ability to work and consume their way to significance.

Safety

The need for safety is another factor that may motivate people to inhabit virtual worlds. While we are aware that social encounters in the real world can end in violence, an avatar cannot be physically hurt. In addition, the virtual world simply does not allow the range of illegal acts that are possible in the real world. *Second Life* rules are operationalized as an altered state of physics rather than a governing force because they are not seen but rather taken for granted and accepted. For example, one resident reports an incident in which he attempted to test drive someone else's motorcycle. His attempt was thwarted, not by sirens or police, or a gun-wielding owner, but by a message that simply said, "This does not belong to you," and his avatar was immediately booted from the motorcycle's saddle (Seryte and Storgaard 2007). Avatars are also free from other physical dangers. The needs potentially satisfied by virtual worlds do not involve physical things like shelter or food, but do involve the safety of virtual goods and an emotional safety component as well.

Safety is also operationalized in the virtual world in the way that users can engage in many types of social interaction without the fear of negative repercussions. The computer screen acts as a buffer that can abrogate what might be a negative social situation. If your avatar is rejected in *Second Life*, it is likely to be less traumatic. They didn't reject you, they rejected your avatar. If you find yourself in a situation that is unpleasant, you have the option to teleport to another place or log off entirely. You can always log in somewhere else. If you do something that will cause people to not desire your company in the virtual world, you can change the appearance of your avatar or create an entirely new one (Castronova 2001). Socially, a player cannot lose in *Second Life*. For people who fear social rejection, *Second Life* provides an opportunity to socialize without the risks associated with real-world interaction.

A concept that is closely related to emotional safety is anonymity, which is a significant draw to *Second Life* (Seryte and Storgaard 2007). Throughout history, people have hidden their true identities through masquerade balls, pen names, CB radio handles, and chat room IDs (Hemp 2006). Many have longed to experience being someone else, and virtual worlds provide a medium where this is possible, safe, and easy. The quest for anonymity in the technology of *Second Life* serves as a response to the privacy concerns associated with technology elsewhere. Our privacy is increasingly at risk through credit card records, buyer loyalty programs, and Internet tracking (Deighton 2005). The anonymity provided in *Second Life* may provide a counterbalance to the elimination of avenues of anonymity in the real world.

The sense of safety in the virtual world appears to be more of a freeing force than a motivator of social capital production. According to Baumeister and Leary (1995), all individuals will be motivated to belong to groups and engage in social capital-generating activities. The perception of increased safety in the virtual world removes factors that may deter a resident from engaging in traditional forms of social capital production.

Second Life and Virtual Consumer Behavior Implications

In the introduction to this chapter we showed the size and the growth statistics for the virtual world of *Second Life*. Throughout the body of the chapter we have outlined factors that may be driving individuals to seek social capital from the virtual world. This growing phenomenon has implications for both marketing practitioners and consumer behavior researchers. Residents have virtual currency and spend it to enhance the appearance and position of their avatar. The amount of consumption has led to the creation of *Second Life* entrepreneurs who sell to others, in some cases, making profits large enough to be useful in the real world. Real-world marketers are also increasingly positioning virtual versions of their goods in *Second Life* as a type of product placement similar to that seen in many films and TV programs. In this section, we will address consumer behavior within *Second Life* and its implications for research and marketing practice.

For Marketing Practitioners

One of the most compelling aspects of the *Second Life* virtual world is the fact that a user can capture another user's descriptive profile with a simple right click. This profile is a mixture of self-reported information and information about the virtual groups to which the avatar belongs. The self-reported information is important in socializing as it is expected that other users will read your profile prior to a socialization attempt. The self-reported information is subject to the same issues and biases that all self-report information faces, but grouping information is automatically placed on the profile when a user joins a group. It is possible that a virtual retailer could generate scanner-type data to link purchases with profile types. This information would be different from traditional scanner data because it would link products to the personally projected information that is generated in an effort to socialize. This type of information may be more useful than the demographic information gathered by most customer loyalty programs. The key to the success of this concept will be the level of involvement that users have with *Second Life* and the importance of their profiles in achieving their in-game goals.

Although audio plays an auxiliary role in *Second Life,* there is no taste, feel, or smell in the virtual world. Product experiences are mainly visual. As such, visual aesthetics are paramount in the attractiveness of a given product and may offer opportunities for design research (Bloch, Brunel, and Arnold 2003). The virtual world could be manipulated to act both as an incubator and a test bed for visual product design. Some real-world manufacturers are already using designs that have been adapted from prototypes first introduced in the virtual world (Hemp 2006). The measurement of affective responses to aesthetic design holds particular promise in the virtual world. As discussed above, the virtual world is built on hedonism, ideals, and wants. By stripping away role requirements, expectations, and associated social baggage, the virtual world may give a snapshot of a user's true affective response to an aesthetic design.

A variety of real-world forces are making face-to-face interaction both more expensive and less attractive. Factors such as an increased distance between business partners due to globalization, the threat of terrorism and its associated hassles, and concerns over carbon footprints are all decreasing the appeal of marketing-related travel. Virtual worlds could potentially host a wide range of marketing activities that have traditionally required people to travel to the same location. Social business networks, auctions and reverse auctions, conferences, training demonstrations, sales presentations, dispute resolution—the list of virtual world applications in a marketing setting is practically infinite. Several companies are already moving forward with activities in the virtual world (Rubin 2007; Hemp 2006). An adequate understanding of consumer behavior in the virtual world will be required for this technology to be fully embraced by business.

Second Life offers high levels of consumption at low cost to the consumer. A surprising finding from a study of related MMORPGs found that players' age averaged in the late twenties, making them a highly attractive target for marketers in the real world (Yee 2006). Placing real products inside of *Second Life* has become an attractive communications option for marketers seeking to reach this young, technology-savvy segment (Hemp 2006; Rubin 2007). It is also assumed that the time spent in *Second Life* is time away from exposure to other forms of promotion. In other words, product placement in *Second Life* may be a useful defense against losing awareness among these consumers who may be spending less time consuming traditional forms of media. If the residents of virtual worlds are insulating themselves from traditional marketing communication channels, then the virtual world will become a powerful medium for the disbursement of marketing messages. Interestingly, marketing activities within *Second Life* may be more effective than rival efforts in traditional media. The residents of *SecondLife* are highly engaged with the virtual environment and many are looking to consume virtual products. This is especially true if these products will facilitate social interaction in the virtual world. Thus, virtual worlds offer marketers the opportunity to cheaply create a sustained, realistic involvement that exceeds virtually anything else that can be found in the real world (Hemp 2006).

For Consumer Behavior Researchers

The virtual world allows a researcher to minimize the obtrusiveness of gathering information about product preference and choice. The medium of *Second Life* is wide open for experiments that can be seamlessly built into the setting, and *Second Life* management has agreed to take a hands-off approach to in-game marketing and research (Castronova 2004; Yee et al. 2007; Hemp 2006). For example, alternative product designs could be offered to *Second Life* consumers or as a prize for completing a gaming element that the experimenter would build into the virtual world. Dichotomous scale questions may be built into the virtual world as aspects of a gaming element. Initial tests on the generalizability of the virtual world have been promising as concepts like interpersonal distance seem to hold in both the virtual and real worlds (Yee et al. 2007). Goffman (1959) posited that choreographed performances can be studied to learn about human interaction.

These concepts will need to be thoroughly tested, but the virtual world may present an opportunity to experiment on a virtually unlimited pool of subjects.

Listings on eBay indicate that a Linden dollar, the currency of *Second Life,* has a US$ exchange rate of approximately 200:1. Because virtual products in *Second Life* are priced in relative parity with real-world dollars, this exchange rate allows people who are not wealthy to purchase items for their avatars that they could not dream of in real life. Because there are no physical needs in the virtual world, almost all of the consumption that takes place in *Second Life* can be viewed as discretionary or even as conspicuous consumption. The *Second Life* website reports that more than one million U.S. dollars change hands every day in the game, and there were almost 23 million transactions in the virtual world in October 2007. Nearly all of these transactions are made for either self-expression or display in the pursuit of social capital (Seryte and Storgaard 2007). Avatars and their operators seem to be engaging in a form of hedonistic cyber-materialism that is aimed at impressing others in the virtual world. Similar to real life, status seems to be conveyed to those individuals who own "cooler stuff." As status is a building block of social capital, there is a direct and obvious link between an individual's virtual material goods and his ability to generate social capital. One qualitative research project in *Second Life* bemoaned the difficulty of socializing in-world before the participant successfully "jazzed up" his avatar (Seryte and Storgaard 2007).

Past consumer research has suggested that there is a clear distinction between affective preferences (wants, ideals) and cognitive reasoned preferences (shoulds, oughts) (Shiv and Fedorikhin 1999; Dhar and Wertenbroch 2000; Pham and Avnet 2004). Holbrook and Hirschman (1982) argued that consumption may be primarily experiential and focused on symbolic meanings, hedonic responses, and aesthetic criteria. These aspects of the consumption process may be particularly well suited to study within *Second Life.* The virtual world may provide a cultural vacuum that results in choices made strictly on hedonic grounds. The ability to separate the hedonic element of a consumption decision from the mundane may prove useful in further studies of consumer behavior. Additionally, the consumption practices in the *Second Life* world can inhabit all four dimensions involved in Holt's (1995) Typology of Consumption Practices. The autotelic actions of *consuming as experience* and *consuming as play* are obvious when considering the virtual world. The instrumental actions of *consuming as integration* and *consuming as classification* are quite clear when one considers the social aspects that permeate the use of virtual worlds.

Deighton (2005) identified five degrees of buyer identity: anonymity, transitory identity, persistent identity, role-specific identity, and self-expressive identity. There are benefits associated with each level of buyer identity, but there are several tradeoffs that must be made in moving from one level to the next. Virtual worlds may be able to bridge the gap between self-expressive identity and anonymity. This allows a player to receive the benefits associated with sharing self-related information with other avatars through self-expressive consumption without losing the benefits associated with anonymity. In this way, the virtual world is able to combine two powerful forces in the world of consumer motivation. The medium of the virtual world may provide researchers with the ability to study consumer behavior without the confounding moderation of anonymity or self-expressive factors.

Sociologists and consumer behavior researchers have described desire as "a state of enjoyable discomfort" (Belk, Ger, and Askegaard 2003; Campbell 1987). This comment suggests that desire is not a state that is thrust upon consumers; rather consumers in a low state of desire may view higher levels as a pleasurable condition. Consequently, exploration may be used as a way of seeking objects or experiences that will become the focus of desire. The *Second Life* medium gives users the ability to seek desire in a context that is disconnected from the real world. Because desire without the possibility of fulfillment is simply envy, the virtual world may be preferable to the real world in terms of desire as it offers earning power for virtual money and tremendous purchasing power for real-world money.

Desire is generally thought to be an emotion that only comes alive in a social context (Belk, Ger, and Askegaard 2003; Wilk 1997). We define ourselves by what we desire and by what we despise. The act of consumption is an expression of our wish for social recognition. Holt (1995) describes consumption as a type of social action in which people make use of consumption objects in a variety of ways. The virtual world gives researchers a tool that may not be as confounded as in real-world society. There is little doubt that virtual worlds will develop a culture of their own that will affect studies of social action, but the recent incarnation of these worlds along with a common interest in community growth will ensure that these factors remain somewhat transparent. Envy controlling and envy restricting mechanisms that are prevalent in the real world are not as pronounced in the virtual world. The virtual world does not have philosophical, religious, or cultural norms that tell residents that they shouldn't strive to obtain all that they covet (Douglas and Isherwood 1979). The anonymity of a player may combine with the dogmatic rules of the virtual world to allow researchers to see more directly the factors that are driving consumer desire.

CONCLUSION

Baumeister and Leary (1995) contend that the need for social interaction has been bred into the all humans to some degree. It is not surprising that recent cultural changes have outpaced individuals' ability to fulfill their "need to belong." The gap between the ideal social interaction level and actual levels has created a market for products and services designed to facilitate social interaction and the creation of social capital. The search for social interaction appears to be the most salient motivator of entry into a virtual world. This chapter examined the phenomenon of

Second Life and proposed four forces that drive the quest for interaction in *Second Life*. Users turn to the virtual world because relationships are easy to create and inexpensive in both time and effort. *Second Life* users also go virtual in an effort to leave their real lives behind by adopting roles and role-related behaviors that more consistently mirror their true wants and desires. The lack of accountability in the virtual world endows users with power and choice at levels that are not found in the real world. Lastly, the virtual world of *Second Life* offers safety in both physical and emotional terms. This level of safety allows users to interact in ways they may not be capable of in real life.

This chapter highlighted several aspects of *Second Life* that are of interest to marketers. The virtual world of *Second Life* offers access to a different form of information than that which is currently harvested from traditional sources. Some companies have already experimented with visual product design in the virtual world. The increasing costs and hassles associated with marketing-related travel make it more likely that some forms of business will actually take place "virtually" in the future. Participation in virtual worlds has grown to the point that virtual residents may themselves be considered a market segment. Product exposure in the virtual world may be seen as a hedge against this segment's attrition from the consumption of more traditional media.

The virtual world offers many attractive attributes to researchers wishing to study consumer behavior. *Second Life* may separate the "want" from the "ought" of consumption by allowing people to adopt their desired roles and behaviors. Consumption is considered an element of the social context so the fairly new, stripped down society of *Second Life* may be seen as a cultural vacuum that has fewer confounds than a real-world society. With a little creativity, useful experiments and surveys can be conducted in the game. If in-game users will sit in a chair for five minutes to gain what translates to a fraction of a cent, these players would certainly run through an experiment or survey for a more substantial reward, especially if the survey/experiment were built into a gaming element. The potential for marketing research in the virtual world is practically limitless. As the influence of virtual worlds grows, so will the need to understand how and why these environments attract so many users.

REFERENCES

Aronson, Elliot. 1992. "The Return of the Repressed: Dissonance Theory Makes a Comeback." *Psychological Inquiry* 3 (4): 303.

Baumeister, Roy F., and Mark R. Leary. 1995. "The Need to Belong: Desire for Interpersonal Attachments as a Fundamental Human Motivation." *Psychological Bulletin* 117 (3): 497–529.

Beard, Jacob G., and Mounir G. Ragheb. 1983. "Measuring Leisure Motivation." *Journal of Leisure Research* 15 (3): 219.

Belk, Russell W., Guliz Ger, and Soren Askegaard. 2003. "The Fire of Desire: A Multisited Inquiry into Consumer Passion." *Journal of Consumer Research* 30 (3): 326–351.

Bloch, P. H., F. Brunel, and T. Arnold 2003, "Individual Differences in the Centrality of Visual Product Aesthetics: Concept and Measurement," *Journal of Consumer Research* 29 (4): 551.

Brown, Rupert. 2000. "Social Identity Theory: Past Achievements, Current Problems and Future Challenges. *European Journal of Social Psychology* 30 (6): 745.

Campbell, Colin. 1987. *The Romantic Ethic and the Spirit of Modern Consumerism.* London: Blackwell.

Castronova, Edward. 2001. "Virtual Worlds: A First-Hand Account of Market and Society on the Cyberian Frontier." *CESifo Working Paper Series No. 618.* Available at SSRN: http://ssrn.com/abstract=294828.

———. 2004. "The Price of Bodies: A Hedonic Pricing Model of Avatar Attributes in a Synthetic World." *Kyklos* 57 (2): 173.

Coleman, James S. 1988. "Social Capital in the Creation of Human Capital." *American Journal of Sociology* 94: 95.

Deci, Edward L., and Richard M. Ryan. 2000. "The 'What' and 'Why' of Goal Pursuits: Human Needs and the Self-Determination of Behavior." *Psychological Inquiry* 11 (4): 227.

Deighton, John. 2005. "Consumer Identity Motives in the Information Age." In *Inside Consumption: Consumer Motives, Goals and Desires,* ed. S. Ratneshwar and David Mick. New York: Routledge.

Dhar, Ravi, and Klaus Wertenbroch. 2000. "Consumer Choice Between Hedonic and Utilitarian Goods." *Journal of Marketing Research* 37 (1): 60–71.

Douglas, Mary, and Baron Isherwood. 1979. *The World of Goods: Towards an Anthropology of Consumption.* New York: Norton.

Ellison, Nicole, Charles Steinfield, and Cliff Lampe. 2007. "The Benefits of Facebook 'Friends': Social Capital and College Students' Use of Online Social Network Sites." *Journal of Computer-Mediated Communication* 12 (4): 1143.

Enders, Albrecht, H. Hungenberg, H. Denker, and S. Mauch. 2008. "The Long Tail of Social Networking. Revenue Models of Social Networking Sites. *European Management Journal* 26 (3): 199.

Goffman, Erving. 1959. *The Presentation of Self in Everyday Life.* Garden City, NY: Doubleday Anchor.

Grayson, Kent. 1999. "The Dangers and Opportunities of Playful Consumption." In *Consumer Value: A Framework for Analysis and Research,* ed. Morris B. Holbrook. New York: Routledge.

Hagerty, Michael R. 1997. "Testing Maslow's Hierarchy of Needs: National Quality-of-Life Across Time." *Social Indicators Research* 46 (3): 249.

Hemp, Paul. 2006. "Avatar-based Marketing." *Harvard Business Review* 84 (6): 48–57.

Holbrook, Morris B., and Elizabeth C. Hirschman. 1982. "The Experiential Aspects of Consumption: Consumer Fantasies, Feelings, and Fun." *Journal of Consumer Research* 9 (2): 132.

Holt, Douglas B. 1995. "How Consumers Consume: A Typology of Consumption Practices." *Journal of Consumer Research* 22 (1): 1.

Holzwarth, Martin, Chris Janiszewski, and Marcus M. Neumann. 2006. "The Influence of Avatars on Online Consumer Shopping Behavior." *Journal of Marketing* 70 (4): 19–36.

Kim, Kuoung H., J.Y. Park, D.Y Kim, H.I. Moon, and H.C. Chun. 2002. "E-Lifestyle and Motives to Use Online Games." *Irish Marketing Review* 15 (2): 71.

Maslow, Abraham H. 1948. "Higher and Lower Needs." *Journal of Psychology* 25: 433.

Mathwick, Charla, and Edward Rigdon. 2004. "Play, Flow, and the Online Search Experience." *Journal of Consumer Research* 31 (2): 324.

McClelland, David C. 1982. "The Need for Power, Sympathetic Activation, and Illness." *Motivation and Emotion* 6 (1): 31.

Moon, Youngme. 2000. "Intimate Exchanges: Using Computers to Elicit Self-Disclosure from Consumers." *Journal of Consumer Research* 26 (4): 323.

Nowak, Kristine L., and Frank Biocca. 2003. "The Effect of the Agency and Anthropomorphism on Users' Sense of Telepresence, Copresence, and Social Presence in Virtual Environments." *Presence: Teleoperators and Virtual Environments* 12 (5): 481.

O'Guinn, Thomas, and Albert Muñiz, Jr. 2005. "Communal Consumption and the Brand." In *Inside Consumption: Frontiers of Research on Consumer Motives, Goals, and Desires,* ed. David Glen Mick and S. Ratneshwar. New York: Routledge.

Pham, Michel Tuan, and Tamar Avnet. 2004. "Ideals and Oughts and the Reliance on Affect versus Substance in Persuasion." *Journal of Consumer Research* 30 (4): 503–518.

Putnam, Robert D. 2000. *Bowling Alone: The Collapse and Revival of American Community.* New York: Touchstone.

Rhee, Kenneth S., and T. H. Sigler. 2005. "Science versus Humankind: The Yin and Yang of Motivation Theory." *International Journal of Organization Theory and Behavior* 8 (3): 313.

Rubin, Jonathan. 2007. "Hacking Your Brain: How Video Games Are Going Beyond Product Placement to Impart Messages. *Medill Reports Chicago,* http://news.medill. northwestern.edu/chicago/news.aspx?id=66611 (accessed October 31, 2007).

Seryte, Jovita, and Lasse Storgaard. 2007. *"Second Life,* Second Chance." Unpublished master's thesis, Lund University.

Shiv, Baba, and Alex Fedorikhin. 1999. "Heart and Mind in Conflict: The Interplay of Affect and Cognition in Consumer Decision Making." *Journal of Consumer Research* 26 (3): 278.

Simonson, Itamar, and Stephen Nowlis. 2000. "The Role of Explanations and Need for Uniqueness in Consumer Decision Making: Unconventional Choices Based on Reasons." *Journal of Consumer Research* 27 (1): 49.

Sirgy, Joseph, M. 1982. "Self-Concept in Consumer Behavior: A Critical Review," *Journal of Consumer Research* (pre–1986) 9 (3): 287.

Vorderer, Peter, Tilo Hartmann, and Christoph Klimmt. 2003. "Explaining the Enjoyment of Playing Video Games: The Role of Competition." Proceedings of the Second International Conference on Entertainment Computing, Pittsburgh, May 9–10.

Weitz, Barton A. 2006. "Electronic Retailing." In *Retailing in the 21st Century,* ed. M. Kraft and M. Mantrala. Berlin: Springer.

Wilk, Richard. 1997. "A Critique of Desire: Distaste and Dislike in Consumer Behavior." *Consumption, Markets and Culture* 1 (2): 19.

Yee, Nick. 2006. "The Demographics, Motivations, and Derived Experiences of Users of Massively Multi-User Online Graphical Environments." *Presence: Teleoperators and Virtual Environments* 15 (3): 309–329.

Yee, Nick, and Jeremy Bailenson. 2007. "The Proteus Effect: The Effect of Transformed Self-Representation on Behavior." *Human Communication Research* 33 (3): 271–290.

Yee, Nick, Jeremy Bailenson, Mark Urbanek, Francis Chang, and Dan Merget. 2007. "The Unbearable Likeness of Being Digital: The Persistence of Nonverbal Social Norms in Online Virtual Environments." *CyberPsychology and Behavior* 10 (1): 115–121.

CHAPTER 4

I Don't Know You, But I Trust You

A Comparative Study of Consumer Perceptions in Real-Life and Virtual Worlds

JAMES E. BROWN AND TRACY L. TUTEN

> The notion of community has been at the heart
> of the Internet since its early days.
> —*Armstrong and Hagel (1996)*

As the world shifts into new expanses of communicative ability, led by the ever-evolving force of technology, the opportunity to seek and attain knowledge and understanding expands as well. Currently, a new medium of communication and interaction has grown in popularity and begs to be examined: computer-mediated environments (CMEs), otherwise known as virtual worlds.

Much like the famous saying from the television show *The Twilight Zone,* this realm is not made up of sight or sound, but of mind. CMEs, as they have come to be known, are environments designed by individuals using computers and programming scripts to create a new world online. The environment of CMEs is intangible, with no sense of touch, no *real* images or sounds. CMEs are a product of the application of a resident's mind spurred forward by a dream of creating a world where anonymity reigns and characteristics such as appearance can be controlled to fit any whim or desire. They are unlike any electronic medium to come before, made unique by the fact that consumers entering these worlds acquire an additional identity to their own in reality. Thus, a resident can be both the creator and the consumer of his or her world, if he or she so desires.

The adaptation and acceptance of brands in these worlds is an area of research that only recently gained popularity in the scholarly community; this book serves as a perfect example of that trend. The topic has drawn the interest of many within the research community because such worlds offer marketing researchers the opportunity to explore consumer behavior on a new plane.

What if the relationship between a brand and customer could be enhanced by nurturing it on both planes—reality and virtual? Is brand loyalty enhanced when consumers with dual identities interact with brands in their first and second lives? CMEs enable brands to connect with users on a psychological level free of social aspects such as the peer pressure found in reality. However, if this subconscious level is able to be reached, what course of action should brands take to connect to it? Is it as simple as existing within the CME, or must they be promoted as rigorously as real-world products? If promotion is necessary, how will those messages be received? Finally, if brand messaging is received positively within virtual worlds, will it carry over into the real world?

A troubling aspect of virtual research is that in the majority of cases the true characteristics of study respondents (their real-world traits) are unknown to the researcher. For instance, a beautiful woman being interviewed in *Second Life* may in fact be a middle-aged male in real life. Anonymity has essentially granted him the ability to change form, traits, habits, and even thoughts on certain subjects if he so desires. Can research concerning his perceptions be trusted, or are they skewed by the mendacity anonymity has created?

Research on socially desirable responding patterns for participants in online studies suggests that the enhanced perception of anonymity online results in more truthful responses. The same phenomenon may occur in virtual world interaction in that people may feel protected by the anonymity granted by identity representation in the form of an avatar. If so, consumers in virtual worlds may even respond differently to forms of social influence than they would in a real-world environment. For instance, as this study explores, residents in worlds such as *Second Life* may be more receptive to trusting advice or recommendations from others within the virtual world than they would be in real life. As they personally respond to others in a more open or honest way, even if only on a subconscious level brought on by the comfortable ambiguity of their true identity, they may expect the same type of behavior from others. Thus, during interactions where a brand is being promoted, the messaging residents receive may be viewed as sincere and perceived as trustworthy.

If brand-consumer communications are perceived as more sincere when exchanged in a CME, marketers have yet another reason to develop a brand presence in-world. As Wilson (2008) succinctly stated in *Mediaweek,* "a virtual world has the promise of being able to tell you exactly which customers see your campaign, how long they spend with it, how they talk about it and, ultimately, if they act on it by purchasing a virtual or even a real product."

In this study, we explore brand- or product-specific word-of-mouth communication between residents and compare those interactions to other forms of communication. We seek to answer these questions: Do the influence of communication and recommendations within virtual worlds mean more to consumers than those taking place in other venues? Are in-world interactions perceived as trustworthy? Here we take a first step toward comparing the impact of consumer advice and recommendations in a virtual world to that in the real world. In an exploratory context, the following research will assess the impact of virtual-world recommendations upon consumers, and then compare it to other forms of recommendations. These other forms will be real-life friends, real-life salespeople, and web-based recommendation agents. As a result, we hope to develop a greater understanding of the role virtual-world communication can play upon brand perception and acceptance in other residents.

A BACKGROUND ON THE IMPACT OF COMMUNICATION IN VIRTUAL ENVIRONMENTS

As previously mentioned, the popularity and growth of virtual worlds is a fairly new trend. However, concerning virtual *communities* (i.e., forums or message boards), much research has been conducted over the last decade. Although they sound similar, the difference between the two virtual platforms is fairly significant. Virtual communities are static groups that meet online in order to share information with one another. Virtual worlds, on the other hand, are dynamic environments where members associate with one another through digital face-to-face encounters. Essentially, virtual communities are information posting areas; virtual worlds are virtual realities. However, as both involve virtual interaction and information sharing in some form, exploration into the research of virtual communities serves well as a basis for developing an understanding of the root from which the virtual consumer has grown.

According to Rheingold (1993), a virtual community is an association of like-minded individuals who maintain extended discussions mixed with enough feeling to develop deeper relationships online. However, the basis for such aggregation has been debated. Some research has claimed participation stems from a need for sharing interests and discussing issues (Armstrong and Hagel 1996; Rheingold 1993). Another belief is that the importance of finding an information source draws people into joining a community (Muñiz and O'Guinn 2001).

Whatever be the case, Shang, Chen, and Liao (2006) illustrated that participation in virtual communities may lead to a heightened level of brand loyalty. Thus, it was determined that brands should promote the creation of communities pertaining to their products and attract consumers to participate (Shang et al. 2006). This is due to the gravity of peer recommendations in the context of the decision-making process.

As reported by *Brand Strategy* ("Consumer Trust" 2007), 78 percent of global consumers rate their trust of other people's recommendations for products and services higher than any other medium, such as newspapers, conventional, and online advertising. This has allowed word-of-mouth (WOM) and web-based word-of-mouth (eWOM) communication to reach the top two ranks as trustworthy sources of information for consumers ("Consumer Trust" 2007).

eWOM, the form of communication within virtual communities, has not always been so recognized. Until recently, research has focused primarily on the reality-based, person-to-person form of communication (normal WOM), or consumer's task/selection criteria for WOM sources (Duhan et al. 1997; Gershoff, Broniarczyk, and West 2001; Smith 2002). The resulting research has since shown WOM to be an influential factor during a consumer's purchase decision (Hutton and Mulhern 2002; Katz and Lazarsfeld 1957; Silverman 1997; Whyte 1954).

As the Internet grew in popularity, eWOM became the topic of conversation in many works of market research (Bickart and Schindler 2001; Chen, Fay, and Wang 2002; Godes and Mayzlin 2004; Hennig-Thurau et al. 2004). The advent and success of review sites such as Amazon and Epinions brought eWOM further into the spotlight (Smith 2002). Since this shift, research has emerged on the positive impact that online recommendation can have on consumers if there is a correlation between consumer preferences and reviewed attributes (Saranow 2005). Additionally, research has indicated that consumers tend to purchase an item specifically if the item had been recommended to them, online or off (West et al. 1999). This only added to an increase in desire to design online recommendation agents for the many different forms of online communities (Tsai 2004).

What is still widely debated is how, or why, consumers can put such a great amount of trust in the word of other individuals. The strong impact of reality-based recommendations, in a face-to-face setting, is understandable, but how are credibility or expertise judged when dealing with online agents?

INVESTIGATING THE CREDIBILITY OF eWOM

Credibility has been defined as a combination of expertise and trustworthiness (Kelman 1961), and expertise as the reliability of the source to deliver the correct answer (Senecal and Nantel 2004; McGuire 1969). The online recommendation agent may indeed identify the best solution to a consumer's problem. However, under what conditions will the consumer trust in the recommendation? This question is largely unanswered in the literature.

Research has acknowledged trust in a person as trust in the person's competence, benevolence, and integrity (Komiak, Wang, and Benbasat 2004; McKnight, Choudhury, and Kacmar 2002). The recognition of these qualities is perhaps the most integral step that occurs between a consumer and a salesperson during the decision-making process (Morgan and Hunt 1994; Swan, Bowers, and Richardson 1999). However, that pertains to actual face-to-face interactions, not communication through eWOM. Therefore, one must ask what consumers use as a basis to judge virtual communication/recommendation sources.

This is a critical question, as there is an absence of cues for consumers to employ (McKnight, Choudhury, and Kacmar 2002). In real-life interactions, consumers may pick up on hints of intent from a salesperson. An example of this could be purchases where salespeople earn their wage from commissions (i.e., car sales). A recommendation that the consumer purchase an expensive car may signify that a salesperson is looking out for himself and not the consumer's interests. However, the body language or tone of voice of the salesperson while he explains the reasoning behind his recommendation could either assuage or support a consumer's suspicion. These subtle cues do not come across in virtual communication. Thus, the basis for this trust seems to stem from a feeling of similarity between the individual and the virtual salesperson—which can be an identified company representative discussing the product (i.e., record company description of a compact disk on Amazon) or regular consumers supporting a product (i.e., consumer reviews about the same CD on Amazon). If this feeling occurs, studies have shown a positive correlation between trust in virtual salespeople and a consumer's willingness to shop online (Gefen, Karahanna, and Straub 2003; McKnight et al. 2002; Wang and Benbasat 2005; Cassell and Bickmore 2000; Komiak, Wang, and Benbasat 2004).

A study by Komiak, Wang, and Benbasat (2004) investigated the differences between consumer trust in virtual and real-life salespeople. They concluded that, on average, customers will trust a virtual salesperson more than a human salesperson.

How can this be possible? It would seem a valid case to argue that nothing can replace face-to-face interaction, granting the consumer the ability to render intent through body language or verbal cues. However, the research seems to argue otherwise. One can derive explanations of this behavior from two theories of consumer behavior: the Theory of Social Responses to Computers, concerning human/computer interface interaction (Reeves and Nass 1996), and the Trust-TAM model, which illustrates the judgment placed on computerized agents by consumers (Wang and Benbasat 2005).

Research concerning the behavior of society toward computers has shown that people frequently treat their computers as though they were human and apply social rules to them. However, this behavior is not realized by the individual (Wang and Benbasat 2005). This includes applying characteristics to computers or text-interfaces such as friendliness (Reeves and Nass 1996). Thus, when consumers encounter eWOM (i.e., reading reviews) it seems as though they are likely to assign a personality to the reviewer, which could either strengthen the review (if assigned a positive personality) or cause it to be disregarded (if the judgment is negative). Granted, it must be taken into consideration that the messages viewed are created by human actors with personality traits, individual characteristics, and specific motivations. This strengthens the argument that while computers do not have "life," the messages found on them already do and do not need further personality assignment. However, the qualities of the writer are generally unknown to the reader, and must be inferred unless explicitly revealed. Thus, the translations are most often completed with subtle hints—sentence structure, seemingly disingenuous statements, wording that the reader can relate to—or simply by instinct. The subtle cues or instinct could lead to the reader correctly guessing the personality and motives of the writer, but they could also create a misinterpretation, thereby causing the reader to take a like-minded consumer's review and reject the opinion as untrustworthy or meaningless.

The Trust-TAM model is a variation of the Technology Acceptance Model, first posed by Davis (1989). The Trust-TAM model differs from the original TAM in that trust is identified as a key determinant of one's interpretation of the usefulness and value of technology. Experimentation based upon the Trust-TAM model has shown that consumers encountering online recommendation agents perceive human characteristics, such as benevolence or integrity (Wang and Benbasat 2005). Adding to these findings, Trust-TAM was found to explain online recommendation acceptance. Furthermore, the study revealed the importance of a consumer's initial trust in relation to other aspects of TAM. This includes the perceived usefulness or the perceived ease of use of the product (Wang and Benbasat 2005).

Thus, by applying these paradigms to the previous research concerning trust in virtual salespeople compared to real-life salespeople, it seems as though the choices are placed on a level field where location of interaction plays little role during the trust/acceptance phase. What is interesting is that in both the Theory of Social Response to Computers and Trust-TAM, it seems as though individuals attribute personality traits to the interfaces, thereby humanizing the otherwise lifeless technology or messaging. Thus, it could be argued that individuals view advice found on sites such as Epinions only as regular people, not corporate agents, whereas real-life salesmen have an employer to please. However, it would be logical that trepidation does exist in the mind of consumers over whether the online recommender was genuine in their motivation, particularly when positive messages appear to push for a purchase.

The creation and population of virtual worlds has opened an arena to further examine the differences in consumer perception of virtual and real-life recommendation sources. Thus far, the literature has focused exclusively on virtual *communities,* an all-encompassing term referring to web-based recommendation agents such as Epinions or Amazon reviews, rather than on virtual worlds. The communities studied have been static sources of information, where users post reviews or provide information for others to read. Consumers may indeed assign personalities and traits to the handles of those providing information, resulting in some sense that the reviews are offered by a real, trustworthy person. However, in a virtual world, the traits of the person offering a recommendation is enhanced with visual components, much as they would be in the real world. In essence, the virtual world enables a type of hybrid with the visual cues present in the real world delivered via a web-based platform.

The question that has yet to be addressed by research is how opinions within these worlds rate when compared to other sources. As displayed in Komiak,

Wang, and Benbasat (2004), virtual agents can rank higher than real-life agents in terms of the perceived level of trustworthiness in the eyes of consumers. Taking this into account, and the findings from the research on the Theory of Social Response to Computers and Trust-TAM model experiments, would virtual-world recommendations rank higher in trustworthiness than real salespeople as well? Additionally, how do the ratings of trust differ in regards to the opinions of virtual *world* residents compared to virtual *community* residents? Finally, if the recommendations of virtual-world residents are found to be more trustworthy than both real salespeople and virtual communities, how do they compare to real-life friends? It is the intent of the following research to address these questions.

METHOD

The research approach is an exploratory one, relying upon limited responses to an online survey. *Second Life* (SL) residents (*n* = 19) responded to a survey that included a series of questions designed to elicit valuable information for addressing the research questions posed above.

SAMPLE

Participants were recruited by identifying areas of SL with traffic, and then visiting those locations to invite participation in the online survey. In this regard, recruitment was much like the real-world equivalent used to recruit for intercept surveys.

We focused on less populated areas rather than massively inhabited islands (such as the free-money or sex-centric islands), as we felt it would be easier to reach residents who were not looking for some form of reimbursement for taking the survey (such is the case on many of the larger islands). Additionally, we focused on attracting participants from a variety of interest islands in order to collect a sample with several virtual interests and backgrounds.

The 19 participants answered a questionnaire containing 21 questions. The questions were mostly open-ended, although some were closed-ended but contained a field for participants to explain their response. The survey included an introductory section, and questions on real-life (RL) stores, online stores, *Second Life* product reviews, and trust in forms of online WOM communication. Section 1 asked participants basic introduction questions, covering topics such as: when they joined SL, how they found out about SL, and whether they consulted other people before joining.

Section 2 asked the participants questions about their shopping habits in real life. These questions included topics such as whether they research products before deciding to buy, if they ask friends for advice, and if they ask salespeople for advice. Additionally, they were asked whether they tended to purchase an item especially if a friend recommended it, and how they feel about a salesperson's opinion compared to their friend's. Section 3 covered online stores. Questions included whether they shopped online, where they shopped online, if they read reviews, and what they thought of reviews.

Section 4 was the heart of the study, concerning participant perceptions of other residents in *Second Life*. To gauge this perception, participants were asked about product recommendations in SL, their sense of community in SL, trust, and impact of another resident's opinion in-world and out.

Finally, Section 5 asked participants to rate their level of trust of four sources of advice and recommendations: (1) RL friends, (2) RL salespeople, (3) online reviews/recommendations, and (4) SL residents. The rating was based on a 4-point scale using percentages of trustworthiness, meaning that participants would choose a rating of "1" if they completely (100 percent) trusted the source. A rating of "4" would signify only a small degree, or lack, of trust (25 percent). In other words, trust levels ranged from very little to unconditional trust in the source.

RESULTS

The survey produced interesting information concerning the varied levels of perception that consumers have of the different sources.

Section 1

The majority of the sample joined SL in 2007 (73 percent), while the others ranged from the newest member joining in 2008, to the oldest having joined in 2004. Additionally, the majority (73 percent) discovered the virtual world through referrals, both in online and real-life communities. Their favorite islands in-world (in order to gauge their avatar's interests) were diverse, explained by the fact that recruitment was conducted in a variety of locations throughout SL.

Section 2

Similar to the response concerning their favorite islands, the participants' RL favorite stores were diverse as well. This inquiry was done to pair avatar interest with RL interest, and research showed similar tastes in-world and out. Furthermore, 67 percent said they research a product before they go to a store in RL. Nearly all participants (89 percent) said they frequently check with friends before making a purchase decision, and of these, 74 percent said they would purchase the item after receiving a friend's approval. Only 50 percent said they referred to salespeople as well for advice.

Section 3

Eighty-three percent of participants reported that they frequently shopped online. Common stores were Amazon and eBay, mentioned specifically in 85 percent of respondents' lists of favorite stores. Eighty-two percent said they read reviews online and nearly all (92 percent) of these respondents felt "safer" buying a product with positive recommendations attached to it.

Additionally, 94 percent admitted to having purchased a product online without ever having seen it in person. Of this group, 76 percent said the review of the product by other consumers played a major role in their purchase decision. However, the majority of respondents (82 percent) also reported being suspicious of product reviews composed by someone other than a regular consumer, perhaps a paid employee of the manufacturing company.

Section 4

The majority of participants (75 percent) said they have been recommended products in *Second Life* as well. These products included clothes or other appearance-based items. Eighty-one percent also stated that they had specifically asked other residents for advice or recommendations. This included both product recommendations and general life recommendations, up to even high trust issues such as relationship advice.

A strong majority (81 percent) also felt as though there was a true feeling of community shared by all residents in SL. More importantly, 88 percent said that they "trust" other SL residents, as if they were regular friends in RL. Surprisingly, when asked whether they had ever had an experience in SL where another member recommended something that influenced both their second and their real life, over a third (37 percent) said they had.

Section 5

Of the four sources of personal recommendations, RL friends ranked above all others with an average rank of 1.3. SL residents followed, with an average ranking of 2.3. Third were online recommendations at 2.4, and the lowest on the scale were RL salespeople, with an average rank of 2.9.

DISCUSSION AND CONCLUSION

Overall, data suggest that the opinions of residents within virtual worlds such as *Second Life* can be influential, and seem to be trusted more than online recommendation agents or real-life salespeople. While virtual world residents only rank slightly higher than virtual communities, what is of interest is the concentration of responses within a certain rank. *Second Life* users and online recommendations had an average ranking of 2.3 and 2.4, respectively; however, while 94 percent were split between 2 and 3 for online recommendations, 80 percent chose 2 only for other *Second Life* residents. Thus, while the mean may be similar, the confidence in choice is greatly divergent.

This exploratory study contributes to the research and practice of understanding consumer behavior in virtual worlds, particularly in the area of variations in trust. In a similar vein as studies conducted over the past decade concerning eWOM from virtual *communities,* this research catches a glimpse of the perception of eWOM from virtual *worlds,* thereby allowing future perception-based work to build off this foundation.

The popularity of worlds such as SL is increasing at a steady rate, and each day an exponential amount of people are taken into a world where text and digital imagery come together to form a hybrid experience—one that is nothing more than a by-product of a mind wishing to express itself through digital code. However, for many experiencing the product of that genesis, the virtual world's beauty doesn't come from a skillfully designed code but instead from the livelihood given to each resident. Every entrant into the virtual world is granted an escape from whatever life they have in the real world, and a shield of anonymity allows them to openly express themselves and be more receptive to the expressions of others as well.

This escape also grants them the ability to run, dance, sing, shop, laugh, and love others just like them. These interactions, although only virtual, may indeed create a stronger bond between residents than each had intended on experiencing. However, the understanding of these bonds, and what they mean, is only beginning to be developed. Thus, further research on this subject may prove to be highly influential in order to create effective brand communication and answer the unknowns presented with current explorations such as this.

Concerning the research presented, one aspect that must be resolved with later work is whether the lack of large-island inhabitants skewed the data toward higher trust of virtual-world residents. The respondents, being from less populated areas bound by similar interests, may have been preconditioned to a level of trust associated with smaller communities. This is a characteristic those who frequent larger islands may not experience. Additionally, if a larger sample is used, future research should monitor the proportion of new residents to old residents on the smaller islands. The less populated areas may attract more experienced residents who no longer wish to associate with the "newbies" who frequent the larger islands. If these members compose the majority of a sample, the data may not accurately reflect the virtual world as a whole, as they may be more likely to respond favorably to questions concerning their comfort with the population around them.

Additionally, much of this behavior may be operating on an unconscious level, which we, as researchers, can only glimpse. Future research will need to dig deeper into the mind of virtual world residents in hopes of uncovering stronger evidence. Moreover, it is worth exploring to what extent the visually interactive nature of virtual worlds could be a mitigating factor in the perceptions of avatars. This could be investigated by comparing static and dynamic messaging within a virtual world, and judging the differences in a resident's trust for each form of communication. Finally, this study focused on gauging the perceived levels of trust for various recommendation agents, but only hinted at the extent to which the residents acted upon the recommendations. Future work should explore this aspect by attempting to track and compare the actual success rates of each recommendation source.

In regards to practice, much like previous research, which urged companies to promote virtual communities, a possible implication of this research is that promotion of consumer involvement in virtual worlds is also positive. Interaction with brand advocates, whether disguised or not, may indeed result in heightened brand loyalty, as participants have shown a greater trust in residents than RL salespeople or online community messaging. Residents may experience heightened response to narrative when it is coupled with digitally enhanced visual cues.

In conclusion, while friends in real life still reign supreme in terms of trust, virtual-world members are more trusted than other sources of WOM/eWOM information. Taking into account the higher rating of SL residents to RL salespeople, it stands to reason that while the RL salesperson and SL resident may be the same person, consumers will believe the avatar more than the person behind it. This may be due to the unique characteristics of virtual worlds, such as the interactive abilities and individual identities granted to users, coupled with paradigms such as Trust-TAM.

REFERENCES

Armstrong, A., and J. Hagel. 1996. "The Real Value of Online Communities." *Harvard Business Review* 74: 134–141.

Bickart, B., and R. Schindler. 2001. "Internet Forums as Influential Sources of Consumer Information." *Journal of Interactive Marketing* 15: 31–40.

Blackwell, R.D., P.W. Miniard, and J.F. Engel. 1993. *Consumer Behavior.* New York: Dryden Press.

Cassell, J., and T. Bickmore. 2000. "External Manifestation of Trustworthiness in the Interface." *Communications of the ACM* 43 (12): 50–56.

Chen, Y.B., S. Fay, and Q. Wang. 2002. "Online Consumer Product Reviews: What Can We Learn?" Working paper, June, University of Florida.

"Consumer Trust: Word of Mouth Rules." 2007. *Brand Strategy* (November): 40–41.

Davis, F.D. 1989. "Perceived Usefulness, Perceived Ease of Use, and User Acceptance of Information Technology." *MIS Quarterly* 13: 319–340.

Duhan, D., S. Johnson, J. Wilcox, and G. Harrell. 1997. "Influences on Consumer Use of Word-of-Mouth Recommendation Sources." *Academy of Marketing Science* 25: 283–295.

Gefen, D., E. Karahanna, and D.W. Straub. 2003. "Trust and TAM in Online Shopping: An Integrated Model." *MIS Quarterly* 27: 51–90.

Gershoff, A., S. Broniarczyk, and P. West. 2001. "Recommendation or Evaluation? Task Sensitivity in Information Source Selection." *Journal of Consumer Research* 28: 418–438.

Godes, D., and D. Mayzlin. 2004. "Using Online Conversations to Study Word-of-Mouth Communication." *Marketing Science* 23: 545–560.

Hennig-Thurau, T., K.P. Gwinner, G. Walsh, and D.D. Gremler. 2004. "Electronic Word-of-Mouth Via Consumer-Opinion Platforms: What Motivates Consumers to Articulate Themselves on the Internet?" *Journal of Interactive Marketing* 18: 38–52.

Hutton, J.G., and F.J. Mulhern. 2002. *Marketing Communications: Integrated Theory, Strategy and Tactics.* Hackensack, NJ: Pentagram Publishing.

Katz, E., and P.F. Lazarsfeld. 1957. *Personal Influence.* Glencoe, IL: Free Press.

Kelman, H.C. 1961. "Processes of Opinion Change." *Public Opinion Quarterly* 25: 57–78.

Komiak, S., W. Wang, and I. Benbasat. 2004. "Trust Building in Virtual Salespersons Versus in Human Salespersons: Similarities and Differences." *E-Service Journal* 3.3: 49–63, 103–105.

McGuire, W.J. 1969. "The Nature of Attitudes and Attitude Change." In *The Handbook of Social Psychology,* ed. G. Lindzey and E. Aronson, 137–314. Reading, MA: Addison-Wesley.

McKnight, D.H., V. Choudhury, and C. Kacmar. 2002. "Developing and Validating Trust Measures for e-Commerce: An Integrative Typology." *Information Systems Research* 13: 334–359.

Morgan, R.M., and S. Hunt. 1994. "The Commitment-Trust Theory of Relationship Marketing." *Journal of Marketing* 58: 20–38.

Muñiz, A.M., and T.C. O'Guinn. 2001. "Brand Community." *Journal of Consumer Research* 27: 412–431.

Reeves, B., and C. Nass. 1996. *The Media Equation: How People Treat Computers, Television, and New Media Like Real People and Places.* New York: Cambridge University Press.

Rheingold, H. 1993. *Virtual Community: Homesteading on the Electronic Frontier.* Cambridge, MA: The MIT Press.

Saranow, J. 2005. "It's a Match! As Buyers Head to the Web for Research, Car Makers Are Trying to Make Sure They Find What They Want." *Wall Street Journal,* July 25, R4.

Senecal, S., and J. Nantel. 2004. "The Influence of Online Product Recommendations on Consumers' Online Choices." *Journal of Retailing* 80: 159–169.

Shang, R., Y. Chen, and H. Liao. 2006. "The Value of Participation in Virtual Consumer Communities on Brand Loyalty." *Internet Research* 16: 398.

Silverman, G. 1997. "How to Harness the Awesome Power of Word of Mouth." *Direct Marketing* (November): 32–37.

Smith, D.M. 2002. Trust me, would I steer you wrong? The influence of peer recommendations within virtual communities. Ph.D. dissertation, University of Illinois at Chicago.

Swan, J.E., M.R. Bowers, and L.D. Richardson. 1999. "Customer Trust in the Salesperson: An Integrative Review and Meta-Analysis of the Empirical Literature." *Journal of Business Research* 48: 93–107.

Tsai, M. 2004. "Online Retailers See Improved Site Search as Sales Tool." Dow Jones News Service, August 20.

Wang, W., and I. Benbasat. 2005. "Trust in and Adoption of Online Recommendation Agents," *Journal of the Association for Information Systems* 6: 72–101.

West, P.M., D. Ariely, S. Bellman, E. Bradlow, J. Huber, E. Johnson, B. Kahn, J.D.C. Little, and D. Schkade. 1999. "Agents to the Rescue?" *Marketing Letters* 10: 285–300.

Whyte, W.H. Jr. 1954. "The Web of Word of Mouth." *Fortune* 50: 140–143.

Wilson, M. 2008. "Virtually Engaged." *Mediaweek* 18 (February): 6.

CHAPTER 5

Social Interaction with Virtual Beings

The Technology Relationship Interaction Model and Its Agenda for Research

KATHY KEELING, DEBBIE KEELING,
ANTONELLA DE ANGELI, AND PETER MCGOLDRICK

There is a significant move toward the use of "robot avatars," that is, representations of virtual humans, real or imaginary objects acting as virtual salespeople, on e-tail websites and retail stores in virtual worlds. De Angeli, Lynch, and Johnson (2001, p. 198) characterize avatar representations as "social agents," "intentionally designed to be human-like, to show a sense of personality and attitude, and to involve the user in social relationships." Although robot avatar actions and communication are likely generated from a database rather than a human, there is a stream of international research indicating that human–avatar interactions in e-tailing can induce feelings of trust or liking within users and even influence users' decisions (Wood, Solomon, and Basil 2005; Holzwarth, Janiszewski, and Neumann 2006; Luo et al. 2006; Keeling, McGoldrick, and Beatty 2007).

Nevertheless, there is a lack of systematic research concerning the fundamental building blocks to our understanding of behaviors in such interactions. Consumers are human and so inherently social beings sensitive to the meanings of actions and expressions of other beings (Mead 1934), even other avatars found in virtual worlds (Donath 2008). Introducing explicit social presence to the interface will invoke social reactions and expectations concerning the nature of such interactions. So, during interactions with avatars, customers theoretically will react as though with a "real" person, though it is not by any means clear exactly how far the analogy holds and what the boundaries are to the illusion of reality.

Thus, questions arise surrounding social interaction content suited for salesperson-customer interactions, as well as the potential to produce self-awareness in consumers, leading to social comparison and ultimately, challenges to consumer self-esteem and identity. Reflecting concerns for customer relationship building in the e-world, questions can also be asked about whether relationships can be built between robot avatar salespeople and customers. Further, Hemp (2006) argues that in creating a new avatar, consumers, in effect, create new personae for themselves, taking on the identity of their self-created avatar. Such situations create new dilemmas for the personalization of marketing communications.

As social beings we cannot divorce ourselves from our own socialization processes; so considering humans as inherently social beings, we derive an explanatory model indicating how and why specific aspects of an interaction with an avatar are related to customer behavioral intentions. To generate the general framework, we first discuss some background features of interactions with avatars, including the role of relational schema. Having established prima facie the operation of schema or scripts during interactions, and, therefore, that performance expectancy could be active, we introduce Expectancy Violation Theory. This is followed by discussion of communication competence, relational devaluation, and social allergens, chosen on the grounds of theoretical association with perceived relationship quality, self-perceptions, and self-esteem. A possible negativity bias is also explored.

After defining the theoretical model, a preliminary test is presented. Finally, a research agenda is proposed considering individual differences and situational aspects that may moderate the effects of the concepts within the model. This knowledge will be instrumental in driving technology design and marketing strategies for a new-generation user experience, where virtual bodies will mediate the interaction with real and virtual beings.

BACKGROUND: ADVANTAGES AND DRAWBACKS OF USING AVATARS IN E-TAILING

A major advantage of introducing human–avatar interaction for facilitating effective communication is an increased perception of social presence by the users. When anthropomorphic features of an interface increase, people develop a greater sense of telepresence (Qiu and Benbasat 2005). E-tailing research so far establishes the perception of social presence as benefiting trust building, engagement, and persuasion (e.g., Cyr et al. 2007). One strategy replaces face-to-face interactions with an avatar that encourages website users to interact with it. If artificial representations possess properties such as language and personality, users often show automatic social responses (Lee and Nass 2003). Avatars need not be either realistic or human to invoke responses and collaboration; users show social reactions to a wide range of depictions of humans, animals, or even animated objects.

Automatic social responses are likely to invoke established "social rules" and dynamics from offline interactions (Reeves and Nass 1996) so that they are transferred to online interactions with avatars. Thus, these characters could offer a smoother and more familiar style of interaction and make a website more engaging and motivating (De Angeli, Lynch, and Johnson 2001). Avatars therefore offer the potential for greater information and entertainment value on e-tail websites; other advantages can be surmised, such as 24/7 availability without becoming fatigued, thus offering the same level of service at all times.

Yet such strategies are also fraught with hazard. Cassell et al. (2000) conclude that processing of interfaces with avatars requires more effort than using nonpersonified interfaces. Social interaction relies on smooth synchronization, which can be difficult to achieve in online communication. Further, an avatar presence may lead users to expect the system to be as flexible and intelligent as a human assistant (Dehn and van Mulken 2000), a level of expectations that technology is as yet far from reaching. Moreover, not all interactions go smoothly, and there is increasing empirical evidence of the dark side of such interactions, describing some disturbingly aggressive and abusive reactions (De Angeli and Brahnam 2008).

THE SOCIAL NATURE OF AVATAR INTERACTION

The literature on social interaction suggests that adverse reactions may be strongly connected to perceptions of relationship status and self-esteem implications of interaction outcomes, especially those falling short of the expectations of normative social exchanges. Leary (2002) maintains that "interactions between individuals may be viewed as interactions between the selves of those individuals, with each person's perceptions of and responses to the other filtered through and mediated by his or her self-perceptions." Maintaining positive self-perceptions is important because humans are essentially social animals needing the support of others to survive; self-esteem functions as a "sociometer" of the degree to which we are valued by other people and ourselves as socially acceptable (Leary et al. 1995).

Consequently, in offline interactions, one well-established outcome of interpersonal communication is the perception of the strength of interpersonal attraction (e.g., McCroskey, Hamilton, and Weiner 1974; Duran and Kelly 1988). Depending on such perceptions, people make judgments of character and attributions of motive toward the other interactant and use these in decisions to continue or discontinue a relationship. Importantly, this seems to occur whether the interaction is face-to-face or mediated by computer (Burgoon et al. 2000; Martin, Heisel, and Valencic 2001).

Relational Schema

Interaction behavior depends on goals (Fiske 1992), but the precise form of the behavior is dependent on "societal norms, roles, understandings, and customs"

(Berscheid 1994) organized into expected interaction patterns resulting from past experiences. These "relational schema" or "performative scripts" represent expectations of the content and nature of interactions (Berscheid 1994). There is evidence in the literature to surmise that relational schema are active outside intrahuman interaction. First, research on social reactions to computers (Reeves and Nass 1996) indicates the activation of relational schema in human-computer interactions. Extrapolating those findings to human interactions with avatars strongly suggests such interactions will also activate relational schema. Second, there appears to be a tendency for human observers to endow even inanimate objects with the characteristics of living organisms in certain circumstances. For example, when objects or groups of objects move systematically, people perceive them as characters having beliefs and desires. This effect is enhanced when these objects have the appearance and behavior of social agents that initiate interaction with users, thereby exhibiting what looks like social competence, personality, and intelligence (Hayes-Roth et al. 1995).

If activated, relational schema have at their core the premise that relationships have implicit social "rules" that allow them to function, such as not being rude or abrupt; being more than only task-oriented; displaying positive regard, praise, and honesty (Mottet and Richmond 1998); not imposing on others' time; fairness; respecting privacy and refraining from criticism (Argyle 1992). These constitute part of the "scripts" for pro-social interactions, which the intentionally social design of the avatar interaction is likely to activate. Indeed, in that context, Miller (2004) describes such schema as "etiquette" informed by offline interactions that aid more pleasant, polite, and cooperative interactions when present. Conversely, when etiquette is violated, interactions are perceived as "insulting, exploitative, and unpleasant" (Miller 2004, p. 32).

Expectancy Violation Theory

Burgoon and Walther (1990) define interaction expectations as "cognitions about the anticipated communication behavior of specific others" (p. 236). In naturalistic situations, schema and goal activation is often automatic. Hence, interactions meeting expectations and norms of a relational schema move along relatively automatically as exchanges that fit with expectancies have little need for conscious monitoring. However, when expectancies are violated, more conscious consideration of the interaction is triggered and resources are re-allocated to monitoring exchanges (Bargh and Chartrand 1999).

A further consequence of expectancy violation is a sense-making phase. Burgoon and Hale (1988) posit that disconfirmation of social interaction expectancies activates a process of evaluation involving attributions of intention and motive regarding the norm violation that results in attachment of positive or negative valence. They term this Expectancy Violation Theory. Negative expectation violations will decrease the attractiveness of the avatar as a future interactant.

Social Competence: Pro-Social Competence and Sociability

The ability to engage in and successfully adhere to relational schema is part of social competence. Griffin and Langlois (2006) posit that social competence consists of two related subdomains: pro-social competence and sociability. Pro-social competence consists of the tendency toward cooperation and helping others, whereas sociability is the tendency to want to interact with others (e.g., being friendly). Minimum levels of pro-social and sociable behavior are expected and necessary for smooth interaction that does not violate communication norms. Communication competence is associated with perceived task and social attractiveness (Duran and Kelly 1988). Consequently, the activation of relational schema during human–avatar interaction, resulting in user evaluation of the social competence of the avatar, present one explanation for acceptance or rejection of future avatar interaction.

> P_1: Perceptions of avatar social competence (pro-social competence and sociability) are positively related to perceptions of relationship quality and intentions regarding avatar use.

Relational Devaluation

As discussed above, certain minimum levels of pro-social behaviors are expected in interactions. When these are not present, then expectancy violations influence judgments of a violator's social attractiveness (Afifi and Burgoon 2000). In particular, perceived insincerity or inappropriate responses show a negative association with social attractiveness (Martin, Heisel, and Valencic 2001). The process behind this negative linkage may be the attributions people make about the status of interpersonal relationships based on their interpretation of the behavior of other people toward them. Kowalski (2000) argues that the presence of explicit negative behaviors is attributed by the recipient of such behavior as indicative of "relational devaluation." Kowalski (2000) describes two types of behavior: First, there are those behaviors perceived as directed at the "victim" and termed as direct aversive behaviors, such as betrayal of friendship or dishonesty. These are depicted as direct and malicious. The second type is inappropriate behavior attributed to the personality of the perpetrator, for example, arrogance, rudeness, dominating the conversation. These are termed "indirect" aversive behaviors. At the extremes, stealing and betrayal (dishonesty), offensive remarks, inconsiderate behavior (inappropriate behavior) result in negative reactions, for example, aggression (Bushman and Baumeister 1998).

> P_2: Perceptions of social allergens (dishonesty/ insincerity and/or inappropriate responses) during interactions with an avatar are negatively related to perceptions of relationship quality and intentions regarding avatar use.

Emotional Valence, Spiraling Negativity, and Social Allergens

According to Expectancy Violation Theory, user perceptions of negative expectancy violations are likely to result in negative emotional valence. Early attachment of negative valence can prejudice following evaluations, including person perception (Fiske 1980; Skowronski and Carlston 1989), and so precipitate "spiraling negativity." Explaining this, Cunningham et al. (2005) use the analogy of social allergens—that is, once a person is sensitized to unpleasant behaviors, repeated experiences lead to increasingly negative reactions, as with a physical allergen. These are accompanied by attributions of "relational devaluation" (Kowalski 2000), that is, the receiver believes that the perpetrator does not care about the relationship, is ill-mannered, or, worse, intentionally insulting. Hence, even relatively mild one-sided aversive behaviors can produce extreme reactions if repeatedly performed. Baumeister et al. (1990) describe how the offended party often initially stifles anger but finally responds explosively to an accumulation of aversive behaviors. The escalation of negative evaluations and reactions appears to be a recurrent finding in studies of human behavior whether in close relationships or work relationships (Andersson and Pearson 1999). Direct violations are considered a voluntary and deliberate act and so the perpetrator is considered more responsible than for indirect violations. Hence, direct violations are thought more diagnostic of relational devaluation and produce more negative evaluations than indirect behaviors (Skowronski and Carlston 1989).

> P$_3$: Perceptions of the dishonesty/insincerity dimension of social allergens will show a stronger association than the inappropriate responses dimension with ratings of relationship quality and intentions regarding avatar use.

Negativity Bias

Research consistently indicates a negativity bias in decision making. According to Expectancy Violation Theory (Burgoon and Hale 1988), violation of expectation leads to increased cognitive effort to understand the cause and meaning, and this is more likely to happen for negatively valenced violations (Pratto and John 1991). Cognitive processing research provides strong evidence that people weigh negative information more heavily than positive when forming impressions of others (Fiske 1980; Skowronski and Carlston 1989). Thus, there is a double impact of greater awareness plus greater weighting for negative information.

> P$_4$: The negative associations of social allergens will be stronger than the positive association of social competence with intention and relationship quality.

Relationship Quality and Para-Social Relationships

A gauge of felt relationship quality with virtual or fictional characters can be found in the strength of perception of "para-social" relationships. A para-social relationship or pseudo-friendship (Perse 1990) is formed when there is an illusion of a face-to-face relationship (such as might be found after interaction between the avatar and a customer) and/or the viewer identifies with people or fictional characters (Rubin and McHugh 1987). The theory of relational schemas suggests that people will attribute motivation, personality, and emotion to the avatar as result of interactions. Perse and Rubin (1989) conclude that the same cognitive constructs utilized in building actual social relationships are implicated in para-social relationships. We argue that the perceived quality and depth of the relationship itself are reflected in the perception of the strength of the para-social relationship.

Further, Rubin and McHugh (1987) found that para-social interactions follow a path from (a) social and task attraction to (b) para-social interaction. Hence, we can surmise that perceptions of para-social relationships will be positively impacted by perceptions of communication competence and negatively impacted by perceptions of social allergens. Rubin and Step (2000) find a positive association between listening behaviors and para-social interaction with a talk show host, thus we may also suppose a positive relationship between perceptions of para-social relationships and intentions to interact with the avatar.

P5: Perceptions of para-social relationship quality are positively related to intentions regarding use of the avatar.

Following the discussion and propositions above, a model of the foregoing propositions is presented in Figure 5.1, showing the relationships between perceptions of social competence, social allergens, relationship quality, and intentions toward use of a "robot" avatar acting as a virtual salesperson in online retailing.

EXPLORING THE PROPOSITIONS

Exploratory research to examine the feasibility of these propositions was carried out. Data were collected via questionnaire from sixty-six respondents after an interaction with one of three 2D avatars representing a series from realistic human to cartoon animal to abstract concept. A range of representations was chosen to help control for effects specific to one level of depiction, such as raised expectancies for human-like avatars. The human respondent was not represented as an avatar but interacted directly with the 2D representation through text boxes on an ordinary computer interface. As a first test of the model it was appropriate to use 2D avatars for two reasons: first, if the proposed effects apply in situations with minimum reality cues such as afforded by interactions with 2D representations,

Figure 5.1 **Proposed Relationships in the Technology Relationship Interaction Model**

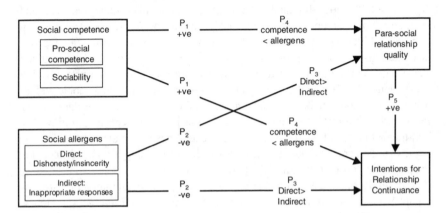

then this tests the lower boundaries within which the effects operate; second, given that many people are unfamiliar with the use of virtual worlds, potential respondents are likely to be more familiar and comfortable with regular website environments. Hence, steep learning curves for use are avoided and respondent reactions to interactions with avatars are less likely to be modified by effects from unfamiliar settings. Moreover, in this situation, the attention of the respondent is more focused on the interaction with the avatar as the human interactant is not represented as an avatar and so does not have to expend mental effort on controlling the actions of an avatar as well as making social responses. Recruitment of participants from a limited geographical area was necessary for practical reasons, in order that participants could be interviewed face-to-face. A purposive sample of people with at least two years' regular Internet experience was recruited via a university website, where e-mails to all staff alert them to particular news items and provided the necessary link. A core of original respondents was used to "snowball" a further sample to reach participants beyond the university.

The Sample

Of the people recruited, 25 (38 percent) were male and 41 (62 percent) female, the age range was between 18 and 65; 53 percent were between 18 and 35 years old and 47 percent above 35 years old, with no systematic bias between gender and age. Respondents had a wide variety of occupations.

Avatars in This Study

Suitability for a "family audience" ruled out a number of avatars for this study but, after some searching, three were found that satisfied that requirement, as well as a capability for real-time dialogue between the avatar and the respondent, a substantial interaction repertoire, and interaction with some task-fulfillment content. The avatars chosen for the study represent a series from realistic human to cartoon animal to abstract concept. Lucy was a realistic human representation responding to questions about work opportunities in the United States for health care professionals. She is dressed in green and has limited movement of her head and shoulders. The onscreen "buddy" was a cartoon purple ape with entertainment, search, and selling functions. The logo is one representation of an onscreen interactive help function and represents an abstract construct that nevertheless displays some reactions and actions during a textual interaction providing a help function for a word-processing software package.

Measures Used

Among other tasks, respondents completed questionnaires regarding perceptions of avatar social competence, social allergens in the interaction, relationship quality, and future use. The measures were constructed as follows.

Social competence consists of pro-social competence and sociability. Sociability means friendliness, politeness, and positive regard (Argyle 1992; Mottet and Richmond 1998). Immediacy is the communication of approachability, positive regard, and closeness (Mehrabian 1966) that might be termed friendliness or sociability. As a measure of sociability, perceptions of immediacy manifested in the avatar were measured by three items derived from the Relational Communication Scale (Burgoon and Hale 1987) (alpha = .74).

The pro-social behavior of cooperative and helping communication behaviors, including collaborating in the management of an efficient interaction, is covered by three items from the receptivity subscale (alpha = .59) of the Relational Communication Scale (Burgoon and Hale 1987).

Dishonesty/insincerity was measured by the four-item Salesperson Sincerity Scale (Campbell and Kirmani 2000) (alpha = .73) modified for the avatar interaction context.

Perceptions of conversational inappropriateness were determined using a two-item subset of the Conversational Appropriateness Scale (Canary and Spitzberg 1987) (alpha = .75) that fitted with the onscreen context.

Relationship quality, as discussed above, can be found in the perception of the strength of "para-social" relationships. With suitable amendments, four items appropriate for the avatar context were included from the Parasocial Interaction Scale (Rubin, Perse, and Powell 1985) to assess the level of relationship (alpha = .77).

Intentions to continue the relationship were measured by three variables derived from the literature and the interview data: would not use the avatar if given a free choice (reversed), would stay longer on website, likely to revisit the website (alpha = .68).

A MECHANISM FOR REACTIONS TO AVATARS: TOWARD THE TECHNOLOGY RELATIONSHIP INTERACTION MODEL?

The means for the constructs in Table 5.1 reveal that overall, respondents perceived no strong sense of immediacy or receptivity, the means being 3.33 and 3.12 respectively, which are near the middle of the 1–5 scale on which these perceptions were rated. Overall, most users rated dishonesty in the interaction just below the mid-point (59 percent below, 26 percent above, mean = 2.78) and inappropriate responses a little above the mid-point (26 percent below, 49 percent above, mean = 3.31). Reflected in this are the low ratings for para-social relationships (1.93) and intentions (2.05) on the same scale. The avatars used in this exploratory research were 2D representations with some interaction capabilities but rather limited in their range of movement and facial expression. Indeed, there is none of the latter in the case of the logo; thus, it is not surprising that this avatar, displaying the least range of movement and expression, is given a significantly lower rating for immediacy than the other two. Perhaps because the buddy occasionally tried to sell services and products to the users, it was given a significantly higher rating for dishonesty and insincerity than the other two.

In the interests of refining our model, we conducted a preliminary analysis consisting of two multiple regression analyses (see Table 5.2) to assess the strength of relationships—first, for interaction competence and social allergens with relationship quality (model 1), and subsequently, the relationships between these three variables with intentions (model 2).

We examine each proposition in turn, identifying the degree to which our exploratory research supported (or otherwise) these propositions.

Proposition 1 is only partially upheld: for perceptions of pro-social competence (receptivity) there is a significant relationship with intentions (use by choice/likely to visit/stay longer) (see Table 5.2). However, there is no significant relationship with relationship quality. On the other hand, sociability (immediacy) only shows a significant relationship with para-social relationship quality and is not significantly related to intentions.

Proposition 2 shows a similar pattern: dishonesty/insincerity has a direct negative relationship with intentions but no significant association with relationship quality. Inappropriate responses, however, are negatively related to relationship quality but not significantly related to intentions (see Table 5.2). Thus, there is only mixed support for Propositions 1 and 2.

Proposition 3 also has mixed support. The dishonesty/insincerity (direct allergen) dimension of social allergen path to intentions is stronger than the inappropriate response path (indirect allergen) as proposed (see Table 5.2). However, the inappropriate response (indirect allergen) dimension of social allergens to perceptions of relationship quality path is stronger than the corresponding path for the dishonesty/ insincerity (direct allergen) dimension, the opposite of Proposition 3.

Table 5.1

Means and Standard Deviations for Constructs in the Model

Perceptions of . . .	Mean	Standard deviation	Overall mean	Standard deviation	
Immediacy (sociability)			3.33	.771	p < .01 Logo lower than others
Logo	2.81	.650			
Buddy	3.78	.666			
Lucy	3.35	.638			
Receptivity (pro-social competence)			3.12	.660	ns
Logo	3.12	.518			
Buddy	3.13	.806			
Lucy	3.10	.617			
Inappropriate response (indirect allergen)			3.31	.823	ns
Logo	3.24	.890			
Buddy	3.27	.765			
Lucy	3.47	.846			
Dishonesty (direct allergen)			2.78	.712	p < .01 Buddy higher than others
Logo	2.45	.617			
Buddy	3.21	.655			
Lucy	2.56	.588			
Para-social relationship			1.93	.742	ns
Logo	1.66	.629			
Buddy	2.10	.756			
Lucy	2.05	.802			
Intentions			2.05	.850	ns
Logo	1.95	.727			
Buddy	1.93	.913			
Lucy	2.39	.871			

Table 5.2

Multiple Regression Results for Perceptions of Relationship Status and TRI Model

Model 1. Dependent Variable: Parasocial Perceptions	
Perceptions of . . .	Standardized coefficient
Immediacy (sociability)	.357**
Receptivity (prosocial competence)	.045
Inappropriate response (indirect allergen)	-.336**
Dishonesty (direct allergen)	-.105
Adj R^2	.21

Model 2. Dependent Variable: Intentions	
Perceptions of . . .	Standardized coefficient
Immediacy (sociability)	.077
Receptivity (pro-social competence)	.295*
Inappropriate response (indirect allergen)	-.178
Dishonesty (direct allergen)	-.307**
Para-social relationship	.273*
Adj R^2	.41

**Significant at 0.01 level.
*Significant at the 0.05 level.

Figure 5.2 **Multiple Regression Results for Technology Relationship Interaction Model**

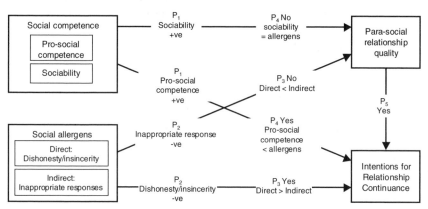

Proposition 4: As proposed, direct allergens have a stronger path to intentions than social competence (see Table 5.2). Nonetheless, sociability and indirect allergens have nearly equal path strength for parasocial relationship quality.

Overall, the results of the two multiple regressions indicate that, as shown in Table 5.2), it is possible to conclude a model of the pattern of relationships as shown in Figure 5.2. We term this the Technology Relationship Interaction Model (TRIM).

The pattern of partial support for Propositions 3 and 4 is consistent; moreover, it is consistent in a clear direction, that is, for the paths to intention there is support for Propositions 3 and 4, but not for paths to para-social relationship quality. Hence, for these data, the original conclusions drawn for intentions from the literature about the relative effects of direct and indirect allergens and a negativity bias on future behavior seem justified (see Table 5.2 and Figure 5.2). On the other hand, the similar conclusions drawn for para-social relationship quality are not supported by these data. One conclusion from these findings is that the antecedents of para-social relationships with an avatar are not necessarily the same as those for intentions to use that avatar (see Table 5.2 and Figure 5.2). Just as in the real world, not all interactions are with "friends," and the social, friendly benefits of interaction are not the only motivation for an interaction. Furthermore, it is also conceivable that the meaning of sociability itself may be different when applied to a machine, and people may expect virtual agents to respect different social norms than human beings (e.g., to take a servile role). Hence, perceptions of sociability need not be a strong antecedent of intentions for future use if there are other advantages to be gained. Further, pro-social competence (showing the skills required to carry on a competent conversation that is focused on the user needs) is more important than sociability in creating user intentions to use the avatar. Conversely, when forming "friendships," sociability skills and cues are more fitting. Attendant on sociability skills, and a strong heuristic cue of the value placed on the relationship by the other interactant, will be the presence of (in)appropriate responses within the interaction, and indeed, such is the case displayed here (see Table 5.2 and Figure 5.2).

While sociability skills might not be crucial in decisions to use an avatar, perceptions of honesty are paramount. The strongest determinant of (negative) future intentions is the perception of dishonesty/insincerity (see Table 5.2 and Figure 5.2). It is important for human participants to be able to trust any information given through the avatar interaction; without such trust, there is little reason for human participants to use the avatar beyond curiosity, novelty, or purely social motivations. This finding is consistent with the importance of the concept of information reality (Shapiro and McDonald 1992) and user sophistication in distinguishing genuine information and sincerity (Rubin, Perse, and Taylor 1988).

Proposition 5 finds support in the significant association between relationship quality and intentions. Thus, perceptions of the para-social relationship quality are one antecedent of intentions. Further, para-social relationship quality mediates the effects of sociability and inappropriate responses. These two variables only have an indirect effect on intentions through para-social relationship quality (see Table 5.2 and Figure 5.2).

Potential social allergens have a stronger effect on intentions than pro-social competence; this is consistent with the attachment of negative valence and a negativity bias. However, the negativity bias may only hold for direct allergens; sociability seems to have an equal effect to indirect allergens on para-social relationship quality. Alternatively, perhaps a lack of sociability and friendliness also has a negative valence attached and so matches the effects of indirect allergens. Certainly, in everyday interactions, a minimum level of politeness and positive regard between interactants is expected. The lack of such "social graces" is considered discourteous and disrespectful (and hence, inappropriate) by many interactants.

Overall, the results from this preliminary assessment of the avatar-human interaction model are consistent with relational devaluation in that interactions judged to be unfriendly and/or to contain indirect social allergens will have a negative effect on perceptions of para-social relationship quality.

CONCLUSIONS AND IMPLICATIONS

The study of reactions to various expectancy violations may help understanding of engagement (or not) with avatars. There are three potential paths to negative appraisals: first, through the attributions following perceptions of "direct" aversive behaviors (such as dishonesty); second, through the perceptions of repeated minor, "indirect" aversive behaviors (such as inappropriate responses or behavior and other politeness norm violations) (Baumeister et al. 1990; Cunningham et al. 2005); and last, but not least, through perceptions of low sociability and pro-social competence. The results of the study of user reactions to avatars reported here lend support to the proposal that direct social allergens have a strong negative impact on future engagement with a particular avatar. Support is also found for a negativity bias in behavioral decision making.

An important consequence of "social allergen" perceptions is the attachment of negative attributions of cause and intention to the other interactant, in this case an avatar. Such negative attributions can lead to feelings of relational devaluation. Hence, expectancy violation and attributions of relational devaluation attached to aversive social behaviors present one potential explanation for the evaluation of relationship quality and consequent interaction with avatars.

Furthermore, Serenko (2007) demonstrates that while individuals often expect software to fail, negative attributions are heightened in situations where the agent is perceived to have a higher level of autonomy. Nonetheless, the antecedents leading to perceptions of a para-social relationship appear to be different to those for a more utilitarian use, though use is also impacted by para-social relationship perceptions.

Therefore, the principal lesson from these preliminary results is that humans act on two distinct but interrelated levels in assessing the avatar use. On the one hand, on a relationship level, even within the artificial context of a textual interaction with an avatar, the human propensity toward sociability (Mead 1934) is a powerful driver; though in this case users reported little relationship developing with an avatar. Consequently, issues regarding user self-esteem must be considered when developing robot avatar interactions. Any hint of relational devaluation, whether through social allergens or poor sociability, will result in negative user perceptions of the value of the relationship and, ultimately, affect returns for future interactions.

On the other hand, users have a highly developed sense for sincerity and honesty during interactions and seem to make more concrete judgments of the usefulness of information as a result of such assessments. Such judgments have a direct effect on the influence of the avatar and are influential in determining intentions to use the avatar again or not, though perhaps with some lack of enthusiasm for unfriendly, less socially cooperative avatars that create negative feelings and threaten self-esteem. The reverse is also likely to be true: avatars with greater social competence will attract users to return for future interactions.

An Agenda for Future Research: Application of the Model for Avatar Interaction Design

The framework presented here could be the basis for systematic research on customer interactions with salespeople, whether online or offline, whether a 2D or 3D avatar or even an offline robot. An initial wave of research might consider manipulating the levels of the constructs in the model—for example, can an avatar be too friendly? Does over-friendliness arouse suspicion? What exactly constitutes dishonesty and at what level of inappropriate behavior are negative effects triggered? A comparison of effects of such manipulations between different media and offline and online interactions will highlight distinctions and similarities across interaction locations.

A reasonable extension to the model is the extent and role of felt emotions stemming from the interaction. However, the primacy of emotion or cognition, that is, whether the emotion-cognition model (Zajonc 1984) or cognition-emotion model (Lazarus 1984) best fits this situation, is yet to be established through research.

Other variables might also be added to the model. These are of three kinds: product/service factors, situational factors, and individual difference factors. Product/service factors include the product/service classification within the search-experience-credence continuum (Girard, Silverblatt, and Korgaonkar 2002). It is clearly important to understand whether the product or service category alters the impact of avatar interaction on customer patronage intentions.

As regards situational factors, research on offline shopping finds both the prior mood of the customer before entering the store and customer perceptions of the store atmosphere to moderate customer responses and purchase intentions. Spies, Hesse, and Loesch (1997) suggest this is because a pleasant store atmosphere reminds customers of other positive experiences, which in turn induce positive moods on the part of customers. Beyond the store environment, other situational factors are suggested by work on triggers of aggressive responses and whether the outcome of public events have a stronger effect on self-esteem than private events.

Individual difference variables fall into two categories. First are those that help illuminate complex relationships and lead to better requirements capture for personalized website responses. These variously include gender differences in reactions to certain features of social interaction or individual differences in involvement with the product (Zaichkowsky 1985; Laurent and Kapferer 1985; Higie and Feick 1988); individual differences in hedonic and utilitarian shopping values (Babin, Darden, and Griffin 1994); and differences in propensity to seek help when shopping based on risk reduction strategies (Mitchell and McGoldrick 1995). Cultural differences also assume a fundamental importance, as customers will hold different social norms in mind when interacting with social agents.

For other individual differences, the researcher might wish to control for their effects to separate out background effects due to the natural differences between people. For example, pertinent to the model are low or high self-esteem, as low self-esteem is likely to result in more extreme reactions to relationship devaluation (Leary 2002). Other variables in this category are "individual" information-processing differences in interpreting social and situational cues such as attention to social comparison information (Bearden and Rose 1990), susceptibility to interpersonal influence (Burkrant and Cousineau 1975), self-concept clarity (Campbell et al. 1996), and general sentiment toward the marketplace—for example, consumer alienation from the marketplace (Allison 1978). Other questions concern how the physical appearance of the avatar may affect perceptions of the interaction, perhaps through setting higher or lower expectations or even creating a halo effect of physical attractiveness. What avatar representation (e.g., human, animal, or abstract construct) is most appropriate in difference situations or for different products?

The model should also be useful in considering appropriate interaction content for different contexts. Norms and requirements are likely to differ across disparate situations such as a virtual doctor–human patient interaction compared to a virtual shop assistant–human customer interaction. To this end, conversation analysis should also be performed to help clarify conversational rules and norms driving interactions in the particular case of human–avatar interaction. Such research may also help shed light on the human interactant view of the status of the avatar; for example, are such interactions considered as between a servant (avatar) and master (human), or on an equal footing?

Consideration can additionally be given to the tailoring of service provision, particularly providing choice of avatar agents (and the likely range and nature of avatars to be provided). This might even include a choice of personality of the agent.

Limitations

The sample of users for this study was limited by geography to one region of the UK, hence this study invites replication with a wider group of users, and the findings should be interpreted with care. Nonetheless, one contribution of this exploratory research is the model derived from theory and analysis that can provide the basis for future research and can be tested in future work such as suggested in the agenda for future research.

A further limitation is that this study relied upon user self-report. Future research on user reactions might consider the use of observational data collection, including biometrics such as eye-tracking, electroencephalography, breathing rate, and heart rate alongside protocol interviews to gain some measure of emotional reactions from the human partner that may accompany avatar interactions. Insight on the emotional correlates of behavior should help refine appropriate interaction programming for avatars in particular situations.

ACKNOWLEDGMENTS

We thank all respondents and the EPSRC grant number R66890/01 for supporting this research.

REFERENCES

Afifi, W.A., and J.K. Burgoon. 2000. "The Impact of Violations on Uncertainty and the Consequences for Attractiveness." *Human Communication Research* 26 (2): 203–233.

Allison, N.K. 1978. "Psychometric Development of a Test for Consumer Alienation from the Marketplace." *Journal of Marketing Research* 15: 565–575.

Andersson, L., and C. Pearson. 1999. "Tit for Tat? Spiraling Incivility in the Workplace." *Academy of Management Review* 24 (3): 452–471.

Argyle, M. 1992. *The Social Psychology of Everyday Life.* London: Routledge.

Babin, B.J., W.R. Darden, and M. Griffin. 1994. "Work and/or Fun: Measuring Hedonic and Utilitarian Shopping Value." *Journal of Consumer Research* 20: 644–656.

Bargh, J., and T. Chartrand. 1999. "The Unbearable Automaticity of Being." *American Psychologist* 54 (7): 462–479.

Baumeister, R.F., A. Stillwell, and S.R. Wotman. 1990. "Victim and Perpetrator Accounts of Interpersonal Conflict: Autobiographical Narratives About Anger." *Journal of Personality and Social Psychology* 59: 994–1005.

Bearden, W.O., and R.L. Rose. 1990. "Attention to Social Comparison Information, an Individual Difference Factor Affecting Consumer Conformity." *Journal of Consumer Research* 16: 461–471.

Berscheid, E. 1994. "Interpersonal Relationships." *Annual Review of Psychology* 45: 79–130.

Burgoon, J.K., J.A. Bonito, B. Bengtsson, M. Lundeberg, and L. Allspach. 2000. "Interactivity in Human Computer Interaction: A Study of Credibility, Understanding, and Influence." *Computers in Human Behavior* 16 (6): 553–574.

Burgoon, J.K., and J.L. Hale. 1987. "Validation and Measurement of the Fundamental Themes of Relational Communication." *Communication Monographs* 54: 19–41.

———. 1988. "Nonverbal Expectancy Violations: Model Elaboration and Application to Immediacy Behaviors." *Communication Monographs* 55: 58–79.

Burgoon, J.K., and J.B. Walther. 1990. "Nonverbal Expectancies and the Consequences of Violations." *Human Communication Research* 17: 232–265.

Burkrant, R.E., and A. Cousineau. 1975. "Informational and Normative Influence in Buyer Behavior." *Journal of Consumer Research* 2: 206–215.

Bushman, B.J., and R.F. Baumeister. 1998. "Threatened Egoism, Narcissism, Self-Esteem and Direct and Displaced Aggression: Does Self-Love or Self-Hate Lead to Violence?" *Journal of Personality and Social Psychology* 75: 219–229.

Campbell, J., P.D. Trapnell, S.J. Heine, H.M. Katz, L.F. Lavalee, and D.R. Lehman. 1996. "Self Concept Clarity, Measurement, Personality Correlates and Cultural Boundaries." *Journal of Personality and Social Psychology* 70 (1): 141–156.

Campbell, M.C., and A. Kirmani. 2000. "Consumers' Use of Persuasion Knowledge: The Effects of Accessibility and Cognitive Capacity on Perceptions of an Influence Agent." *Journal of Consumer Research* 27 (1): 69–83.

Canary, D.J., and B.H. Spitzberg. 1987. "Appropriateness and Effectiveness Perceptions of Conflict Strategies." *Human Communication Research* 14: 93–118.

Cassell, J., J. Sullivan, S. Provost, and E. Churchill. 2000. *Embodied Conversational Agents.* Cambridge, MA: MIT Press.

Cunningham, M., S. Shamblen, A. Barbee, and L. Ault. 2005. "Social Allergies in Romantic Relationships: Behavioral Repetition, Emotional Sensitization, and Dissatisfaction in Dating Couples." *Personal Relations* 12: 273–295.

Cyr, D., K. Hassanein, M. Head, and A. Ivanov. 2007. The Role of Social Presence in Establishing Loyalty in e-Service Environments." *Interacting with Computers* 19 (1): 43–56.

De Angeli, A., and S. Brahnam. 2008. "I Hate You! Disinhibition with Virtual Partners." *Interacting with Computers* 20 (3): 302–10.

De Angeli, A., P. Lynch, and G. Johnson. 2001. "Personifying the e-Market: A Framework for Social Agents." In *Human-Computer Interaction: Interact '01,* ed. Michitake Hirose, 198–205. Amsterdam, IOS Press.

Dehn, D.M., and S. van Mulken. 2000. "The Impact of Animated Interface Agents: A Review of Empirical Research." *International Journal of Human-Computer Studies* 52: 1–22.

Donath, J. 2008. "Giving Avatars Emote Control." *Harvard Business Review* 86 (2): 31–32.

Duran, R.L., and L. Kelly. 1988. "The Influence of Communicative Competence on Perceived Task, Social, and Physical Attraction." *Communication Quarterly* 36: 41–49.

Fiske, S.T. 1980. "Attention and Weight in Person Perception: The Impact of Negative and Extreme Information." *Journal of Personality and Social Psychology* 38: 889–906.

———. 1992. "Thinking Is for Doing." *Journal of Personal and Social Psychology* 63: 877–889.

Girard, T., R. Silverblatt, and P. Korgaonkar 2002. "Influence of Product Class on Preference for Shopping on the Internet," *Journal of Computer-Mediated Communication* 8; 1–22.

Griffin, A.M., and J.H. Langlois.2006. Stereotype Directionality and Attractiveness Stereotyping: Is Beauty Good or is Ugly Bad? *Social Cognition* 24(2); 187–206.

Hayes-Roth, B., E. Sincoff, L. Brownston, R. Huard, and B. Lent. 1995. "Directed Improvisation with Animated Puppets." In *Proceedings of CHI '95 Conference on Human-Computer Interaction,* Denver (May 7–11), NewYork, ACM Press 79–80.

Hemp, P. 2006. "Avatar-based Marketing." *Harvard Business Review* 84 (6): 48–57.

Higie, R.A., and L.F. Feick. 1988. "Enduring Involvement: Conceptual and Methodological Issues." *Advances in Consumer Research* 16 (1): 690–696.

Holzwarth, M., C. Janiszewski, and M.M. Neumann. 2006. "The Influence of Avatars on Online Consumer Shopping Behavior." *Journal of Marketing* 70 (4): 19–36.

Keeling, K.A., P.J. McGoldrick, and S. Beatty. 2007. "Virtual Onscreen Assistants: A Viable Strategy to Support Online Customer Relationship Building?" *Advances in Consumer Research* 34: 138–144.

Kowalski, R., ed. 2000. *Aversive Interpersonal Behaviors.* 2nd ed. Washington, DC: APA.

Laurent, G., and J-N. Kapferer. 1985. "Measuring Consumer Involvement Profiles." *Journal of Marketing Research* 22: 41–53.

Lazarus, R.S. 1984. "On the Primacy of Cognition." *American Psychologist* 39 (2): 124–129.

Leary, M.R. 2002. "When Selves Collide: The Nature of the Self and the Dynamics of Interpersonal Relationships." In *Psychological Perspectives on Self and Identity,* vol. 2, ed. A. Tesser, J. Wood and D. Stapel, 119–145. Washington, DC: APA.

Leary, M.R., E.S. Tambor, S.K. Terdal, and D.L. Downs. 1995. "Self-Esteem as an Interpersonal Monitor: The Sociometer Hypothesis." *Journal of Personality and Social Psychology* 68: 518–530.

Lee, K.M., and C. Nass. 2003. "Designing Social Presence of Social Actors in Human Computer Interaction. In *Proceedings of the CHI 2003 Conference on Human Factors in Computing Systems*, Ft. Lauderdale (April 5–10), New York, ACM Press 289–296.

Luo, J.T., P. McGoldrick, S. Beatty, and K.A. Keeling. 2006. "On-Screen Characters: Their Design and Influence on Consumer Trust." *Journal of Services Marketing* 20 (2): 112–124.

Martin, M.M., A.D. Heisel, and K.M. Valencic. 2001. "Verbal Aggression in Computer-Mediated Decision Making." *Psychological Reports* 89 (1): 24.

McCroskey, J.C., P.R. Hamilton, and A.N. Weiner. 1974. "The Effect of Interaction Behavior on Source Credibility, Homophily, and Interpersonal Attraction." *Human Communication Research* 1: 42–52.

Mead, G.H. 1934. "The Social Foundations and Functions of Thought and Communication." In *Mind, Self, and Society from the Standpoint of a Social Behaviorist: Works of George Herbert Mead,* ed. Charles W. Morris, section 33, 253–260. Chicago: University of Chicago. Available at http://spartan.ac.brocku.ca/~lward/Mead/pubs2/mindself/Mead_1934_33.html.

Mehrabian, A. 1966. "Immediacy: An Indicator of Attitudes in Linguistic Communication." *Journal of Personality* 34: 26–34.

Miller, C.A. 2004. "Human-Computer Etiquette: Managing Expectations with Intentional Agents." *Communications of the ACM* 47 (4): 30–34.

Mitchell, V., and P. McGoldrick. 1995. "Consumer Risk Reducing Strategies: A Review and Synthesis." *International Journal of Retail, Distribution and Consumer Research* 6 (1): 1–33.

Mottet, T.P., and V.P. Richmond. 1998. "An Inductive Analysis of Verbal Immediacy: Alternative Conceptualization of Relational Verbal Approach/Avoidance Strategies." *Communication Quarterly* 46 (1): 25–40.

Perse, E.M. 1990. "Media Involvement and Local News Effects." *Journal of Broadcasting and Electronic Media* 34: 17–36.

Perse, E.M., and A.M. Rubin. 1989. "Attributions in Social and Parasocial Relationships." *Communications Research* 16: 59–77.

Pratto, F., and O.P. John. 1991. "Automatic Vigilance: The Attention-Grabbing Power of Negative Social Information." *Journal of Personality and Social Psychology* 61: 380–391.

Qui, L., and I. Benbasat. 2005. "Online Consumer Trust and Live Help Interfaces: The Effects of Text-to-Speech Voice and Three-Dimensional Avatars." *International Journal of Human-Computer Interaction* 19 (1): 75–94.

Reeves, B., and C.I. Nass. 1996. *The Media Equation: How People Treat Computers, Television, and New Media Like Real People and Places.* Stanford, CA: CSLI Publications and Cambridge University Press.

Rubin, A.M., E.M. Perse, and R.A. Powell. 1985. "Loneliness, Parasocial Interaction, and Local Television News Viewing." *Human Communication Research* 12 (2): 155–180.

Rubin, A.M., E.M. Perse, and D.S. Taylor. 1988. "A Methodological Examination of Cultivation." *Communication Research* 15 (2): 107–134.

Rubin, A.M., and M.M. Step. 2000. "Impact of Motivation, Attraction, and Parasocial Interaction on Talk Radio Listening." *Journal of Broadcasting and Electronic Media* 44 (4): 635–654.

Rubin, R.B., and M.P. McHugh. 1987. "Development of Parasocial Interaction Relationships." *Journal of Broadcasting and Electronic Media* 31: 279–292.

Serenko, A. 2007. "Are Interface Agents Scapegoats? Attributions of Responsibility in Human-Agent Interaction." *Interacting with Computers* 19: 293–303.

Shapiro, M.A., and D.G. McDonald. 1992. "I'm Not a Real Doctor, But I Play One in Virtual Reality: Implications of Virtual Reality for Judgments About Reality." *Journal of Communication* 42 (4): 94–114.

Skowronski, J.J., and D.E. Carlston. 1989. "Negativity and Extremity Biases in Impression Formation: A Review of Explanations." *Psychological Bulletin* 105: 131–142.

Spies, K., F. Hesse, and K. Loesch. 1997. "Store Atmosphere, Mood and Purchasing Behaviour," *International Journal of Research in Marketing* 14: 1–17.

Wood, N.T., M.R. Solomon, and B.G. Englis. 2005. "Personalisation of Online Avatars: Is the Messenger as Important as the Message?" *International Journal of Internet Marketing and Advertising* 2 (1/2): 143–161.

Zaichkowsky, J.L. 1985. "Measuring the Involvement Construct." *Journal of Consumer Research* 12: 341–352.

Zajonc, R.B. 1984. "On the Primacy of Affect." *American Psychologist* 39 (2): 117–123.

CHAPTER 6

Personalized Avatar

A New Way to Improve Communication and E-Service

DAVID CRETE, ANIK ST-ONGE, AURELIE MERLE,
NICOLAS ARSENAULT, AND JACQUES NANTEL

Many consumers use the Internet as a search tool prior to many purchases. More than 93 percent of consumers will seek information on the Internet before buying electronic appliances (Hallerman 2006), and 39 percent of consumers confirm that the Internet influenced their purchasing decisions (CEFRIO 2006). In addition, U.S. online sales for the year 2007 were expected to reach $131.3 billion, a 20.8 percent increase compared to the previous year. Sales of apparel, footwear, and accessories were expected to reach $22.1 billion in 2007, a 21 percent increase over 2006 (Grau 2007). Today, U.S. shoppers spend more on online shopping for apparel than for computers, allowing that market to become the largest online retail sales category (excluding travel). Consequently, many retailers try to claim their share of the market by enhancing their retailer websites in order to give their online consumers the best experience possible and to increase the conversion rate (Childers et al. 2001).

In this context, the tendency to customize the content of web pages through interactive tools will soon become a standard in the development of retailer websites. A new form of customization of information is emerging in the apparel industry: the use of an avatar that reflects the consumer's body. An avatar is a 2D or 3D virtual image that represents the user and/or the customer service representation (Qiu and Benbasat 2005). New forms of avatars are distinctive in that users can input information regarding measurements, body shape, hair style, and so forth and create a virtual model to visualize and "try on" clothing using a body similar to their own (Calhoun, Lyman-Clarke, and Ashdown 2007). We refer to this as a personalized avatar.

Many studies have been carried out concerning interactivity and data processing (Ariely 2000; Häubl et al. 2004; Häubl and Trifts 2000; Steckel et al. 2005;

Wang and Lin 2002), website customization (Wind and Rangaswamy 2001), and avatars (Keeling et al. 2004; Holzwarth, Janiszewski, and Neumann 2006; McGoldrick, Keeling, and Beatty 2008; Wood, Solomon, and Englis 2005, 2008). However, to the best of our knowledge, little is known about the influence of the customization of information involving the use of a *personalized* avatar on online behavior and on perceptions of a website.

The goal of this research is also to determine the influence of customization of information by means of a personalized avatar on perceived quality, attitude, and stickiness of a website. In addition, the issue of information level is important on the Internet. Walsh, Mitchell, and Frenzel (2004) pointed to the possibility of "overload e-confusion" related to the increasing assortment of e-tailers. Some authors claimed that personalization could help consumers to reduce the overload of information and to facilitate choice in larger assortments (Kahn 1998; Schubert and Ginsburg 1999). Consequently, we decided to examine our results according to the level of assortment provided on the website. In other words, is the use of a personalized avatar a relevant way to increase the consumer's positive perception of the website, regardless of the level of assortment? This chapter also contributes to a better understanding of the impact on website perception of customization of information through the use of a personalized avatar.

LITERATURE REVIEW

Avatars and e-Customerization

Customerization is an advanced form of personalization that is carried out by the customer (Wind and Rangaswamy 2001; Cöner 2003). In an interactive environment where the quantity of information is overwhelming, it becomes particularly interesting to customize the contents of web pages. The customization of information consists of providing a quantity and quality of information that corresponds to the individual preferences of the consumers. One of the objectives is to limit their exposure to too much information and to offer them information that precisely meets their needs (Peppers and Rogers 1993; Wind and Rangaswamy 2001). Many websites use avatars to customize information, although few studies have investigated this phenomenon. Holzwarth, Janiszewski, and Neumann (2006) maintain that avatars are virtual characters that can be used as company representatives, personal shopping assistants, or website guides. In the same vein, McGoldrick, Keeling, and Beatty (2008) identified three potential roles of an avatar: friend, personal shopper, and helper. In fact, consumers have considerable reluctance to shop online; obstacles include impersonal service and lack of staff to answer their questions if they need help. The use of avatars enables retailers to humanize the consumer's relationship with the website (Trogemann 2003), facilitate communication with users of the website (Salem and Earle 2000; Wood, Solomon, and Englis 2005), and increase user confidence (Qiu and Benbasat 2005). Here, we focus on personalized avatars.

Website Quality

Academic and commercial research has demonstrated that e-quality is a constant preoccupation. Zeithaml, Parasuraman, and Malhotra (2002) argue that companies must first understand how customers perceive and evaluate online service. They maintain that E-SQ (electronic service quality) is the extent to which a website facilitates efficient and effective shopping, purchasing, and delivery of products and services. In addition, Bressolles and Nantel (2007) identify five dimensions related to perceived website quality: layout, information, ease of use, security/privacy, and reliability. We focus here on the first two since we assume that both of them can be improved with the use of a personalized avatar.

The literature reveals that offering entertainment content to consumers should have a positive impact on the perception of the retailer's product and the company (Brown and Stayman 1992; MacKenzie and Lutz 1989; MacKenzie, Lutz, and Belch 1986). Holzwarth, Janiszewski, and Neumman (2006) support the assertion that the use of an avatar leads to more entertainment value. Hence, avatars can be used to increase shopping pleasure and improve the aesthetics of web design. Beautiful interfaces are generally better rated by consumers (Tractinsky 1997). As Norman (2004) asserts, because attractive things are believed to work better, aesthetics should command a higher priority in design. Today, designers have the ability to make a product attractive and appeal to users' emotions (Jordan 2000). Therefore, we hypothesize the following:

H_1: Use of a personalized avatar contributes to increasing the perceived design quality of a website.

In addition, customization makes it possible for organizations to improve the quality of information customers require and hence present products that correspond to the consumers' specific needs (Peppers, Rogers, and Dorf 1999; Freund 2003). This is undoubtedly one of the most important advantages for the customer. Through customization, the consumer can process only the data that is relevant to his/her needs without being overexposed to data. Hart (2002) described this notion of relevance on the web as the ability of a site to present information that meets the user's needs immediately. By having access to personalized information, websites are able to reduce considerably the cost of information searches to potential customers (Ray 2003; Häubl et al. 2004). Customers are thus able to make more enlightened decisions (Huang 2000). Therefore, we posit that the use of a personalized avatar will result in a higher perception of the quality of information.

H_2: Use of a personalized avatar contributes to increasing the perceived quality of information on a website.

Attitude Toward the Website

Many researchers state that one of the key advantages of customization over the web is the development of customer loyalty (Peppers, Rogers, and Dorf 1999). An organization can improve each interaction with customers because it has the capacity to present products in a manner that corresponds to their needs. It thus becomes increasingly difficult for a competitor to achieve the same level of customization. Attitude toward the website is analyzed as an antecedent of website loyalty (Donthu 2001). This concept is defined as "a person's predisposition to respond to a website in a consistent manner" (Chen and Wells 1999) and is seen as an indicator of website efficiency (Elliott and Speck 2005). According to Ray (2003), consumers who shop on customized websites have greater confidence in the organization. In addition, the literature has suggested that the main value of the customization of a website is the positive impact on website attitude and purchasing intention (Stevenson, Bruner, and Kumar 2000). In consequence, hypothesis H_3 can be stated.

H_3: Use of a personalized avatar contributes to increasing positive consumer attitude toward a website.

Stickiness

Today, many websites are an extension of the brick and mortar business. Web interfaces allow retailers to go beyond commercial communications and offer consumers many online services. Additionally, the Internet continues to influence sales in offline channels, strengthening traditional store brands as well as catalogues. Due to the importance of the relation between consumers and websites, many companies want their website to be as attractive as possible in order to attract, retain, and sell products to consumers. It is important to remember that consumers are free to surf the Internet as they please, and are never more than a click away from exiting the site and not coming back (Oxley and Miller 2000).

To measure the performance of websites, many specialists evoke the term "stickiness." We define this concept as the retention of consumers on the website or the ability to attract and hold a visitor's interest (Bhat, Bevans, and Sengupta 2002). Stickiness can be measured by the average time a user spends on a site, the number of pages visited, and the frequency of his or her visits to the site (Guenther 2004). Thus, these indicators provide excellent insight into the performance of the site, and its evaluation and retention by consumers. The more attractive the site is, the more time people will spend there, hence the more the opportunity for companies to deliver messages to users (Bhat, Bevans, and Sengupta 2002) and to encourage consumers to buy products. In the same way, we argue that customizing a website with the help of a personalized avatar will have a positive impact on navigation time and the number of visited pages, leading to hypotheses H_4 and H_5.

H_4: Use of a personalized avatar contributes to increasing the total navigation time on a website.

H_5: Use of a personalized avatar contributes to increasing the total number of pages visited on a website.

Assortment

Offering a wide variety of products or items is a frequent strategy to increase the probability that each consumer will find a product that meets her/his needs. The Internet provides an interesting platform for every firm for whom assortments and variety are part of the business. In this chapter, we define the concept of assortment as "the total set of items offered by a retailer, reflecting both the breadth and depth of offered product lines" (Simonson 1999). Grewal et al. (1999) recall that assortments are a strategic positioning tool to attract and retain core customers. They provide several benefits to consumers. According to Betancourt and Gautschi (1990), they allow consumers to find the products they are looking for, at a relatively low search cost. They also contribute to reducing uncertainty and provide relevant information to decision makers (Ross and Creyer 1992; Simonson 1999). Assortments can also enhance the enjoyment of shopping (Babin, Darden, and Griffin 1994).

However, this strategy can have a "dark" side. Large assortments and complexity are likely to increase consumer dissatisfaction and frustration. For example, too much information can lead to information overload (Jacoby, Speller, and Berning 1974). Researchers have shown that such dissatisfaction with the shopping process is largely attributable to retailers. This lack of satisfaction is thus likely to impact store traffic and the number of consumers that make a purchase (Fitzsimons, Greenleaf, and Lehmann 1997). Furthermore, Chernev (2006) asserts that consumers are often less confident in choices made from larger rather than smaller assortments. The author maintains that people often cannot predict their need for variety and they overrate the attractiveness of large assortments. In addition, several researchers (Jacoby, Speller, and Berning 1974; Malhotra 1982; Keller and Staelin 1987) found evidence that increasing the number of alternatives or attributes in a choice set leads to a decline in the quality of consumers' choices.

However, when choosing among assortments, consumers opt for the variety offered by larger assortments (Chernev 2006). Oppewall and Koelemeijer (2005) affirm that larger assortments are rated more positively. They also claim that larger assortments are generally preferable to smaller ones, even if the smaller one contains the preferred or favorite alternative. This finding is contrary to the belief that people with strong prior preferences will value smaller assortments more than consumers with no such preferences. Researchers have argued that people often do not have clear and stable preferences (Bettman, Luce, and Payne 1998). Simonson (1999) maintains that this finding is consistent with the idea that in many situations, people construct their preferences when faced with a specific purchase decision, rather than retrieve preformed evaluations of product features and alternatives. It is also important to let consumers choose from a large assortment, rather than restricting them to a smaller one. The use of a personalized avatar can be seen as a way to help the consumer in a large assortment setting. By trying the products on their own body, consumers can make better choices. We also argue that using a personalized avatar can result in more positive attitude and higher stickiness when the level of assortment is high. Indeed, consumers have a greater need for such virtual tools to help them in this type of environment. In consequence, we can state hypotheses H_6, H_7, H_8, and H_9.

H_6: When the level of assortment offered on a website increases, the use of a personalized avatar increases too.

H_7: When the level of assortment offered on a website increases, the use of a personalized avatar increases the total navigation time on the website (interaction effect).

H_8: When the level of assortment offered on a website increases, customizing the use of a personalized avatar increases the total number of visited pages on the website (interaction effect).

H_9: When the level of assortment offered on a website increases, the use of a personalized avatar contributes to improving consumers' attitude toward the website (interaction effect).

CONCEPTUAL FRAMEWORK

To summarize the constructs and the hypotheses presented in the previous section, Figure 6.1 portrays our theoretical model of the impact of a personalized avatar on the perceived quality, attitude toward, and stickiness of a website. We hypothesized a moderating role of the level of assortment on the relationships between the use of a personalized avatar and two out of the three dependent variables: attitude toward the website and stickiness.

METHODOLOGY

Our study used an experimental website constructed in collaboration with two companies, Home Shopping Network (HSN.com) and My Virtual Model (MVM.com). The pages were hosted on a university server. HSN is an online retailer selling different categories of products, while MVM technology can be used to create virtual 3D models according to a user-specified profile. Users manipulate twelve bits of information (e.g., size, measurements, weight, hair color) to give a model the desired appearance and can recreate a virtual representation of themselves. This model lets customers try on clothes before buying them on retailers' sites (Nantel 2004).

Figure 6.1 **Conceptual Framework**

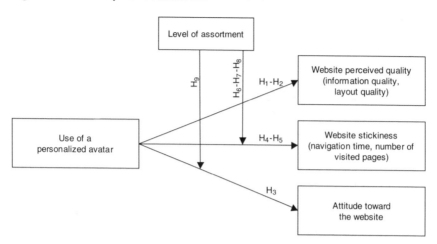

Sampling and Procedure

Participants were recruited through a mass e-mail sent to 45,000 individuals. A drawing for a $500 prize served as an incentive. As virtual models primarily target women, we retained only female subjects for the analysis. Of the 45,000 e-mails that were originally sent, 400 female subjects agreed to participate (84 percent of them were between 19 and 54 years old). The study design involved a 2 × 3 between-subject experimental design (2 being use of a personalized avatar: personalized avatar proposed or not; 3 being level of assortment: 10, 20, or 30 blouses). Each participant was randomly assigned to one of the six experimental conditions and was exposed to the fictitious website. We asked each of them to buy a blouse, with no time constraint. We offered to 193 out of 400 participants the option of using the virtual model. Of the 193 subjects, 56 did not use it and were eliminated. After the task completion, subjects were directed to the questionnaire site. Then, they were thanked. Table 6.1 shows each cell composition. A total of 344 participants are included in the analysis.

Measures

Only the measures used in the analysis are described here. Perceived design and information quality were measured on a 7-point scale developed by Bressolles and Nantel (2007). This scale, NetQual, measures five dimensions related to perceived website quality: information, ease of use, layout, security/privacy, and reliability. For this study, we measured only the layout and information dimensions. The mean of the three items was used (Cronbach's alpha = 0.92 for layout dimension and 0.90 for information). Attitude toward the website (Awebsite) was measured on

Table 6.1

Cell Composition

		Personalized avatar use		
		Yes	No	Total
	10 blouses	43	74	117
Level of assortment	20 blouses	53	70	123
	30 blouses	41	63	104
	Total	137	207	344

a 5-point scale bounded from "Definitely disagree" to "Definitely agree" (Chen and Wells 1999). The last item was anchored from "One of the worst" to "One of the best." The mean of the six items was used (Cronbach's alpha = 0.92). Stickiness was measured according to experimental navigation data: task duration and number of visited pages.

RESULTS

Analysis is reported here only for the two major issues mentioned earlier: (1) whether customization influences the perceived quality and the attitude toward the website, and (2) whether customization influences stickiness (duration and number of pages visited). To test the effects of customization on the dependent variables, a one-way ANOVA test was conducted.

Website Quality

Customization is likely to improve perceived layout quality. Analysis shows that participants who used the virtual model had a better opinion of the design quality of the site than those who did not use it ($F[1, 338] = 3.320, p < .05$). H_1 was thus supported. Furthermore, our findings show that using a virtual tool provides more in-depth information about the product proposed ($F[1, 338] = 3.039, p < .1$). H_2 was thus marginally supported.

Attitude Toward the Website

Customization had a mixed effect on the attitude toward the website. The results point in two directions. First, use of the virtual model does not influence Awebsite ($F[1, 338] = 1.617, p > .05$). It does not make the attitude more positive; H_3 was not supported. However, an interaction effect existed between the number of blouses and the use of the virtual model ($F[2, 338] = 4.550, p < .05$), which demonstrated that as the number of alternatives increases, the impact of the use of a personalized avatar on the attitude varies. However, this effect (interaction)

Table 6.2

Attitude Toward the Website (Interaction)

Level of assortment	Difference in means	T	Df	Sig.
10 blouses	−0.115	−0.598	92.477	0.276
20 blouses	−0.564	−3.106	113.032	0.001
30 blouses	0.255	1.247	72,813	0.108

Table 6.3

Descriptive Statistics Task Duration

Use of a personalized avatar	Level of information	Mean	SD	N
Yes	10 blouses	118.63	92.62	43
	20 blouses	172.11	94.32	53
	30 blouses	239.17	155.14	41
	Total	194.23	118.35	137
No	10 blouses	175.96	161.96	74
	20 blouses	171.26	119.02	70
	30 blouses	157.35	83.20	63
	Total	168.71	127.22	207
Total	10 blouses	176.94	140.05	117
	20 blouses	171.63	108.64	123
	30 blouses	189.61	123.00	104
	Total	178.87	124.22	344

seems to obtain for a certain amount of information only. The highest attitude score is reached at 20 blouses and the lowest at 30 pieces of clothing. Once again, the level of assortment acted as a moderating factor. H_9 was thus supported. A t-test showed that using a personalized avatar has a significant influence on attitude toward the website only for 20 blouses ($t = -3.106$, $p < .001$) (see Table 6.2).

Stickiness

Results demonstrated that the use of a personalized avatar has the potential to influence navigation patterns. Analysis revealed that subjects who used this tool took more time to complete the task ($F[1, 338] = 4.375$, $p < .05$); H_4 was thus supported. Moreover, the amount of information presented has an impact on task duration. Table 6.3 shows descriptive statistics, reporting level of customization (personalized avatar use), level of information (number of blouses), task duration, mean scores, and standard deviations.

First, there was a significant interaction between the number of blouses and the use of the virtual model ($F[2, 338] = 3.682$, $p < .05$). Customizing the information had a balanced effect on total task duration according to the level of assortment

Table 6.4

Descriptive Statistics Visited Pages

Personalized avatar use	Level of assortment	Mean	SD	N
Yes	10 blouses	11.28	4.65	43
	20 blouses	11.09	4.21	53
	30 blouses	12.88	6.83	41
	Total	11.75	5.29	137
No	10 blouses	9.42	4.27	74
	20 blouses	9.81	4.85	70
	30 blouses	8.73	3.28	63
	Total	9.34	4.22	207
Total	10 blouses	10.10	4.49	117
	20 blouses	10.37	4.61	123
	30 blouses	10.45	5.40	104
	Total	10.30	4.81	344

proposed. The analysis showed that using the virtual model results in a longer task duration only when 30 blouses are offered. It is worth noting that subjects who chose from among 30 blouses used the virtual model 2.71 times compared with 1.58 times for those who had a choice of 20 blouses ($F[1, 338] = 7.076$, $p < .05$). This increased use explains the variation in the task duration and shows that the level of assortment acted as a moderating factor. Therefore, the results support H_6 and H_7.

Second, use of a personalized avatar had an impact on pages visited. Table 6.4 shows descriptive statistics of this dependent variable, reporting level of customization (virtual model use), level of information (number of blouses), pages visited, mean scores, and standard deviations. Subjects who used the personalized avatar visited more pages to complete the task ($F[1, 338] = 23.627$, $p < .000$). H_5 was thus supported. As for the task duration, there was a significant interaction between the number of blouses and the use of the virtual model ($F[2, 338] = 3.277$, $p < .05$). This interaction showed that as the number of blouses offered increases, the influence of the use of a virtual model on the number of visited pages increases too. Consequently, H_8 was supported.

Overall, the results regarding task duration and visited pages indicate that using a "customization tool" such as a virtual model can positively influence users' navigation patterns.

DISCUSSION AND CONCLUSIONS

Given the growth of Internet purchases and the strong competition between retailers, it is important to determine what factors attract and retain consumers, motivate their purchases, and favor their loyalty. The quality of online service delivery is a major component in the influence of consumers' online behavior (Zeithaml, Parasuraman, and Malhotra 2002). Our research examined the impact of an innovative way to shape the perceptions of a website: the use of a personalized avatar created by the consumer. Based on an experimental study, we identified the impact of using this kind of avatar on the perceived quality, attitude toward, and stickiness of a website. Although research has been conducted on avatars and customization, we conducted, to the best of our knowledge, the first study concerning the merits of using an avatar specifically related to the consumer's self-image (i.e., virtual model) to enhance communication and consumers' experience on a website.

Our findings suggest that the use of a personalized avatar influences users' perceptions of the layout of the website. Norman (2004) asserts that an interface that is more aesthetically pleasing will leave customers with a better impression and can increase customer retention and loyalty. Consequently, using this kind of personalized avatar could be an asset for a website. However, this implies that the personalized avatar is perceived as attractive/esthetic by the consumer. In other words, since the virtual model is a reflection of the consumer's body, she/he has to perceive herself/himself as good-looking. In this sense, further studies should introduce self-image, or self-esteem, as a moderating factor. How will the consumer react if she perceives herself as an unattractive person? In addition, the results of this study show that consumers using a personalized avatar have a more positive perception of the information generated by the website. This result is particularly interesting because we know that one of the main reasons consumers shop online is to obtain in-depth information on the product (Li, Cheng, and Russell 1999; Swaminathan, Lepkowska-White, and Rao 1999). If the consumers do not perceive the information provided on this site in a positive way, they are likely to favor other websites or traditional stores. Further, our results are congruent with previous studies, which demonstrate that when consumers obtain more personalized information, the cost associated with information retrieval is reduced (Ray 2003; Häubl et al. 2004), and this personalized information helps consumers complete their purchases. Other objectives of this study were to explore the impact of customization on website stickiness and attitude. Following the manipulation of the level of assortment, we observed several significant variations in the behavior and attitudes of the respondents.

Customizing the information presented on a website by using a personalized avatar contributed to increasing total navigation time as well as the number of pages visited. However, our results suggest that it is only starting from a certain level of assortment (30 blouses) that the customization of the personalized avatar interferes with navigation patterns, especially in terms of the total navigation time and number of pages visited. In fact, the major difference between the group with the personalized avatar and the group without is significantly higher among the respondents who are exposed to 30 blouses. The longer navigation time and substantial number of pages visited may well be related to a process of effective navigation that includes several features of interest to consumers. When the consumers are exposed to a certain extent of assortment (i.e., 30 blouses) and can use a personalized avatar, their interest is sustained and they thus continue analyzing the information presented. Further, "stagnation" of time spent on information analysis is probably observed among users that did not have access to a personalized avatar. Scholars suggest that an interesting website will retain people longer and customers will thus be more likely to consume and process the information on the site (Bhat, Bevans, and Sengupta 2002).

Thus, using an interactive system such as a personalized avatar can lead to a state of mind in which consumers lose track of time (i.e., flow state) (Belleman et al. 2004). Consequently, consumers are likely to visit more pages and spend more time on the website. In this study, it is possible that respondents who used a personalized avatar spent more time on the site because of the enjoyment of "trying on" the clothing offered, whereas those who did not have access to the tool did not put forth the same effort in analyzing all the blouses. However, this influence is significant only for the higher assortment condition (30 blouses). The use of a virtual model is conceivably a relevant service that influences stickiness only when the level of assortment is high. If assortment is lower, consumers may not need such a service. Nevertheless, given that websites tend to increase their level of assortment, personalized avatars could be a very worthwhile tool for retailers. Indeed, the more consumers spend time navigating on a transactional website, the more they will tend to make purchases (Huang 2000). We have also observed that when the amount of information presented on a website increases, customizing this information helps and improves the users' attitude. Indeed, we showed that when consumers are exposed to a certain amount of information (i.e., 20 blouses), they develop a form of gratitude toward businesses that try to facilitate information processing through the use of an interactive tool. The scope of this observation is especially important as we assume that a positive attitude toward a transactional site can have a definite influence on the desire to return and, consequently, on purchasing intentions.

Nonetheless, these results suggest that up to a certain level of information (30 blouses), the benefits of using a personalized avatar on the attitude toward the website is no longer significant. It is probable that at this stage, other factors contribute to this result. The greater the quantity of information available, the more consumers can make choices adapted to their needs (Russo 1974). This finding is consistent with Jacoby, Speller, and Berning (1974), who affirm that the degree of consumer satisfaction increases proportionately with the abundance of information, even if a loss of efficiency in the decision-making process is observed. Thus, when a retailer has a large assortment, as in this case, although consumers spend more time on the site and visit more pages, they might nonetheless find that 30 blouses is an overly large assortment. They may become slightly discouraged at the thought of having to try all of these blouses on their avatar. In fact, even though consumers say they prefer a wide range of products, when there is an increase in the quantity of information it becomes increasingly difficult to identify items that are truly relevant, which results in higher research costs for the consumer (Klapp 1986).

In conclusion, it appears that using a personalized avatar plays an important role in e-commerce because it positively influences online consumer behavior, and thus favors online product purchasing.

LIMITATIONS AND FURTHER RESEARCH

This article possesses several methodological limitations. First, the sample employed for this study consists of consumers who had already used the My Virtual Model website. As a result, the fact that respondents had already used this site, and probably had a good impression of it, may have biased the data. Second, it would have been useful to examine considerably more than three levels of assortment, notably a higher level of assortment, that is, more than 30 blouses. This study demonstrates that a self-image avatar contributes to increasing website navigation time and the number of pages read, but only when the assortment comprises at least 30 blouses. A higher level of assortment would have increased our internal validity. Finally, this research studied the influence of the use of a personalized avatar on perceptions of a website. A further step will be to take into account several other variables related to the experience on a website, like experiential value satisfaction. It would also be interesting to conduct this study with men and adolescents in order to improve the external validity of our findings.

ACKNOWLEDGMENT

The authors thank the RBC Financial Group Chair of Electronic Commerce for its technical and financial support.

REFERENCES

Ariely, Dan. 2000. "Controlling the Information Flow: Effect on Consumers' Decision Making and Preferences." *Journal of Consumer Research* 27 (2): 233–248.

Babin, Barry J., William R. Darden, and Mitch Griffin. 1994. "Work and/or Fun: Measuring Hedonic and Utilitarian Shopping Value." *Journal of Consumer Research* 20 (3): 644–656.

Belleman, Steve, Eric J. Johnson, Gerald L. Lohse, and Naomi Mandel. 2004. "Designing Marketplaces of the Artificial: Four Approaches to Understanding Consumer Behavior in Electronic Environments." Paper presented at the MIT conference on Marketing and the Internet, June 21.

Betancourt, Roger, and David Gautschi. 1990. "Demand Complementarities, Household Production, and Retail Assortments." *Marketing Science* 9 (2): 146–161.

Bettman, James R., Mary Frances Luce, and John W. Payne. 1998. "Constructive Consumer Choice Processes." *Journal of Consumer Research* 25 (3): 187–217.

Bhat, Subodh, Michael Bevans, and Sanjit Sengupta. 2002. "Measuring Users' Web

Activity to Evaluate and Enhance Advertising Effectiveness." *Journal of Advertising* 31 (3): 97–106.

Bressolles, Gregory, and Jacques Nantel. 2007. "Toward a Typology of Web Sites for Consumers." *Revue française du marketing* 213: 41–56.

Brown, Steven P., and Douglas M. Stayman. 1992. "Antecedents and Consequences of Attitude Toward the Ad: A Meta Analysis." *Journal of Consumer Research* 19 (6): 4–51.

Calhoun, E.L., Lindsay Lyman-Clarke, and Susan Ashdown. 2007. "Virtual Fit of Apparel on the Internet: Current Technology and Future Needs." The 2007 World Conference on Mass Customization and Personalization, MIT Cambridge/Boston, October.

CEFRIO (Centre Francophone de Recherche en Informatisation des Organisations). 2006. NETendances.

Chen, Qimei, and William D. Wells. 1999. "Attitude Toward the Site." *Journal of Advertising Research* 39 (5): 27–38.

Chernev, Alexander. 2006. "Decision Focus and Consumer Choice Among Assortments." *Journal of Consumer Research* 33 (1): 50–59.

Childers, Terry L., Christopher L. Carr, Joann Peck, and Stephen Carson. 2001. "Hedonic and Utilitarian Motivations for Online Retail Shopping Behavior." *Journal of Retailing* 77 (4): 511–536.

Cöner, Altan. 2003. "Personalization and Customization in Financial Portals." *Journal of American Academy of Business* 2 (2): 498–504.

Donthu, Naveen. 2001. "Does Your Web Site Measure Up?" *Marketing Management* 10 (4): 29–32.

Elliott, Michael T., and Paul Surgi Speck. 2005. "Factors That Affect Attitude Toward a Retail Web Site." *Journal of Marketing Theory and Practice* 13 (1): 40–51.

Fitzsimons, Gavan J., Eric A. Greenleaf, and Donald R. Lehmann. 1997. "Decision and Consumption Satisfaction: Implications for Channel Relations." Marketing Studies Center.

Freund, Robert J. 2003. "Mass Customization and Personalization." E-Learn Conference, China, March 21–23.

Grau, Jeffrey. 2007. "Apparel E-Commerce." *E-Marketer,* August.

Grewal, Dhruv, Michael Levy, Anuj Mehrotra, and Arun Sharma. 1999. "Planning Merchandising Decisions to Account for Regional and Product Assortment Differences." *Journal of Retailing* 75 (3): 405–424.

Guenther, Kim. 2004. "Pull Up a Chair and Stay Awhile: Strategies to Maximize Site Stickiness." *Online* 28 (6): 55–57.

Hallerman, David. 2006. "Search Marketing: Spending and Metrics." *E-Marketer,* March.

Hart, Geoff. 2002. "Nice Web Site—But Is It Relevant?" *Computer World Canada* 18 (1).

Häubl, Gerald, and Valerie Trifts. 2000. "Consumer Decision Making in Online Shopping Environments: The Effects of Interactive Decision Aids." *Marketing Science* 19 (1): 4–21.

Häubl, Gerald, Benedict G. C. Dellaert, Kyle B. Murray, and Valerie Trifts. 2004. "Buyer Behavior in Personalized Shopping Environments." Insight from the Institute for Online Consumer Studies. Amsterdam: Kluwer Academic Publishers, 207–223.

Holzwarth, Martin, Chris Janiszewski, and Marcus M. Neumann. 2006. "The Influence of Avatars on Online Consumer Shopping Behavior." *Journal of Marketing* 70 (4): 19–36.

Huang, Ming-Hui. 2000. "Information Load: Its Relationship to Online Exploratory and Shopping Behavior." *International Journal of Information Management* 20: 337–347.

Jacoby, Jacob, Donald E. Speller, and Carol Kohn Berning. 1974. "Brand Choice Behavior as a Function of Information Load: Replication and Extension." *Journal of Consumer Research* 1 (1): 33–42.

Jordan, Patrick W. 2000. *Designing Pleasurable Products. An Introduction to the New Human Factors.* London: Taylor & Francis.

Kahn, Barbara E. 1998. "Dynamic Relationships with Customers: High-Variety Strategies." *Journal of the Academy of Marketing Science* 26 (1): 45–53.

Keeling, K., S. Beatty, P.J. McGoldrick, and L. Macaulay. 2004. "Face Value? Customer Views of Appropriate Formats for ECAs in Online Retailing." *Hawaii International Conference on System Sciences,* 1–10.

Keller, Kevin Lane, and Richard Staelin. 1987. "Effects of Quality and Quantity of Information on Decision Effectiveness." *Journal of Consumer Research* 14 (2): 200–213.

Klapp, Orrin E. 1986. *Overload and Boredom: Essays on the Quality of Life in the Information Society.* Westport, CT: Greenwood.

Li, Hairong, Kuo Cheng, and Martha G. Russell. 1999. "The Impact of Perceived Channel Utilities, Shopping Orientations and Demographics on the Consumers' Online Buying Behavior." *Journal of Computer Mediated Communication* 2: 1–23.

Mackenzie, Scott B., and Richard J. Lutz. 1989. "An Empirical Examination of the Structural Antecedent of Attitude Toward the Ad in an Advertising Pretesting Context." *Journal of Marketing* 53 (2): 48–65.

Mackenzie, Scott B., Richard J. Lutz, and George E. Belch. 1986. "The Role of Attitude Toward the Ad as a Mediator of Advertising Effectiveness: A Test of Competing Explanations." *Journal of Marketing Research* 23 (2): 130–143.

Malhotra, Naresh K. 1982. "Information Load and Consumer Decision Making." *Journal of Consumer Research* 8 (4): 419–430.

McGoldrick, P.J., K.A. Keeling, and S.F. Beatty. 2008. "A Typology of Roles for Avatars in Online Retailing." *Journal of Marketing Management* 24 (3–4): 433–461.

Nantel, Jacques. 2004. "My Virtual Model: Virtual Reality Comes into Fashion." *Journal of Interactive Marketing* 18 (3): 73–86.

Norman, Donald A. 2004. *Emotional Design: Why We Love (or Hate) Everyday Things.* New York: Basic Books.

Oppewal, Harmen, and Kitty Koelemeijer. 2005. "More Choice Is Better: Effects of Assortment Size and Composition on Assortment Evaluation." *International Journal of Research in Marketing* 22 (1): 45–60.

Oxley, Martin, and Jeff Miller. 2000. "Capturing the Consumer: Ensuring Website Stickiness." World Advertising Research Centre, 21–24.

Peppers, Don, and Martha Rogers. 1993. *The One to One Future.* Doubleday: New York.

Peppers, Don, Martha Rogers, and Bob Dorf. 1999. "Is Your Company Ready for One-to-One Marketing?" *Harvard Business Review* 77 (1): 151–160.

Qiu, Lingyun, and Izak Benbasat. 2005. "Online Consumer Trust and Live Help Interfaces: The Effects of Text-to-Speech Voice and Three-Dimensional Avatars." *International Journal of Human-Computer Interaction* 19 (1): 75–94.

Ray, A. 2003. "Personalization Is Vital for Response." *Marketing* 29: 27.

Ross, William T. Jr., and Elizabeth H. Creyer. 1992. "Making Inferences About Missing Information: The Effects of Existing Information." *Journal of Consumer Research* 19 (1): 14–25.

Russo, Edward J. 1974. "More Information Is Better: A Reevaluation of Jacoby, Speller and Kohn." *Journal of Consumer Research* 1 (3): 68–72.

Salem, Ben, and Nic Earle. 2000. "Designing a Nonverbal Language for Expressive Avatars." In *Proceedings of Collaborative Virtural Environments (CVE),* 93–101. New York: ACM Press.

Schubert, Petra, and Mark Ginsburg. 1999. "Virtual Communities of Transaction: The Role of Personalization in Electronic Commerce." 12th International Bled Electronic Commerce Conference, Slovenia, June.

Simonson, Itamar. 1999. "The Effect of Product Assortment on Buyer Preferences." *Journal of Retailing* 75 (3): 347–370.

Steckel, Joel H., Russell S. Winer, Randolph E. Bucklin, Benedict G.C. Dellaert, Xavier Dreze, Gerald Häubl, Sandy D. Jap, John D.C. Little, Tom Meyvis, Alan L. Mongomery, and Arvind Rangaswamy. 2005. "Choice in Interactive Environments." *Marketing Letters* 16 (3/4): 309–320.

Stevenson, Julie S., Gordon C. Bruner II, and Anand Kumar. 2000. "Web Page Background and Viewer Attitudes." *Journal of Advertising Research* 20 (1): 29–34.

Swaminathan, Vanitha, Elzbieta Lepkowska-White, and Bharat Rao. 1999. "Browser or Buyers in Cyberspace? An Investigation of Factors Influencing Electronic Exchange." *Journal of Computer-Mediated Communication* 5 (2).

Tractinsky, Noam. 1997. "Aesthics and Apparent Usability: Empirically Assessing Cultural and Methodological Issues." In *Proceeding CHI*. New York: ACM Press, 115–122.

Trogemann, Georg. 2003. "Mit Hand und Fuß: Die Bedeutung der Nonverbalen Kommunikation für die Emotionalisierung von Dialogführungssystemen." *Avatare-Digitale Sprecher für Business und Marketing,* 267–290.

Walsh, G., V.-W. Mitchell, and T. Frenzel. 2004. "Consumer E-Confusion on the Internet." *Thexis* 17–21.

Wang, Jyun-Cheng, and Juo-Ping Lin. 2002. "Are Personalization Systems Really Personal? Effects of Conformity in Reducing Information Overload." In *Proceedings of the 36th Annual Hawaii International Conference on Systems Sciences,* 222.

Wind, Jerry, and Arvid Rangaswamy. 2001. "Customerization: The Next Revolution in Mass Customization." *Journal of Interactive Marketing* 15 (1): 13–45.

Wood, Natalie T., Michael R. Solomon, and Basil G. Englis. 2005. "Personalisation of Online Avatars: Is the Messenger as Important as the Message?" *International Journal of Internet Marketing and Advertising* 2 (1/2): 143–161.

———. (2008). "Personalization of the Web Interface: The Impact of Web Avatars on Users Response to E-Commerce Websites." *Journal of Website Promotion* 2 (1/2): 53–69.

Zeithaml, Valarie A., A. Parasuraman, and Arvind Malhotra. 2002. "Service Quality Delivery Through Web Sites: A Critical Review of Extant Knowledge." *Journal of the Academy of Marketing Science* 30 (4): 362–375.

■ ———————————————— ■

CHAPTER 7

The Sacred and the Profane in Online Gaming

A Netnographic Inquiry of Chinese Gamers

JEFF WANG, XIN ZHAO, AND GARY J. BAMOSSY

How material possessions influence identity construction has attracted continuous interest in consumer research (Belk 1988, 2001; Arnould and Thompson 2005; Solomon 1983). Previous studies have examined meanings of possessions from different cultures and how they contribute to and extend a sense of self, not only in home settings but also in workplaces (Mehta and Belk 1991; Belk and Watson 1998; Tian and Belk 2005). However, most existing studies have focused on self-extension through tangible material possessions (Belk 1988), or self-presentation (Goffman 1959), or through digital associations on personal web pages (Schau and Gilly 2003). Such theorization of self-extension through possessions emphasizes *having* and *being,* but ignores *doing* as a mode of self-extension (Sartre 1950).

It is unclear how intangible game avatars and virtual possessions in online games extend a sense of self. At the same time, although it has been found that consumers sacralize material possessions they have acquired in the real world/real life (RL) (Belk, Wallendorf, and Sherry 1989), it remains to be explored whether or not consumers construct sacred meanings from and for intangible avatars in the virtual world. We seek to contribute to theories of the sacred and profane in consumer behavior (Belk, Wallendorf, and Sherry 1989), and self-extension (Belk 1988) through a netnographic inquiry (Kozinets 2002, 2006) of the online gaming community in China.

THEORETICAL FRAMEWORK

Extended Self and Online Self-Presentation

One of the most significant findings in consumer research is that material possessions are integral to a person's sense of extended self (Belk 1988). Material possessions are reminders and confirmers of one's identity, and a person's identity resides in objects as much as it does in individuals. However, this theoretical perspective of self-extension (Belk 1988; Tian and Belk 2005) focuses on tangible possessions in the real world, and does not consider (nor, at the time, could this perspective have foreseen) the potential for self-extension and representation via possessions in the virtual world/virtual life (VL) of computer-mediated environments (CMEs).

Consumers also present themselves by manipulating digital elements in CMEs (Schau and Gilly 2003). Personal web pages help to create a telepresence of the self through the construction of a digital self on the Internet. Consumers translate the real-life self into the digital domain by evaluating the original and appropriating various digital elements to construct a digital representation that stands for a physically absent self. The digitally constructed self is often a projection of RL self that is referenced through pictures or created through the use of human-like avatars. The avatar is used to reference the physical body in real life, and some consumers use their avatars to enact relationships with their favorite brands through this digital association. Such digital association constitutes a new form of symbolic possession that does not rely upon actual ownership. However, Schau and Gilly's (2003) focus is on self-presentation, and they examine a relatively static process of self-construction. Avatars in online gaming are more dynamic and actively manipulated by gamers to extend a sense of self. One of the contributions of this study is to examine how consumers use one or more avatars to actively construct an extended sense of self.

The Sacred and the Profane

Durkheim (2001 [1912]) defines as sacred "those things protected and isolated by prohibitions. . . . Religious beliefs are representations that express the nature of sacred things . . . every sacred thing of any importance, constitutes a centre of organization around which a group of beliefs and rites gravitates" (p. 40). The sacred is the opposite of what is ordinary and part of everyday life, and it refers to what is extraordinary and significant (Belk, Wallendorf, and Sherry 1989). The sacred is often beyond rationalization and can only be comprehended through devotion. It evokes momentary ecstatic experiences, in which one temporarily feels he or she stands outside his or her self. The sacred is surrounded by myths and cultural narratives that define sacred status through repetition. The sacred has the power to contaminate or sacralize, and it is often concretized and materialized in objects. Anything can become sacred, and the act of imbuing sacredness is an investment process in which consumers actively seek to separate ordinary objects from the world of the profane and to create sacred meanings in their lives (Belk, Wallendorf, and Sherry 1989). A material object can be sacralized through ritual, pilgrimage, quintessence, gift giving, collecting, inheritance, and external sanction. For instance, an ordinary commodity can become sacred by rituals that help to decommodify the object, in which consumers seek to impose and project their own identities on tangible possessions.

An aspect of experiential consumption can be sacralized through a secular pilgrimage when consumers are away from their everyday world. For example, the distinction between sacred and profane trips can be decided by the destination and purpose of the travel (Bamossy 2005). In other instances, an object can be sacralized through gift giving. Gifts often have special meanings, and selection of gifts to give to others differs from commodity purchases. Lastly, an object can become sacred through sanction by an external authority, as in the enshrinement of a piece in a museum. However, these previously studied processes of sacralization focus on the transformation of existing material objects or places, and have not examined how the virtual could be sacralized within computer-mediated environments such as online games. They emphasize having and being as a mode of experiencing the sacred.

Although it has been noted that the investment of labor plays an important role in transforming the ordinary into the sacred, how such experiences can become sacred is not explored. Likewise, it is unclear whether or not consumers' gaming experiences in the virtual world can be sacred and, if so, whether or not the sacralization of intangible virtual possessions takes similar trajectories. We seek to address these theoretical gaps through netnographic inquiries into the use of avatars in online gaming in China. Online gaming has attracted consumers around the world. It has become an important arena of entertainment and constitutes a major business (see Hemp 2006). A wide variety of online games was introduced into China during 2000, and quickly gained momentum among young gamers. This nascent gaming market also offers a unique opportunity to examine consumers' gaming experiences during its early development.

METHODOLOGY

We conducted in-depth interviews with both hard-core and casual gamers in urban China, participating in extended and multisite ethnographic fieldwork from December 2006 to December 2007. We talked to gamers in Internet cafés, their homes, game sweatshops (in which "professional" gamers take on another gamer's avatar and play on their behalf to raise the player's skill level/status to an agreed-upon level in return for payment), and non-Internet cafés where they often gathered for socializing. We interviewed thirty-five informants, including not only gamers, but also game developers, reporters covering the game for newspapers, and managers of Internet cafés. Our research sites covered a wide region in both southern and northern China, and both coastal areas and inner cities, including Beijing, Changchun, Guangzhou, Nanjing, Shanghai, and Shenzhen. Our informants ranged from fifteen-year-old teenagers and to adults in their late forties. Initial informants were recruited in colleges and more experienced gamers were identified through a marketing research firm based in Guangzhou. Some of our informants were affluent young consumers whereas others were poor and played the game to sell virtual possessions in order to make a living. Although such purposive sampling should not be taken as representative of the population of Chinese gamers, this diversity of gamers helps to enrich our understanding of what it means to participate in the game world. Our informants participated in a wide variety of role-play games (RPG), including not only foreign games such as the globally popular *World of Warcraft* (a highly competitive achievement/ quest/adventure oriented game, played with teams, or "guilds"), but also games with an emphasis on traditional Chinese culture such as the *Journey to the West* (based on a sixteenth-century Chinese novel involving quest-like adventures undertaken during long travel). The interviews started with grand tour questions about personal background, interests, history of online gaming, life objectives, and then were followed by questions about gaming experiences (McCracken 1988; Thompson 1997). We allowed the informants to guide the flow of our conversation to reduce interviewer-induced bias (Thompson, Locander, and Pollio 1989). The discussions were facilitated by probing questions aimed to elucidate how gamers understood their gaming experiences, including their uses of and feelings about the avatars that were part of their gaming activities. The interviews lasted from forty-five minutes to three hours. All interviews were digitally recorded and supplemented by extensive field notes, photographs of gamers playing in Internet cafés, and videos of on-site observations. They were then transcribed and analyzed through a systematic and iterative process (Arnould and Wallendorf 1994; Spiggle 1994). Provisional understandings were formulated, challenged, and revised by moving back and forth between individual transcripts and the entire data set. Each individual interview was taken as an idiographic illustration of a culturally shared system of meanings, an interpretative approach similar to previous research (e.g., Holt 2002; Mick and Buhl 1992; Thompson 1997). Initial analysis has generated rich insights about the nature of what is sacred and profane in VLs, and about self-extension in the virtual world of online gaming in China, to which we now turn.

ANALYSIS AND FINDINGS

In this chapter, we focus on massively multiplayer online role-playing games (MMORPGs). In MMORPGs, gamers play a role and actively interact with others through avatars. Avatars are designed and controlled by gamers, and avatars can be manipulated in the CME to acquire virtual possessions and make virtual money. A gamers' social and economic status is expressed in the virtual world through the avatar and is determined by: (1) *skill level:* each avatar has a particular skill level that determines its appearance, capability, strength, and weakness in the game, and skill levels start at the bottom of the hierarchy; and (2) *position in a guild hierarchy:* most games require the formation of guilds to complete difficult missions, and higher position in the guild is maintained by more skilled gamers.

The Process of Creating Myths and Sacred Avatars

There is often strong and focused emotional attachment to an avatar, especially the first successfully created avatar. This "birth order" myth about one's first avatar emerges in many gamers' experiences. The first avatar is more significant to the creator, and experienced as different from other avatars that a gamer may create in later games. This first avatar is often infused with sacred meaning (Belk, Wallendorf, and Sherry 1989), as seen from the following excerpt:

> Many gamers feel very strongly and emotionally about their first avatar. He never has the same feeling about later avatars as he plays more. The first avatar is very like him- or herself. It is an image of him- or herself. . . . He must go through a lot to build this avatar, battle by battle, and little by little. Later avatars are built after you have become experienced and these avatars don't go through the same difficulty and hardness as the first avatar does. You don't feel that emotional about these later ones. The first avatar isn't necessarily the very first one you have ever played with, but it is definitely the most successful and the one that you have played for the longest time. You go out in the game with this avatar and feel like that this avatar is just you yourself in the game. It represents you and it feels the same as yourself. You meet all kinds of people through the avatar and you cry and laugh with the avatar. You fight with others with the avatar and it does everything for you . . . the more you are involved with the avatar, the more it represents yourself. You experience many, many things through this first avatar. It is just like you are dealing with all kinds of things . . . you really pour your emotion into the first avatar. (Male, early twenties)

As seen here, the "first" avatar that gamers have carefully created and nurtured is experienced as significant, extraordinary, and sacred, much as parents view their firstborn (Belk, Wallendorf and Sherry 1989). The avatar's growing skills, and happy and sad moments, help evoke special meanings. Whereas a gamer's accumulated skills allow faster growth of an avatar, the importance and meaning attached to later avatars diminishes over time. But the hardships and difficulties experienced by the first avatar, and the pains and frustrations felt through the first avatar evoke lasting emotional attachment. An avatar expresses the gamer's emotions by crying, laughing, quarreling, and fighting in the game world. As seen above, the first avatar is seen as a representation of the gamer in real life: "the *more you are involved with the avatar, the more it represents yourself.*" The time and effort spent to empower the first avatar constitute symbolic sacrifices that gamers make in the VL of the game world. In order to obtain ecstatic gaming experiences, gamers sacrifice RL time that could be used in RL social activities. Such hedonistic pleasure seeking in the virtual of world of online games is perhaps not so different from the activities of eighteenth-century consumers who indulged themselves in the fantasy world of romantic novels, as described by Campbell (1987). Sacrifices of time and investment of labor engage gamers to experience the sacred within the virtual world. For many, exploring the game world is a daily ritual that has to be performed. Indeed, even among the more casual gamers, a daily visit to the game site was seen as commonplace. For the more serious gamers, often working in guild-coordinated ventures, game visits can last for up to twenty-four hours or more. These gamers put their computer equipment in the same room to facilitate offline communication among their comrades, stock up on food and drink, and have beds available for short sleep breaks.

Successful creation of the first avatar also marks a gamer's transition from an outsider to a member in the gaming community. It is an important ritual to share stories of each other's first avatar. Similar rituals of initiation and integration into a community are also observed in the context of skydiving, in which first jumps are sacred and are often invoked as a marker of identity transition (Celsi, Rose, and Leigh 1993; Schouten 1991). The first avatar is preserved with ritualistic zeal. Gamers become more involved in the game world as the achievements of the first avatar accumulate over time. The exploration of and experimentation with different identity opportunities in the virtual world of online gaming resonate with the process of neophyte Harley Davison bikers becoming accepted members of the subculture of consumption (Schouten and McAlexander 1995). In this process, the new gamers enter the game at the bottom of a status hierarchy and undergo a process of socialization and transformation. As a gamer's commitment to the game deepens, the avatar become an integrated part of the gamer's daily experiences.

Progressive mastery of the avatar and the learning of new gaming skills over time help to cultivate a strong sense of personal growth. This strengthens the emotional attachments of the avatar by the gamer, and the avatar's achievement can be experienced as the gamer's achievements in real life. Similar personal growth is also seen in the process of learning whitewater rafting (Arnould and Price 1993). Although lacking extraordinary encounters with real-life nature, gamers seek extraordinary encounters with CMEs, and in doing so, create and engage in their own sacred gaming experiences. Experiencing personal growth and constructing a different identity through manipulating the acts of the avatar emphasizes *doing* in this process of self-extension (Sartre 1950; Belk 1988). Doing, and achieving goals, is an active transitional state of the fundamental desire to have or to be, and contrasts with the creation of personal web pages, which extend a sense of self through a more static process of digital presentation (Schau and Gilly 2003). It appears that an avatar in the virtual world is not only for self-presentation, but vicariously acts out the will of the gamer. Material possessions help to maintain a sense of self whereas self-extension through an avatar reveals the importance of *doing* in the creation and extension of self. Avatars also allow the gamer to achieve what seems impossible in real life and to realize his or her desires. One gamer passionately comments:

It is a projection of your desire, or the goals that you cannot achieve in [the] real world. You can achieve all of them in the virtual world and you can develop the avatar into whatever you dream. (Female, early twenties)

As seen here, the strong emotional attachment to an avatar also comes from the idealization of the personal goals that have been embodied in the avatar, and the giving away, retiring of, or disposal of an avatar is highly meaningful to many gamers.

My previous avatars are "tuo fu," or given to my friends. I feel more comfortable and don't feel much sadness that way. I really don't want to delete or kill the avatar. Although it is virtual, it is created and grows with me. I will never sell it either. I only leave it with trusted friends. This way, it is a happy ending for me. (Male, early twenties)

This strong attachment, and the sacredness of the avatar, can also be seen in the question of its disposition when a gamer stops playing a particular game. Disposal of the avatar is not taken lightly but experienced as psychologically painful. If an avatar is an extension of the self, then its disposal is a process of detachment from self, which may be similar to the disposition of material possessions (Price, Arnould, and Curasi 2000) Although virtually constructed, an avatar constitutes a vessel of shared meanings valued by gamers (McCracken 1988). More often, an avatar is treated as a sacred item that the gamer is unwilling to dispose of (Belk, Wallendorf, and Sherry 1989). It is regarded as beyond price and cannot be sold. Similar to other sacred objects, the sacred avatar is set apart and beyond the function of economic gains. This self-imposed "never sell" rule precludes the avatar's entry into the realm of the profane. Similar to consumers who experience a sense of death following the loss of a favorite possession, it is an equally painful process for many to abandon their avatar. Different choices are carefully compared and evaluated. When an avatar is given as a gift, such gift giving helps to sustain its sacredness. Transferring an avatar to trusted friends symbolically transfers the sacred meanings and this is considered to be a better ending. For many, the selling of an avatar would be experienced as contaminating its value and purpose and is thus excluded as a possible method of disposal. Likewise, the trading of an avatar for economic gain would be considered to be a taboo (Belk 2005). Similar fears of "contamination" have been expressed by subjects interviewed about body part donations between donors and recipients (Belk 1988, 2007).

Identifying a good friend who can further extend the ability of the avatar is weighted more important than economic gains of selling the avatar. The word "托付" in Chinese culture is often used in grave situations in which one person leaves important and critical tasks to those who can be trusted. It invokes a scenario in which a person who is unlikely to come back home leaves his family or children to trusted friends. The use of such an emotionally charged word strongly implies the importance of avatars in gamers' life experience. Leaving an avatar with trusted friends is a relief. More importantly, the avatar is valued because it was "created" by the gamer as opposed to being purchased from the marketplace. Such emphasis on creating exemplifies the importance of *doing* in self-extension (Belk 1988). Even though having, doing, and being are interrelated and integrated in self-extension, extending one's self through doing is experienced differently by the gamer discussed below.

Social Ties and the Sacred Avatar

> An avatar or a game is often connected with some friends. Once you delete your avatar, you delete the friendship or the connections. You don't feel the same when you get together and talk about the gaming experiences. At one time, we were all playing the same game and were together all the time. Some people sold their avatars when we quit the game. When we talked about our time spent in the game at a later time, those who had sold their avatars had a hard time fitting in and we didn't feel very close to them. We just couldn't. Most of us keep our avatars, even if we don't play the game any more. The avatar still lives in the game world even if we have left. But if you have sold your avatar, it doesn't belong to you and it is not you any more. We know better about each other through the avatar, but once the avatar is sold, it is a different person and we can't talk about the avatar any more. We don't have any connections with the avatar and with the person. That's why those who sold their avatars can't join the conversation any more. (Male, early twenties)

The avatar embodies the shared experiences among gamers, and selling an avatar is seen as potentially altering and contaminating the shared, sacred gaming experience, as well as altering the nature of the friendships developed during the process. The avatar is a form of digital memory, similar to tourist photography taken to preserve the commodified experiences of travel (Belk 2005). Cherished gaming experiences are represented and embodied within the avatar, through which past experiences can be relived. Gamers are connected through avatars, and possessing an avatar is seen as an authenticating act that defines a person's membership within the gaming community. It also provides the prerequisite that allows a gamer to participate in shared recollections of past gaming experiences. Those who have sold their avatars are not accepted and are excluded from discussions of shared gaming experiences. Once sold, the avatar becomes a stranger and the relationships established through it are severed accordingly. The sold avatar and kept avatar render different gaming recollections, with "preserved" avatars embodying gaming experiences that are sacred, and retained in memory (Belk, Wallendorf, and Sherry 1989).

Similar to gifts (Sherry 1983; Geisler, 2007), avatars preserve and sacralize gaming experience. The game world constitutes a social antistructure that frees gamers from their social roles and engages them within a transcending camaraderie of status equality, or *communitas*. As we can see from the above quote, gamers experience a sense of *communitas* through recollecting and reflecting on previous gaming experiences even long after they have quit the game. The camaraderie is mediated by the avatar, and the avatar is an important means through which the experiences of *communitas* can be recalled. The connections among gamers established during the game are sacred, and the sale of an avatar excludes the gamer from recalling and reliving these experiences with other gamers. Within this context, the "sacred" avatar potentially helps gamers to savor and recollect the gaming experiences at a later time, similar to the way photographs help people recall a trip (Belk 2005). Selling an avatar serves to desacralize the sacred gaming experiences among gamers and is thus disdained. Furthermore, the unexpected loss of an avatar, such as through theft by others, often evokes a profound sadness, comparable to the loss of life for many gamers. While not part of our primary data, this point is dramatically illustrated by Wang (2004), who reports on a gamer whose avatar and its possessions were taken away from him by the gaming software company. The gamer was so distraught over this loss that he set himself on fire at the entrance to the gaming firm's building.

Sacred Vicarious Experience: Game as Life and Life as Game

In Virtual Life (VL), gamers engage in vicarious experiences that would be out of their reach in Real Life (RL). Gamers retrospectively reflect on the meaning of gaming, and experiences in the game are used to understand and live out real-world lives. Scripted gaming is experienced as the same or corresponding to real-life experiences. Gamers freely transplant and project the experiences in the two different realms onto each other.

> The game allows me to experience what I cannot have or experience in real world, such as marriage. One of my best gaming memories is virtual marriage. I got virtually married with another avatar in the game. It was really exciting and I was happy. I still have very fond memories of my marriage in the game even today. (Female, early twenties)

Female players report experiencing emotions of love that are considered very similar to RL feelings of love. Within the virtual context of CMEs, avatar life provides both male and female gamers the freedom to more easily transgress social structures inherent in RL relationships, such as real-world marriage. Whereas in RL, marriage and family are typically stable, in the gaming world, male gamers may also seek to experience a life with multiple wives. Our interview data suggest that there is asymmetry in terms of female and male gamers' expectations about such virtual relationships. At times, virtual marriage in a game is expected to last forever, similar to real life or to compensate for the RL conflicts to this romantic ideal. Some gamers also adopt strategies to maintain multiple marriage relationships in the game. The virtual romantic relationship is a strong compensation for the real-life experience of love and ideals related to love. Although most people have a clear understanding of the differences between the real and the virtual, it is difficult to stay away from deep involvement in VL.

In real life, married couples live together, own things, and raise children. In CMEs, marriage as a contractual relationship is reinterpreted by gamers: obligations and responsibilities are redefined, fidelity is loosened, and breakups are common. Virtual marriage is not bounded by legal and moral stipulations. The pressure of vetting a spouse's kinship, a strong agency in Chinese culture, is nonexistent. Initiation and severing of marriages require few individual concerns or social constraints. Starting a relationship in the game is simple: avatars express their desires directly. The query, "Want to be my wife?" is not uncommon from a male avatar who meets a female avatar for the first time. This differs from face-to-face encounters in Chinese culture, where showing affection too soon is regarded as inappropriate. Avatars express their affection spontaneously and accept rejections with ease. Avatars can get married without matching the RL players' age, gender, and socioeconomic background. Because there are fewer female avatars, they usually benefit more from the relationship in terms of acquiring assets and allies in the game. RL criteria for marriage are abandoned by players and they explore new possibilities in their virtual relationships. One perceived VL advantage in CME marriages is that gamers can switch partners quickly. Although few treat their online spouses as an extension of their RL relationships, most refuse to cultivate deep and intimate relationships with their VL partners. This quick-in and quick-out style gives them game relationships a sense of freshness. In RL, such behavior is not only costly and risky but also morally unacceptable. One's strong ties, especially the mutual ties of spouses, may lobby to repair the damages and avoid breakups. In the game, the impact of social networks is reduced in quantity and quality and virtual-relationship responsibility lacks social consensus. Virtual marriages and other intimate relationships allow people to experience something impossible in RL.

Just as social positions signify status in RL, they do as well in VL. *Guan* in Chinese refers to government officials. Due to China's one-party rule and lack of democracy, becoming a government official is beyond most people's reach. In the game, however, gamers have new identities and can climb the guild hierarchy. Some gamers would rather live in the game, where they occupy powerful and covetous positions. They prefer their virtual-world identities because they have the status and prestige that they can hardly or never accomplish in RL. In CME, they can reach such status more quickly and easily, based on skilled game performance. Virtual wealth and conspicuous possessions also signify one's status in the virtual community. New and fancy possessions are constantly discussed among gamers, who well recognize their values and rarity. Avatars with those possessions often receive praise and envy from fellow avatars. Word of mouth in the VL is quick and news spreads to the entire gaming community. VL provides a stage for an avatar to start with a modest life but end up rich and powerful. If these material desires cannot be fulfilled in RL, avatars make it come true in VL, as seen below:

> Others will think that you are really powerful, say if you are the boss of your guild. It is very difficult to become a *guan* [high-level government official] or to become rich in real life to get respect. But it is very easy in the games. You want to do well in the games. (Male, early twenties)

Negative–Self-Extension in an Avatar

> I have some other avatars that nobody knows are me. I can do whatever I want with those avatars. I can go anywhere I like since nobody would recognize me. I have the major avatar that everyone else knows, but the minor avatars are also necessary. I use these minor ones when I need to sell virtual possessions and when I need to negotiate price or do bad things. This way, I won't be found out and won't be considered to be a cunning businessman. I won't be considered as too worldly and pretentious. (Female, early twenties)

Material possessions associated with an undesired self are often severed, and at the same time the extensions of the self that are evaluated negatively are often disposed to reinforce the ideal self (Belk 1988). RL consumers are found to actively dispose of possessions associated with negatively charged extensions of the undesired self, in garage sales. However, unlike in RL, some gamers surreptitiously maintain an avatar that is associated with a negative self, would be described as "never me." This avatar is also used to experiment with and to experience negative aspects of self that the gamer would never risk with his or her major avatar. As seen here, the minor avatar is invoked to do "whatever I want" and to go "wherever I like," since nobody knows that it is me. The dark-side places that gamers guide the minor avatar to visit are often profane (Belk, Wallendorf, and Sherry 1989), such as the auction site or marketplace where the minor avatar is used to negotiate price or to sell virtual possessions. The fear of negative impression of the major avatar motivates the construction and maintenance of a minor avatar instead of the disposal of avatars that represent negative aspects of the self. Gamers also seek to distance themselves from the minor avatar that is used to experiment and participate in profane gaming experiences.

DISCUSSION AND IMPLICATIONS

Although our exploratory analysis presented here is descriptive, it offers some preliminary insights into the sacred and profane lives of gamers and their avatars in CMEs. Accompanying the rise of consumerism is often a sense of loss (Giddens 1991) and a yearning for the sacred, for which consumption is celebrated as a form of compensation. Different games in CMEs emphasize different values and offer a wide range of psychological remedies for everyday problems faced by Chinese gamers. The variety of experiences sought after in online games go well beyond excitement, novelty, and relaxation. Although avatars may appear insignificant and unimportant to most nongamers, the avatar's sacredness undoubtedly manifests itself to its creator and the many gamers we interviewed.

Gamers construct an avatar by projecting a sacred self and then identify with the idealized character in the game. Alternatively, some gamers also project a dark/profane self, and hold this extended identity incognito. Most often, our interview data present an avatar that is created to embody the gamer's ideal self. The constructed self in the game develops social relationships with others, not only within the game, but by extension expands to the gamers' social network of other gamers in RL.

Accompanying the rapid rise of consumerism there is often a sense of unreality (Leach 1992) and a loss of authenticity (Giddens 1991; Schor and Holt 2000). In this regard, online gaming is a play of conflicting values that claims to be able to offer psychological remedies for a lost sense of achievement and unattainable desirable values in the real world. In contrast, to pursue these values in consumption and in images, gamers seek to enact these desired values and seek sacred experiences through gaming. Online games or video games in general constitute a liminal space through which gamers seek a transcendental sacred experience and in which the rite of passage of identity cultivation takes place in the new CME society (Maffesoli 1996). Gaming provides a place for this initiation ritual, and for many Chinese gamers, to play is to regain or reorder the order lost in their rapidly changing society.

In addition to consumer goods (Belk 1988), gamers seek to use virtual resources to pursue individual identity projects (Schau and Gilly 2003), expressing virtual status through virtual consumption or virtual possession in games. This virtual identity shifts toward the real world through border crossing between the real world and virtual world. Whereas RL identity and distinction are pursued through brands and other consumption acts (Holt 1998, 2002), different strategies of identity construction and expression are likely to be adopted in the virtual world of online gaming. The gaming world becomes an important site through which consumers seek to experience and express norms of the offline social world. It constitutes a utopia of cultural resources unconstrained by brands or consumption acts and social norms present in the real world. It is a playground in which consumers can freely pursue cultural experimentation relatively unconstrained by the social norms of the RL.

CONCLUDING THOUGHTS AND DIRECTIONS FOR FUTURE RESEARCH

At the more macro level of inquiry, our research suggests that in China, the popularity of online gaming has contributed to the creation of a carnivalesque culture (Twitchell 1992) in which a communist creed that represses play in the name of self-sacrifice and hard work has been replaced with the new consumerist ethos that encourages playfulness and an obsession with youthful spontaneity and rebellion. This phenomenon is also seen in in Western marketplaces, such as theme parks, shopping malls, urban architecture, and in advertising themes (Barber 2007). Online games provide an ideal arena for researchers to explore the various forms of compensation inherent in gaming, such as gamers' experience of an idealized past and loss of the sacred. For example, some of the informants in our study (the sweatshop gamers) are in fact working long, tedious hours to provide higher-level possessions/power to more affluent (often Western) gamers. The irony is that the more affluent gamers apparently don't have the time to reach the high levels/skill sets of the game because they are perhaps too busy with their day jobs. So, for some Western gamers it would appear that hiring Chinese gamers is a way to enhance their (Western) play time, while the paid work of sweatshop gamers serves to enhance the play of Western gamers. A cross-cultural and comparative study of the codependency between these subsets of Western and Chinese gamers, as well as their potentially overlapping and conflicting values with regard to the ethos and values in the global world of gaming, provides a rich environment for inquiry.

At a meso level of inquiry, different games can be seen to emphasize different values and offer a wide range of psychological remedies for everyday problems faced by Chinese gamers. Although the gaming ethos and avatar behaviors discussed in this chapter may appear profane and unimportant to many nongamers, the feelings and beliefs regarding the sacredness of one's avatar undoubtedly manifests itself to its creator and many gamers we interviewed. An interesting line of inquiry to explore is the extent to which online gaming is a play of conflicting values that offer psychological remedies for a lost sense of achievement and other desirable values in the real world.

Finally, most studies of online gaming and virtual communities have focused on identities issues and examined how the virtual world has offered unprecedented opportunities for reconstructing identities (Meadows 2008). Barber (2007) suggests a promising and different approach regarding how the marketplace encourages and legitimizes *childishness,* and the online gaming world offers a rich arena for exploring this notion. From American *kidults,* German *Nesthocker,* Italian *Mmmoone,* and Japanese *Ffeeter,* to Indian *zippies* and French *Tanguy,* a rising infantilist ethos that encourages and legitimizes childishness is gaining momentum around the world. This market-generated infantilization induces puerility in adults and preserves a sense of childishness in children trying to grow up. An infantilist culture prefers play over work, instant gratification over long-term satisfaction, feeling over reason, picture over word, easy over hard, simple over complex, and fast over slow. The infantilization of society is tied closely to the demands of a global economy, and its ethos has become the major ideology sustaining consumer capitalism (Barber 2007). However, the nature, causes, and consequences of infantilization have only been examined within Western societies. China's rise toward the most populated consumer society offers an unprecedented opportunity to examine this thesis, especially when the one-child policy has left hundreds of millions of families with their focus on the needs of little emperors.

REFERENCES

Arnould, Eric J., and Craig J. Thompson. 2005. "Consumer Culture Theory (CCT): Twenty Years of Research." *Journal of Consumer Research* 31 (March): 868–882.

Arnould, Eric J., and Melanie Wallendorf. 1994. "Market-Oriented Ethnography: Interpretation Building and Marketing Strategy Formulation." *Journal of Marketing Research* 31 (November): 484–504.

Arnould, Eric J. and Linda L. Price.1993. "River Magic: Extraordinary Experience and the Extended Service Encounter," *Journal of Consumer Research* 20 (June): 24–45.

Bamossy, Gary J. 2005. "Star Gazing: The Mythology and Commodification of Vincent van Gogh." In *Inside Consumption: Consumer Motives, Goals, and Desires,* ed. David Mick and S. Ratneshwar, 309–329. New York: Routledge.

Barber, Benjamin R. 2007. *Consumed: How Markets Corrupt Children, Infantilize Adults, and Swallow Citizens Whole.* New York: W.W. Norton.

Belk, Russell W. 1988. "Possessions and the Extended Self." *Journal of Consumer Research* 15 (September): 139–168.

Belk, Russell W., Melanie Wallendorf, and John F. Sherry. 1989. "The Sacred and the Profane in Consumer Behavior: Theodicy on the Odyssey," *Journal of Consumer Research* 16 (June): 1–39.

———. 2001. *Collecting in a Consumer Society.* London: Routledge.

———. 2005. "Exchange Taboos from an Interpretive Perspective." *Journal of Consumer Psychology* 15 (1): 16–21.

Belk, Russell W., Guliz Ger, and Soren Askegaard. 2003. "The Fire of Desires: A Multi-Sites Inquiry into Consumer Passion," *Journal of Consumer Research* 30 (3).

Belk, Russell W., and Janeen Arnould Costa. 1998. "The Mountain Myth: A Contemporary Consuming Fantasy." *Journal of Consumer Research* 25 (December): 218–240.

Belk, Russell W., and Joel C. Watson. 1998. "Material Culture and the Extended and Unextended Self in Our University Offices." *Advances in Consumer Research* 25, ed. Joseph W. Alba and J. Wesley Hutchinson. Provo, UT: Association for Consumer Research.

Campbell, Colin. 1987. *The Romantic Ethic and the Spirit of Modern Consumerism.* Oxford: Basic Blackwell.

Celsi, Richard, Randall Rose, and Thomas Leigh. 1993. "An Exploration of High-Risk Leisure Consumption through Sky-Diving," *Journal of Consumer Research* 20 (June): 1–21.

Durkheim, Émile. 2001 (1912). *The Elementary Forms of Religious Life,* trans. Carol Cosman. New York: Oxford University Press.

Giddens, Anthony. 1991. *Modernity and Self-Identity: Self and Society in the Late Modern Age.* Stanford, CA: Stanford University Press.

Giesler, Markus. 2007. "Consumer Gift Systems: Insights from Napster," *Journal of Consumer Research* 33 (September): 283–290.

Goffman, Erving. 1959. *The Presentation of Self in Everyday Life.* New York: Anchor Books.

Hemp, Paul. 2006. "Avatar-based Marketing." *Harvard Business Review* (June): 48–57.

Holt, Douglas B. 1997. "How Do Ads Mean? New Directions in Cultural Advertising Research." *Advances in Consumer Research* 24: 98–100.

———. 1998. "Does Cultural Capital Structure American Consumption?" *Journal of Consumer Research* 25 (June): 1–26.

———. 2002. "Why Do Brands Cause Trouble? A Dialectical Theory of Consumer Culture and Branding," *Journal of Consumer Research* 29 (June): 70–90.

Holzwarth, Martin, Chris Janiszewski, and Marcus Neumann. 2006. "The Influence of Avatars on On-Line Consumer Behavior Shopping." *Journal of Marketing* 70: 19–36.

Huizinga, Johan. 1970. *Homo Ludens: A Study of the Play Element in Culture.* New York: Harper & Row.

Kozinets, Robert V. 2002. "The Field Behind the Screen: Using Netnography for Marketing Research in Online Communities." *Journal of Marketing Research* 34 (February): 61–72.

———. 2006. "Netnography 2.0." In *Handbook of Qualitative Research Methods in Marketing,* ed. Russell W. Belk. Cheltenham, UK: Edward Elgar.

Leach, William. 1992. *Land of Desire: Merchants, Power, and the Rise of a New American Culture.* New York: Pantheon Books.

Maffesoli, Michel. 1996. *The Time of the Tribes: The Decline of Individualism in Mass Society.* London, UK: Sage.

McCracken, Grant. 1988. *The Long Interview.* Newbury Park, CA: Sage.

Meadows, Mark Stephen. 2008. *I, Avatar: The Culture and Consequences of Having a Second Life.* Berkeley, CA: New Riders.

Mehta, Raj, and Russell W. Belk. 1991. "Artifacts, Identity, and Transition: Favorite Possessions of Indians and Indian Immigrants to the United States." *Journal of Consumer Research* 17 (March): 398–411.

Mick, David Glen, and Claus Buhl. 1992. "A Meaning-Based Model of Advertising Experiences," *Journal of Consumer Research* 19 (December): 317–338.

Price, Linda, Eric J. Arnould, and Carolyn F. Curasi. 2000. "Older Consumers' Disposition of Special Possessions," *Journal of Consumer Research* 37 (September): 179–201.

Sartre, Jean-Paul. 1950. *Being and Nothingness: A Phenomenological Essay on Ontology.* New York: Philosophical Library.

Schau, Hope Jensen, and Mary C. Gilly. 2003. "We Are What We Post? Self-Presentation in Personal Web Space." *Journal of Consumer Research* 30 (December): 385–404.

Schor, Juliet B., and Douglas B. Holt. 2000. *The Consumer Society Reader.* New York: The New Press.

Schouten, John W. 1991. "Selves in Transition: Symbolic Consumption in Personal Rites of Passage and Identity Reconstruction," *Journal of Consumer Research* 17 (March): 412–426.

Schouten, John W., and James H. McAlexander. 1995. "Subcultures of Consumption: An Ethnogropy of the New Bikers," *Journal of Consumer Research* 22 (March): 43–61.

Sherry, John F. 1983. "Gift Giving in Anthropological Perspective," *Journal of Consumer Research* 10 (September): 157–168.

Solomon, Michael R. 1983. "The Role of Products as Social Stimuli: A Symbolic Interactionism Perspective." *Journal of Consumer Research* 10 (December): 319–329.

Spiggle, Susan. 1994. "Analysis and Interpretation of Qualitative Data in Consumer Research." *Journal of Consumer Research* 21 (December): 491–503.

Thompson, Craig J. 1997. "Interpreting Consumers: A Hermeneutical Framework for Deriving Marketing Insights from the Texts of Consumers' Consumption Stories," *Journal of Marketing Research* 34 (November): 438–455.

Thompson, Craig J., William B. Locander, and Howard R. Pollio. 1989. "Putting Consumer Experience Back into Consumer Research: The Philosophy and Method of Existential-Phenomenology," *Journal of Consumer Research* 16 (September): 133–146.

Tian, Kelly, and Russell W. Belk. 2005. "Extended Self and Possessions in the Workplace." *Journal of Consumer Research* 32 (September): 297–310.

Turner, Victor. [1969]1977. *The Ritual Process: Structure and Anti-Structure*. Ithaca: Cornell University Press.

Twitchell, James B. 1992. *Carnival Culture: The Trashing of Taste in America*. New York: Columbia University Press.

Wallendorf, Melanie, and Eric J. Arnould. 1988. "My Favorite Things: A Cross-Cultural Inquiry into Object Attachment, Possessiveness, and Social Linkage." *Journal of Consumer Research* 14 (March): 531–547.

Wang, Xiaoyi. 2004. "A Young Gamer Burned Himself." *Nanfang Daily*, April 21. Available at www.nanfangdaily.com.cn/jj/20040422/jd/200404210029.asp.

PART III

AVATAR CREATION AND APPEARANCE

CHAPTER 8

Finding Mii

Virtual Social Identity and the Young Consumer

J. ALISON BRYANT AND ANNA AKERMAN

SELF-DEVELOPMENT

Harter (1999) describes how children's thinking about themselves has traditionally been thought to progress in a series of crude developmental stages, inextricably linked to cognitive abilities. While young children often describe themselves without apparent organization in terms of concrete, observable characteristics, material possessions, behaviors, and preferences, this changes as they proceed to middle and later childhood, during which time more trait-like constructs are employed. Harter (1999) explains how this was traditionally associated with the recruitment of a higher organizational system and more sophisticated cognitive skills. The culmination of self-development then occurs in adolescence, when more abstract self-definitions and representations, based on psychological processes involving inner thoughts and motivations, are typically used by individuals to describe and understand the self.

According to this oft-employed model, younger children's self-concept seems to resemble somewhat of a list, consisting of a series of concrete descriptors (e.g., "I have brown hair." "I have a sister"), while older children develop the ability to integrate information about the self into a more generalized definition, less dependent on purely external characteristics (e.g., "I am smart"). This becomes more sophisticated during the school years such that older children become increasingly likely to define themselves in relation to others (e.g., "I am smarter than Joe") and in a more situationally dependent manner (Ruble 1987). Older children begin to report being a certain way in one context (at school, with friends) and a different way in another (at dinnertime, with parents). By adolescence, self-concept is no longer tied to concrete terms, and in addition to being abstract is often concerned with internal processes (e.g., "I am moody") or ideology (e.g., "I am a Democrat"). An important hallmark reached in adolescence is the ability to view the self in an increasingly differentiated and altogether multidimensional manner. The capacity and desire to have, be, describe, and even explore multiple selves is a regularly cited and much researched marker of adolescent development (Erikson 1994 [1968]).

However, this broad-based model, structured largely around Piaget's theory of cognitive development (1972), has been criticized more recently by theorists who insist that characterizing the development of self in this overly rigid, broad way fails to take into account, among other considerations, individual differences, as well as contextual factors (Harter 1999). After all, the social environment of the developing child is certainly worth considering and is itself constantly changing due to, for one, the influx of new technologies rapidly entering the home. While mediums like the Internet and video games are no longer novel, their use among the younger segment of the population is steadily growing while their known impact, particularly with respect to self-development and identity exploration, is still not fully understood.

Regardless, these developmental stages certainly provide us with a useful framework to better understand children's motivations when it comes to understanding themselves and their social worlds. One extremely important change that takes place during middle childhood is the ability to globally evaluate one's self-worth, which typically emerges around age 7 or 8 (Harter 1987). This relates back to the cognitive achievements described prior—most notably, the ability to organize and integrate information, here related to as the *self*. But this milestone is also accompanied by a greater capacity to differentiate the self, which becomes increasingly common and sophisticated in adolescence. Not surprisingly, this differentiation applies to self-evaluations too, such that with age children become better able, and increasingly likely, to judge their adequacy along different competencies (e.g., "I am good at tennis, bad at math class," etc.) (Harter 1990).

Scholars such as Frey and Ruble (1990) have described the growing importance that social comparison begins to take on as children increasingly judge themselves against those around them, most notably their peers, before ultimately settling upon more autonomous, and temporally derived, forms of assessment. They suggest that this shift is linked to older children's growing concern with self-esteem maintenance instead of pure skill mastery, which steadily becomes a less pressing issue.

THE INTERPERSONAL SELF: GENDER CONCEPT AND PEER RELATIONSHIPS

According to Ruble (1987), by age five most children have attained gender constancy such that they understand that their biological sex is immutable and thus unaffected by changes in hairstyle or clothes. Others have argued that a full understanding of immutability does not occur until later (e.g., Ruble and Martin 1998). Regardless, this early learning is associated with an active exploration of the kinds of clothing, activities, toys, and games that are typically associated with members of each sex. Ruble and Martin (1998) describe how until about age 8, children rely quite rigidly on their accrued stereotype knowledge to, for example, make judgments and ascribe attributes to social actors, after which point they are more likely to entertain the possibility of individual variation within gender categories. Not surprisingly, this goes hand in hand with preference for same-sex playmates, which intensifies between preschool and grade school and stays high between 6 and at least 11 years of age (Maccoby 1990).

Sexual attraction to members of the opposite sex develops during adolescence, at which point cross-sex interactions are no longer viewed as undesirable. Despite this, many, like Maccoby (1990), claim that the preference for same-sex friends never really goes away and gender segregation in friendship selection and social interactions continues, even into adulthood. Interestingly, a study by Richards et al. (1998) concluded that although adolescents, especially in the early stages, may not be spending time with members of the opposite sex, they are actively thinking about them by ages 10 and 11. Worth noting is that more flexible thinking about gender categories also occurs during early adolescence (after which it either stabilizes, or, in some cases, declines) (Ruble and Martin 1998). The work of Richards et al. (1998) demonstrates that thoughts about opposite-sex members precede activities with opposite-sex peers. Though both increase later, the most amount of time with the opposite sex is spent in late adolescence, around 17 and 18 years of age.

ELECTRONIC GAMES AND IDENTITY EXPLORATION: NEW OPPORTUNITIES FOR THE DEVELOPING SELF

Von Salisch, Oppl, and Kristen (2006) report how playing computer and video games has become a favorite pastime for children in Western industrialized nations, particularly boys. According to Rideout, Roberts, and Foehr (2005), 8- to 18-year-olds in the United States spend more time with recreational media content in an average day than in years past, with the increase coming from video games and computers. Rideout et al. (2005) report the average amount of time spent with video games and nonschool-related computer activities as 49 and 62 minutes per day respectively (up from 26 and 27, in 1999). We would speculate that these numbers have, if anything, grown since Rideout et al.'s (2005) report, particularly for ages 6–17, and believe that the expansion of time spent with these fairly recent mediums could have implications for the facets of children's social development outlined above. How might children and adolescents' online and video game play affect and, in turn, be affected by their level of self-development? This question, and a host of related issues, will be addressed below.

Numerous communication scholars, like von Salisch et al. (2006), have applied a uses and gratifications model to understand children's selection of and preference for certain media over others. This theoretical framework suggests that children decide to play electronic games, for example, because these particular outlets allow them to get ahead with the specific developmental tasks and/or difficulties they are encountering; the selected medium is chosen for this end. It then follows that the increasingly popular video and computer games must therefore provide children a helpful outlet to "work on" the social developmental issues outlined earlier, which relate to tasks like developing a positive attitude of oneself, getting along with peers, and learning appropriate gender role behavior. In the words of von Salisch et al. (2006), "these [electronic] games allow [children] to gather information, to coordinate social perspectives, and to explore new roles in the safe context of a game, without the risk of being held accountable for the consequences of their actions in the real world" (p. 149).

This emphasis on role exploration is very much in line with the work of Sherry Turkle (1995), an early pioneer in discussing the computer's potential to allow users an unprecedented level of freedom to assume and create new, and sometimes even taboo, identities. Turkle (1995) and others have focused primarily on identity exploration as it pertains to adolescents or adults. The focus on adolescents is not surprising, given how crucial the identity search is to this particular developmental stage. As with middle childhood, adolescence too is associated with a host of specific developmental tasks or concerns. Along with becoming autonomous, dealing with their emerging sexuality, acquiring interpersonal skills to interact with opposite-sex members in the interest of eventual mate selection, and acquiring experiences needed for adult work, adolescents are additionally charged with "resolving issues of identity and values" (Elliott and Feldman 1990, p. 13). If we continue to apply the uses and gratifications model discussed earlier to this new developmental context, we can see how media outlets can serve as an important vehicle to satisfy these stage-specific tasks too.

THE RISE OF AVATARS

An important gaming development that may have elevated the online potential for self-exploration and expression has been the rising use of customizable avatars—digital representations of one's persona, for self-representation. It is increasingly common to have avatar features on multiuser games and instant-message systems, which allow users to visually represent themselves on screen (Nowak and Rauh 2005). The ability to create and subsequently use an avatar provides children and adolescents with an even greater degree of liberty to play and explore their developing sense of self. This freedom to choose and design an avatar of their liking—and the relative lack of accountability that children can feel as they explore their online personae while free of the rules, restrictions, and sanctions that abound in everyday real life—provides researchers with a new window into their inner psychic worlds.

CHARACTER IDENTIFICATION

Previous research has suggested that media characters represent an important socializing agent for children, who are prone to develop strong attachments with favorite television personalities. Hoffner (1996), for example, has illustrated the power of gender as an important precursor for television character identification, defined as "the process by which a viewer shares a character's perspective and vicariously participates in his/her experiences during the program" (Maccoby and Wilson 1957, as cited in Hoffner 1996, p. 390). Her research with 7- to 12-year-olds found that though having same-sex favorites was extremely common, it was much more rampant among boys. And, while girls' identification with their favorite characters relied entirely upon physical attractiveness, boys were more influenced by other features, such as physical strength and activity level. How might studies of television character identification be applied to the world of electronic game characters? Though limited, some research has extended this kind of work to better understand children's connections with online characters.

McDonald and Kim (2001) have suggested that although electronic game characters, similar to television characters, could provide youngsters with a viable outlet for developing their own personalities and sense of self via identification, certain important differences between the mediums also exist. For example, electronic games are more interactive, which might lead game players to identify more strongly with game characters than televised ones. Additionally, electronic games are more portable and, due to this ubiquity, could present more of an opportunity to represent a "surrogate companion" for the gaming child (McDonald and Kim 2001, p. 246). The results of their research in fact suggest that children do have strong identifications with electronic characters and use similar dimensions when describing themselves and online characters that they hold in high regard—often in higher regard than they hold themselves. Liking a character generally led to identification with him/her, which was often followed by modeling and imitation behavior.

What about avatars? How has the use of avatars affected this? While the traditional literature on role modeling and imitation suggests that these often behavioral displays are common ways of "trying out" the characteristics of media characters, the use of avatars represents a more direct experience for safe role play which gives children the relatively simple tools to create online representations that incorporate characteristics they are eager to try out and even adopt. As Thomas (2000) describes, in the online graphical world of avatars where users (in her case 8- to 16-year-olds) represent themselves pictorially and interact with one another using these visual symbols, "It is easier to be 'prettier,' it is easier to be 'in control,' and it is easier to be 'liked.'" (p. 669).

This brings to mind an important question—can the advanced role-play features of avatar-based electronic games in part explain the increased attraction that such games hold for children and adolescents, as indicated by recent reports of media usage? After all, the ability to create and manipulate their on-screen identities in this symbolic fashion grants children in particular new levels of power and control, both of which are often missing in their daily off-screen realities. If so, what are the characteristics of the developing child's chosen online self-representations and how might they differ by age and gender? If, as von Salisch, Oppl, and Kristen (2006) report, children are indeed attracted to electronic figures most similar to them with respect to, not surprisingly, age and gender, how might this play out when they are provided the tools to create characters of their own liking and imagination? And, how might these same utensils be applied during adolescence, the stage of life most commonly associated with identity search and development?

In order to delve into and begin to answer these questions, we present a conceptual framework for looking at how kids and teens adopt and modify their virtual social identities. The data on which this framework are based come from a fifteen-month multiproject research agenda undertaken by the digital research team of the Nickelodeon/MTV Networks Kids and Family Group in the United States.

From November 2006 to March 2008, the research team conducted 34 focus groups, 9 in-home mini focus groups, 16 pair interviews, and 16 in-home individual interviews with 6- to 17-year-olds in 7 markets across the United States. Individuals were recruited either through a market research firm or through the Nickelodeon Research Panel, depending on the specific project they were being recruited for. The discussions were moderated by several different moderators, each of whom focused on a specific subproject.

In each of these qualitative sessions, moderators discussed with kids their use of avatars (or other types of virtual pets), their affinity for and engagement with different types of virtual social identities, and the ways in which these identities integrate into their offline life. Over the course of the fifteen months, trends in the qualitative data began to emerge. Because of the wealth and depth of data presented, and the lack of previous research in this area, we took a *grounded theory* approach to analyzing the data (Glaser 1998). Grounded theory allows us to look at the data through adductive reasoning. As we gathered the data, we began to outline common themes regarding the ways in which the kids and teens talked about their virtual social identities; how they created, used, and identified with their avatars; and noting any age or gender differences that arose. Because we were conducting research across a variety of website types and digital platforms, we also kept track of any differences across context.

FINDINGS: THE STAGES OF VIRTUAL SOCIAL IDENTITY

The more data we collected, the clearer it became that there were significant differences between the different age categories with regard to the types of virtual social identities that they decided to create. (Interestingly, gender and context did not arise as clear factors in their choices.) When we examined how age entered into the virtual social identity equation, we saw that the offline identity and social development corollaries were key to understanding their online selves.

Today, as children and adolescents develop their identity and social personality offline, those who have access to the online world are also developing virtual social identities. The evolution of these online identities is directly related to the developmental needs children are experiencing as they figure out who they are and who they are going to be. Findings reveal that there are four stages of virtual social identity: self-development, identity development, identity projection, and self-representation. These stages occur in a somewhat linear progression from around the age a child enters elementary school until adulthood.

Self-Development: Six- to Nine-Year-Olds

In their early elementary school years, children are in the process of constructing their sense of self, of figuring out who they are in relation to others. They tend to understand themselves in the context of others, particularly their family members and close friends. They are beginning to understand the social dynamics that surround friendship, including concepts such as having multiple friendship circles and feeling empathy for others. As mentioned above, they also tend to describe and understand themselves in very concrete terms (e.g., "I have freckles," "I have a baby brother").

For 6- to 9-year-olds, then, belonging is a critical aspect of their offline identity. Virtual social identities for this age group are tied into this underlying sense of figuring out who they are in the context of their immediate world—of where they belong. We see two main types of virtual social identities for this group—the *nurturer* and the *"concrete" avatar.*

The nurturer identity is an expression of children's growing sense of empathy and a reflection of their recognition that they are part of a larger social group in which people take care of people (just as their parents take care of them). In this nurturing identity, children often have fantastical avatars—cartoon-like depictions of animals or mythical creatures that they must take care of (such as Webkinz, Neopets, or NintenDogs). These pet avatars are an outlet for kids to try out their "adult" skills of taking care of others. This virtual caregiving is parallel to the way that kids play with dolls or stuffed animals in real life. Online, however, the scenario for caregiving is often highly developed in that there are economies surrounding the nurturing of their pet as well as consequences for not caring for them. Although younger kids often do not understand or explore all of the intricacies of these online caregiving worlds, they understand the basic consequences of their actions (or inaction).

Moreover, because their everyday lives are so intertwined and constricted by the adults around them, kids in this age group relish the ability to "take control"

Figure 8.1 **Sample Avatars for the Self-Development Phase**

Webkinz   Club Penguin   Neopets   Nintendo Mii

of everyday, mundane things. They like having a pet and "making" money and "shopping" for items like food for their pet. They also enjoy other opportunities for taking control and being creative, particularly in the form of dress-up play with avatars online. Again, similar to offline play, kids like to dress up avatars of others—especially familiar characters or avatars that look like people they know.

When 6- to 9-year-olds create avatars that resemble themselves, they do so in a very simplistic way, in line with the concrete terms they use to define themselves at this stage—hence our description of these as "concrete" avatars. Similar to the ways in which kids of this age draw pictures of themselves, it takes very little in the way of physical attributes for them to identify an avatar as "like them." It might be as simple as putting a similar hair color on a boy avatar in order for a young boy to identify the avatar as himself.

Interestingly, kids in this age group often describe their interactions with these online characters (both the pets and the "concrete" avatars) as playing *with* them, not *as* them, which is what we see in later years. In this way, they are developing various aspects of their sense of self outside of themselves through role-play.

The opportunities for developing these virtual social identities are numerous, and the virtual places kids can go to do so are both exceptionally popular today and growing in number exponentially. Currently, some of the most popular online websites are Webkinz, Club Penguin, Neopets, Barbie Girls, and MyScene. In addition, the exceptional success of the Nintendo Wii has made its avatar (the Mii) a popular virtual expression of the concrete self for this age group. Figure 8.1 provides examples of pets or avatars from these virtual places.

Identity Development: Ten- to Twelve-Year-Olds

In the "tween" years, when children are negotiating between their "child" and "teen" selves, their virtual social identity also takes on a mixed persona. As children, they were developing their sense of self, which was strongly tied to their sense of belonging. As they move toward becoming a teen and begin developing their own identity, they are counterbalancing that perspective of belonging to a family or social group with a sense of independence, of figuring out who they are outside of those relationships. In addition, instead of simply understanding themselves in concrete terms, they begin to understand themselves more abstractly and in terms of situations or internal processes (e.g., "I am good at playing baseball," "I am frustrated").

For 10- to 12-year-olds, therefore, virtual social identity provides a means for developing one's identity in terms of both fitting in and standing out. These pre-adolescents are still firmly planted in the security of their child selves, who rely on others for a sense of self; but they also want to begin to assert their independence. Offline, they are beginning to choose their own activities to take part in (both in and out of school), they are starting to solidify their social circles or cliques, and they are beginning to spend more time engaging in social activities. Their virtual social identities, therefore, are doing the same. Although there are still some concrete aspects of their sense of self that become part of their online identity, especially in terms of gender and race, tweens are more open to trying on different personas or experimenting with different appearances. We see two main types of virtual social identities for this group—the *explorer* and the *"adapting" avatar.*

The explorer identity is the manifestation of the state of flux that tweens find themselves in. At this age, kids begin to describe their interactions with virtual pets or avatars as playing *as* the characters. These virtual representations move from being primarily playmates to being illustrations of oneself that are malleable, so that they are able to experiment with different clothing, accessories, and so forth that fit the identity that they are working on offline. If they are on a virtual pet site, such as Webkinz or Neopets, they are not only interested in basic caregiving but are also exploring the personalities of their characters and engaging more deeply in the complex economies and narratives in which these characters are set. They are also using their pet as a means of communication with others on the site, mimicking (and sometimes pushing the boundaries of) offline social models and norms.

When 10- to 12-year-olds represent themselves through avatars online, they do so in a way that is both concrete (often looking somewhat like them), but also flexible—the "adapting" avatar. In the words of a 10-year-old girl, "I like creating my own character. It sort of gives you freedom." This flexibility is not simply about the appearance of the avatar, although that is certainly important. It is also about having the avatar represent more individualistic aspects of oneself. As one 12-year-old boy put it, when describing the avatar he would create online, "I would make him more to my personality. More like me. I like to wear jerseys and stuff so I would make my guy wear jerseys and a football team's hat. Fit more like me so it's more like me."

Figure 8.2 **Sample Avatars for the Identity-Development Phase**

Nicktropolis   Virtual Magic Kingdom   Zwinky   Gaia Online

As a result, for tweens, this ability to develop their identity online through an "adapting" avatar increases the importance of customization or personalization. Many tweens, therefore, say that they spend a lot of time setting up their avatars, and that they would tweak their avatar often, changing its clothes to reflect their mood or the game they were playing. This sense of their virtual social identity fitting into a transitory context is very different from the more static, concrete selves they were developing as kids.

Some of the virtual spaces in which tweens are developing their identities today are similar to those that we mentioned above, especially the virtual pets websites (Neopets, Club Penguin, Webkinz). Because tweens are more interested in customizable avatars and online identities at this age, however, other websites—and virtual worlds in particular—gain in popularity. Some of the more popular "adapting" avatar-related sites for this age group are Nickelodeon's Nicktropolis, Disney's Virtual Magic Kingdom, Runescape, Stardoll, Zwinky, and Gaia Online. Figure 8.2 provides examples of some of the avatars from these virtual places.

Identity Projection: Thirteen- to Seventeen-Year-Olds

In their teen years, adolescents are striving for independence. At the same time, they have a relatively clear sense of self, more clearly defined social networks, and are developing their interpersonal skills in order to interact with people they are sexually attracted to. At this age, they are also settling any unresolved issues of identity or personal values.

For 13- to 17-year-olds, therefore, their virtual social identity is about projecting their identities. They are spending much more time on social networking websites, such as MySpace, Facebook, and Bebo, and less time on gaming online. This move toward virtual social spaces is a critical part of identity projection, since these spaces not only allow teens to connect with their offline friends and

Figure 8.3 **Sample Avatars for the Identity-Projection Phase**

| Sims | Yahoo! | Avatar | IMVU |

make new friends, but also to create a representation of their "best possible me." We see two main types of virtual social identities for this group—the *"identical" avatar* and the *"real me."*

Because they are trying to let others know about themselves, teens often veer toward these most realistic of representations—the photograph ("real me") or the highly customized avatar that looks like them (the "identical" avatar). Both of these are opaque depictions of the self from an identity perspective, because the individual can choose exactly what they look like or are wearing (as is the case with the "identical" avatar) or choose the photograph(s) that most closely represent the image they are trying to project. In the words of one 13-year-old girl, "I really like the idea of having an avatar to have something like your identity."

For teens, therefore, the ability to have a wide range of customization for their avatars is paramount. As one teenage girl put it (about why she liked Gaia Online. com), "I love all the character designs, from clothes to hairstyles to piercings." In the same way, lack of customization is the death knell for websites featuring avatars for teens. As one teen girl said disapprovingly of Habbo.com, "I was expecting cooler hairstyles and more face and clothes styles. The clothes are very dull."

At this age, teens also want the avatar to be as realistic as possible, which includes wearing or using the brands that they have high affinity for in real life. When asked what they would want to buy for their avatar, teens generally respond with very specific requests in this arena, such as Nike Air Jordan shoes or Apple Bottoms jeans (or whatever the brand-of-the-moment is). The changes they make to their avatars are more than just a concrete projections of themselves, as we see in younger kids, but are about important social nuances and multidimensionality, and brands are an important part of this both offline and online.

As mentioned earlier, most of the time teens spend with their virtual social identities are spent on social networking sites, although there is some time spent in virtual places like the Sims games or massive multiplayer online role-playing games. They also often use avatar generators such as Yahoo!Avatar or IMVU to create depictions of themselves to use on social networking sites or in online communication like instant messaging. Figure 8.3 provides examples of avatars from these virtual places.

Self-Representation: Eighteen and Up

Although this chapter is focused on the young consumer, it is important to point out how virtual social identity formation changes as they reach adulthood. Around the age of 18, higher-order cognitive processes, such as metacognition—the ability understand how one thinks and the ability to monitor, self-regulate, and alter cognition—are in place (Van Evra 2004). In the same way, self-identity is relatively secure, and changes of circumstance and environment are much less likely to have significant effects on an individual's sense of self.

For adults, therefore, virtual social identity is mostly about *self-representation,* using avatars or other online icons as a means to represent oneself, or part of oneself, to others online. Not only do adults tend to use and have affinity for a wider variety of virtual social representations, including avatars, icons, and other graphic representations, but they tend to be more adept at using different representations in different contexts. For example, if they have a profile on a gaming website, they might use the icon of a pair of sunglasses to show that they are an excellent casino game player (the glasses suggest that if they were playing their opponents in real life, they would not have any "tells"). For their profile on a parenting website, on the other hand, they might have avatars that look like their kids. This ability to be flexible in their online identity, and to incorporate context into their virtual social representations, is a hallmark of both higher-order cognition and a more complex, yet static, sense of offline social identity.

CONCLUSION

One of the most interesting findings we've seen in this area of virtual social identity is that there are minimal, if any, gender differences in these stages. When it comes to virtual social identity, the self- and social development that children and adolescents are undergoing through these critical years is the driving factor for the identities they create online. That is not to say that what they do with the manifestations of these identities online is always similar. Girls, for example, are more likely to use them in purely social contexts, whereas boys will use them in more socialized gaming contexts. In addition, there are, of course, variations on specific online identities that are created by each individual child or adolescent, just as there would be in real life; but the consistencies are also incredibly strong, just like in real life.

That is not to say, however, that the generalizations put forth by this stage development model are true for all kids and teens or for all contexts. This model is meant as a starting point for understanding virtual social identity in young consumers. As children and adolescents continue to take their offline self- and social development online, researchers and marketers will need to further understand the role of virtual social identities in kids' lives. Two areas of further inquiry, in particular, come to mind as critical for further understanding this phenomenon.

The first area of future research is the role of context in virtual social identity. For example, kids are more likely to be representing themselves in the context of games or virtual worlds, whereas teens are doing it more in social networking sites. This contextual difference not only affects the way they represent themselves on a particular site, but also their reasons for spending time on the site in the first place. This begs the question of how their choice of online activity is predetermining the ways in which their virtual social identities develop. It also begs the question of how multiple avatars or identities are chosen and used.

Moreover, future research needs to be done in order to better understand how young consumers develop, modify, and utilize their virtual social identities, and how their offline identities are both similar to and different from their virtual ones. For example, there is a need to understand the implications of creating more realistic avatars for online social interactions. As avatars become more realistic, so that customers are able to make very close approximations of their offline selves, will negative social interaction decrease? We have heard a lot over the past couple of years in the press about cyber-bullying, especially with young consumers, so this is a critical area of inquiry. Perhaps interacting with a more realistic representation of someone online will bring back offline social norms, interactions, and rules, so that cyber-bullying can be reduced by websites deliberately using more realistic avatar generators.

As avatars and other virtual social identities become even more commonplace, anyone trying to engage the youth audience, from educators to advertisers, will need to understand both the affinity that kids and teens have for these and the role that they play in self- and social development. With that understanding, we can better engage our youth and provide them with constructive outlets for self-expression and self-exploration.

REFERENCES

Elliott, G.R., and S.S. Feldman. 1990. "Capturing the Adolescent Experience." In *At the Threshold: The Developing Adolescent,* ed. S.S. Feldman and G.R. Elliott, 1–13. Cambridge, MA: Harvard University Press.

Erikson, E.H. 1994 (1968). *Identity: Youth, and Crisis.* New York: W.W. Norton.

Frey, K.S., and D.N. Ruble. 1990. "Strategies for Comparative Evaluation: Maintaining a Sense of Competence Across the Life Span." In *Competence Considered,* ed. R.J. Sternberg and J. Kolligian Jr., 167–189. New Haven: Yale University Press.

Glaser, B.G. 1998. *Doing Grounded Theory: Issues and Discussions.* Mill Valley, CA: Sociology Press.

Harter, S. 1987. "The Determinants and Mediational Role of Global Self-Worth in Children." In *Contemporary Topics in Developmental Psychology,* ed. N. Eisenberg, 219–242. New York: Wiley-Interscience.

———. 1990. "Causes, Correlates, and the Functional Role of Global Self-Worth: A Life Span Perspective." In *Competence Considered,* ed. R.J. Sternberg and J. Kolligian Jr., 67–97. New Haven: Yale University Press.

———. 1999. *The Construction of the Self: A Developmental Perspective.* New York: Guilford Press.

Hoffner, C. 1996. "Children's Wishful Identification and Parasocial Interaction with Favorite Television Characters." *Journal of Broadcasting and Electronic Media* 40 (3): 389–402.

Maccoby, E.E. 1990. "Gender and Relationships: A Developmental Account." *American Psychologist* 45 (4): 513–520.

McDonald, D.G., and H. Kim. 2001. "When I Die, I Feel Small: Electronic Game Characters and the Social Self." *Journal of Broadcasting and Electronic Media* 45 (2): 241–258.

Nowak, K.L., and C. Rauh. 2005. "The Influence of the Avatar on Online Perceptions of Anthropomorphism, Androgyny, Credibility, Homophily, and Attraction." *Journal of Computer-Mediated Communication* 11 (1). Available at http://jcmc.indiana.edu/v0111/issue1/nowak.html.

Piaget, J. 1972. *The Psychology of the Child.* New York: Basic Books.

Richards, M.H., P.A. Crowe, R. Larson, and A. Swarr. 1998. "Developmental Patterns and Gender Differences in the Experience of Peer Companionship During Adolescence." *Child Development* 69 (1): 154–163.

Rideout, V., D.F. Roberts, and U.G. Foehr. 2005. *Generation M: Media in the Lives of 8–18 Year Olds.* Menlo Park, CA: Henry J. Kaiser Family Foundation.

Ruble, D.N. 1987. "The Acquisition of Self-Knowledge: A Self-Socialization Perspective." In *Contemporary Topics in Developmental Psychology,* ed. N. Eisenberg, 243–270. New York: Wiley Interscience.

Ruble, D.N., and C.L. Martin. 1998. "Gender Development." In *Handbook of Child Psychology,* vol. 3: *Social, Emotional, and Personality Development,* ed. W. Damon and N. Eisenberg, 933–1016. 5th ed. New York: Wiley.

Thomas, A. 2000. "Textual Constructions of Children's Online Identities." *CyberPsychology and Behavior* 3 (4): 665–672.

Turkle, S. 1995. *Life on the Screen: Identity in the Age of the Internet.* New York: Simon & Schuster.

Van Evra, J. 2004. *Television and Child Development.* 3rd ed. Mahwah, NJ: Lawrence Erlbaum Associates.

von Salisch, M., C. Oppl, and A. Kristen. 2006. "What Attracts Children?" In *Playing Video Games: Motives, Responses and Consequences,* ed. P. Vorderer and J. Bryant, 147–163. Mahwah, NJ: Lawrence Earlbaum Associates.

CHAPTER 9

Me, Myself, and My Avatar

The Effects of Avatars on SNW (Social Networking)
Users' Attitudes Toward a Website and Its Ad Content

YOUJEONG KIM AND S. SHYAM SUNDAR

Avatars, or pictorial representations of users, are commonly used in chat rooms, video games, and online virtual communities. They not only express users' identities online but also ensure anonymity, allowing users complete freedom to manipulate and manage their online personas. But, does this facility to manage one's self-presentation provide benefits beyond mere impression formation? In particular, does the presence of an avatar as a form of self-representation enhance one's personal investment in the site where the avatar is used? And could this translate to more positive attitudes toward content on the site as well as more sincere appraisal of personally relevant information delivered by the site?

As virtual platforms (e.g., *Second Life* and *There.com*) become increasingly common tools of persuasion, researchers and marketers alike will benefit from an enhanced understanding of the role played by self-created avatars in users' own web experience and information processing, particularly their role in aiding persuasion.

We therefore investigate whether a self-created avatar influences users' persuasive processing of a social networking site and its advertising content. We are especially interested in the degree to which the avatar influences users' processing of health-related public service announcements (PSAs) on such a site. If indeed avatar creation and customization serve to heighten users' concerns about their own health and well-being, we would like to ascertain which psychological variables mediate such an effect.

LITERATURE REVIEW

In a virtual environment, an avatar plays the role of a mirror that reflects a user's identity as well as a window for viewing the world. It is a tool that users choose for communication as well as for self-representation in cyberspace. Self-representation has increasingly become important in social networking sites (SNSs). Regardless of how avatars look and behave, it appears that their presence serves to highlight the self and thereby influence users' information processing and virtual interactions. The control afforded to users in creating and manipulating their avatars is likely to imbue users with a sense of agency. The following sections will address how psychological benefits accrue from the process of avatar creation, use, and customization, with implications for persuasion.

Psychological Benefits of Avatars

Although there are a variety of avatar forms, from objects to animals, the avatar that is most commonly used in video games and virtual communities has human features, such as a face and human body parts.

Thus, users easily identify with these embodied characters and view them as their virtual selves. In particular, when the embodied characters resemble users in appearance, or the virtual environment in which the virtual characters are embedded simulates reality realistically (e.g., virtual reality), users' identification with their self-created characters occurs more readily, while their feelings of actually "being there" also increase. Biocca (1997) conceptualized this psychological state as "self-presence," whereby users are aware of their self-identity inside a virtual environment. Extending the mechanism of self-presence, it may be argued that an avatar's presence will increase a user's sense of self-preservation. The act of routinely seeing one's own representation in the midst of an environment is akin to an out-of-body experience, giving the user a unique perspective on his/her own place in the world. This is likely to influence the user's stance toward stimuli encountered in virtual worlds by replacing the experiential with the phenomenal—that is, the user is able to perceive through his/her senses the interaction between the self (as represented by the avatar) and external stimuli. The user is no longer simply experiencing stimuli, as happens when watching a movie, for example. Instead, the user will see himself or herself in the ongoing narrative of the movie and therefore obtain an extrasensory perception of his/her actions and reactions to events in the virtual world. As a result, the user is likely to develop favorable dispositions toward his/her own avatar, just as we develop favorable dispositions toward protagonists in dramatic portrayals, as suggested by entertainment theorists (e.g., Zillmann 1991).

When watching films and other media portrayals involving heroes and villains, we form strong attitudes toward these characters, such that we experience euphoria when the hero is winning a battle against the villain but experience empathetic distress if the villain is succeeding. That is, we begin to care deeply for the welfare of the protagonist. When we know that danger is lurking behind the hero (as in some suspense films where the camera is the point of view of the villain) or around the corner (when we as viewers have the privilege of an overview or master shot of the scene in which the hero is involved), we find ourselves wanting to help the hero to avoid or otherwise overcome the peril awaiting him or her. Likewise, we can expect a positive disposition toward our own self (as represented by our avatar in a virtual world) to guide our welfare. Therefore, we may hypothesize that avatars increase users' concerns about their physical bodies through their observations of and reflections about themselves. We thus propose that

H_1: Avatar users are more likely to perceive greater potential risks to their physical health than non-avatar users.

The "self-presence" brought about by interacting with one's avatar has been shown to increase users' involvement and enjoyment in the virtual world (Choi, Miracle, and Biocca 2001; Nowak 2000; Skalski and Tamborini 2007). We may attribute this to "implicit egotism," true for all activities in which self-related objects are involved. Pelham et al. (2003) argued that "most people possess positive associations about themselves. For this reason . . . most people should gravitate toward things that resemble the self" (p. 800). In their study, they found that participants showed positive attitudes toward brand names that start with the initial letters of their names and also toward the ad in which the manipulated brand name was embedded. Based on such findings, we can argue that the positive valence induced through self-resembling entities (avatars) would influence users' attitudes toward a website in which their avatars appear, and that these positive attitudes would be transferred to online ads (commercial ads and public service announcements) that are embedded in the website. Therefore,

H_2: Avatar users are likely to evaluate websites and ads (both commercial and public-service advertisements) more positively than non-avatar users.

Technological Benefits of Avatars

The strength of the avatar, technologically, is that users are able to customize their body images by selecting from body features, including skin color, hair, eyes, and even accessories, enabling users to freely create and manipulate their identities.

Customization refers to "adaptive interfaces" that enable people to modify something based on their *individual* needs (Alpert et al. 2003). For example, users customize their web pages by changing colors, fonts, or content. This feature allows each user to be unique and distinct, highlighting his/her sense of self (Sundar 2008). Petty, Barden, and Wheeler (2002) asserted that customization reflects some aspect of one's self by displaying the emotional tone that is consistent with one's personality and by catering to the user's specific cognitive needs and processing styles.

The agency model of customization (Sundar 2008) emphasizes the role of the self as a "creator" and "source" for filtering individual needs and connecting the

Figure 9.1   **Sundar's Agency Model of Customization**

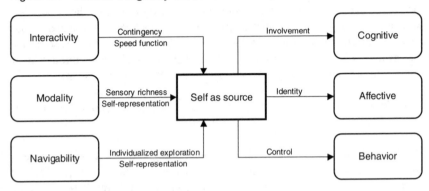

Source: Sundar (2008).

technological affordances (interactivity, modality, and navigability) underlying customization and the resulting psychological outcomes (i.e., cognitive, affective, and behavioral) (see Figure 9.1).

Customization is strongly associated with the interaction between the system and the user. In particular, a system provides contingent response based on a user's input or request. This in turn facilitates a rich dialogue between the system and the user and heightens the "sourceness" of self (Sundar 2008). In addition, the various forms of modalities, such as text, audio, and video, allow users to represent their selves in a richer way. Navigability contributes to the feeling of self-as-source by allowing users to individually and idiosyncratically explore the system, be it a customized portal or a virtual world. All these affordances are likely to play an even stronger role in imbuing a sense of self as source in virtual environments than on portal websites.

Richer modalities, including the availability of facial expressions or movement, facilitate users' self-representation. In addition, by providing idiosyncratic features of the virtual self that are different from others, the user's feeling of "self as source" is likely to be heightened. Furthermore, users have more control over their interaction with the system and with the avatars that they create. And, as mentioned earlier, avatars serve to heighten user involvement with content on the site. In a customizable web portal (e.g., *iGoogle*), for example, users customize their web pages by changing colors, fonts, or content. By doing this, users observe the changes that the computer provides upon their request and experience psychological empowerment while interacting with the system. The capacity to exert control over the system and the subsequent psychological empowerment are critical for developing the sense of agency that we expect from avatar customization (Sundar and Marathe 2006; Zimmerman 1990). Until they are absolutely satisfied with the form of their virtual self, users constantly change skin colors, hairstyles, and clothes. By doing this, users find themselves having control over the system and their avatars as well. It increases their sense of agency and, in turn, influences the avatar creator's persuasive processing.

Identity, control, and involvement are theorized by the agency model to govern the sense of "self as source," with significant psychological benefits. While involvement breeds cognitive attachment with content of the interaction, identity fosters positive attitudes and control contributes to behaviors. Applied to the context of a social networking site on the Web, we may hypothesize, based on this model, that the involvement, identity enhancement, and control derived from avatar customization will result in greater interaction on the site, closer appraisal of contents encountered during this interaction, and more self-preserving and self-enhancing attitudes resulting from perusal of those contents. Therefore, we predict:

H_3: Participants who customize their avatars are more likely to evaluate the website, ad, and PSA positively than participants who are not allowed to customize their avatars or do not have avatars.

Aside from a sense of agency, customization in the portal context is known to influence positive attitudes by breeding a sense of involvement, greater perceived interactivity, and higher perceived novelty (Kalyanaraman and Sundar 2006). If avatars indeed bring about greater involvement with the site as hypothesized, and if this is due at least in part to the novelty of the activity, we can expect user attitudes toward body-related health messages to be mediated by perceived involvement and/or perceived novelty. Alternatively, if the me-ness fostered by interacting via one's avatar underlies our attitudes toward site content, then we would expect perceived agency to be the critical mediator. A third possibility for positive attitudes is the sheer ability of the user to exert control over the interaction through the use of a customized avatar. We investigate these theoretical issues with the help of the following research question:

RQ_1: What are the psychological mediators of the effects of avatar customization on users' attitudes toward websites, ads, and body-related health messages?

METHODS

To explore the effects of avatars on users' attitudes toward a website and its advertising content, a simple three-group comparison experiment was employed, consisting of a customized avatar group, a noncustomized avatar group, and a no-avatar group. The key manipulation was the creation of avatars for representing users' selves on a website, which will be discussed in a later section. Participants ($N = 73$) in the avatar groups (customized avatar group and noncustomized avatar group) created avatars and browsed the website Cyworld.com (www.cyworld.com),

Figure 9.2 **Cyworld Website and Ads That Were Manipulated for the Study**

a Korean online community site similar to Facebook or MySpace. Cyworld has a personal mini-homepage, the so-called Minihompi, on which users are able to post pictures and share them with friends. In addition, this website provides avatars, called "Minimis" for representing the users. Once a user creates an avatar, it appears on the left side of the front page. Participants in the control group (no-avatar group) browsed the website without creating their own avatars. The website had two interactive square ads embedded on the right side of the front page: an advertisement for a shampoo and a PSA for skin cancer (see Figure 9.2). Each ad had multiple tabs allowing participants to interactively explore different layers embedded within it.

Both ads were created for the study and were made identical in size and structure in order to rule out any effects due to formal features of ad design. The positions of the ads were randomly switched from the top of the page to the bottom of the page to rule out position effects.

The ads were chosen based on two criteria: (1) the topics in the ads (shampoo and skin cancer) should be relevant and easily understood by members of our respondent pool; and (2) they should involve an issue or product that concerns the self, in order for us to detect "implicit-egotism" effects of avatar presence and customization that we theorized in the previous section.

Dependent Measures

The dependent measure of attitude toward the website was assessed by asking participants to respond to nine 10-point Likert-type items adapted from Sundar and Kalyanaraman's (2004) "website perceptions" scale, asking participants to indicate how well each of the following adjectives described the Cyworld website: appealing, likeable, entertaining, interesting, attractive, stimulating, trustworthy, honest, and believable. Items were anchored between very poorly and very well. In addition, three questions pertaining to online behavioral intentions were modified from Kalyanaraman and Sundar (2006), and elicited in the form of user agreement with the following statements: "I would bookmark Cyworld as my favorite site," "I would recommend this website to my friends," and "I would revisit this website." These items were measured on a 1–10 scale, ranging from *strongly disagree* to *strongly agree.*

In order to measure users' attitudes toward the ad, ten 10-point semantic differential scales were used (Witte 1998): stimulating, interesting, persuasive, informative, relevant to me, bad/good, appealing, believable, important, and attractive. In addition to these ten items, for measuring users' perceived risks about body-related health, participants were also asked to rate the following questions on a 1–10 scale, with 1 representing *not at all* and 10 representing *a lot:* "How anxious did the shampoo ad make you feel about your hair?" and "How uncomfortable did the shampoo ad make you feel about your hair?"

Lastly, attitudes toward the skin cancer PSA were measured with the same items that were used for the ad (Witte 1998). Ten 10-point semantic differential scales were employed (stimulating, interesting, persuasive, informative, relevant to me, bad/good, appealing, believable, important, and attractive). Also, in order to test the users' perceived risk about body-related health, users were asked two questions using 1–10 scales, with 1 representing *not at all* and 10 representing *a lot:* "How anxious did the 'Don't Toast' skin cancer PSA make you feel about your skin?" and "How uncomfortable did the 'Don't Toast' skin cancer PSA make you feel about your skin?"

Finally, three additional questions asked participants to assess the perceived severity of skin cancer as a potential health problem. They were asked to rate their agreement with the following statements: "skin cancer is a severe health problem," "skin cancer is serious threat to my health," and "skin cancer is a significant disease." These items were measured using a 1–10 scale, ranging from *strongly disagree* to *strongly agree.*

Intervening Variables

Four intervening variables were formally studied in this experiment: perceived novelty, perceived involvement, perceived interactivity, and sense of agency. Questions pertaining to each of these variables were included in order to empirically verify whether these variables mediated the relationship between avatar customization and attitudes toward the website, its ad, and its PSA.

Measures of perceived novelty and perceived involvement were adapted from Kalyanaraman and Sundar's study (2006). Four items were measured for perceived novelty: "This website was typical of most websites you see today," "The website was just like other websites," "You see websites like this all the time; it's the same old thing," and "I've seen a lot of websites like this before." All of the items were reversed for coding. Four items were used for perceived involvement: "I got emotionally involved in this website," "I paid a great deal of attention when going through the website," "I got involved with the information and content on this website," and "I found myself responding strongly to this website."

For perceived interactivity, one item was adapted from Kalyanaraman and Sundar (2006): "the structure of this website was interactive." Three additional items adapted from Sundar and Kim (2005): "this website enabled two-way communication," "this website enabled synchronous communication," and "this website enabled active control." Three items for sense of agency were adapted from concepts recommended by Eagly (1987) and modified for this study: "this website made me feel that I have control over my actions," "this website enabled me to assert myself," and "this website made me feel I have a distinct self."

For the control variable, participants were asked to answer whether they were familiar with avatars in general by responding "yes" or "no."

Procedure

Seventy-three undergraduate students at Penn State University participated in the experiment for extra course credit. The participants were between the ages of 18 and 32 (M = 20.96 years), and 40.3 percent of them were men.

The experiment was administered to groups of participants in a computer lab. As participants arrived in the lab, they were greeted by the experimenter. The experimenter told the participants to have a seat in front of a computer terminal, asked them to read and sign the informed consent form, and directed them to study the instructions on the computer screen, which provided general instructions for the study. By clicking the button that said "click here to go to the next page" after reading the general instructions, participants were randomly assigned to one of the three conditions (CA: customizing avatar, SA: no customizing avatar, or NA: no

Figure 9.3 **The Manipulation of Avatar Creation**

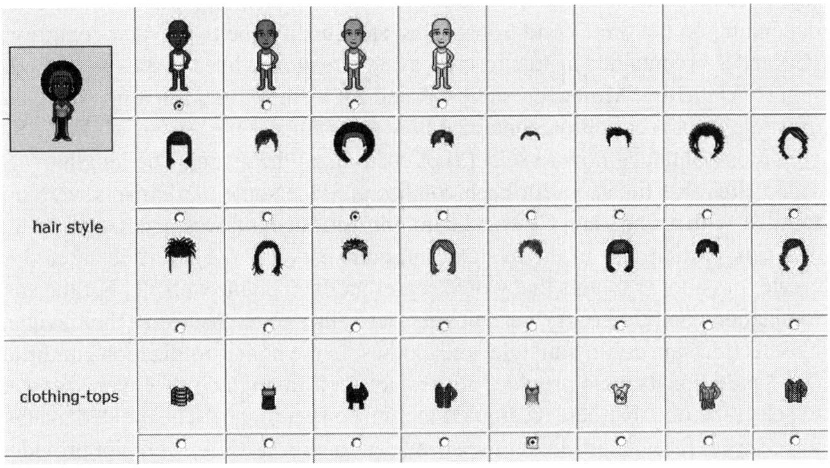

avatar) and were asked to watch a three-minute video clip on the computer screen that introduced Cyworld.com. The content of the video clip was a bit different depending on the three conditions. More specifically, the two avatar conditions (CA and SA) contained instructions for avatar creation, while the no-avatar condition (NA) did not. Moreover, since CA and SA were different in terms of avatar creation, the CA condition contained how to customize the avatar, while the SA condition contained how to select (not customize) the avatar. The length of the video clips was the same for each condition. Since some participants were not familiar with avatars and Cyworld.com, this introduction was necessary.

Then, participants in the avatar conditions (CA and SA) were instructed to create (or choose) avatars that would represent them on the website. For the customization condition (CA), participants were allowed to customize their avatars by selecting skin color, hairstyle, and clothes. In the noncustomization condition (SA), participants were provided several avatars from which they were allowed to select the one that best resembled them (see Figure 9.3). The created avatars were saved. Participants under the no-avatar conditions (NA) were not provided avatars.

In the next section, every participant was asked to browse the manipulated Cyworld.com page for one minute and then evaluate the site. All external links had been disabled for the study, but the two ads (the shampoo commercial and skin cancer PSA) were designed to be interactive so that participants could click on them and receive contingent responses from them. When browsing the website, participants in the avatar conditions (CA and SA) were able to observe the avatar that they created in the previous section. Avatars appeared on the left side of the front page. After one minute, a pop-up window on the screen led participants to the study questionnaire.

To ascertain the degree to which participants paid attention to the ads, participants were asked to write everything that they could recall about the ads and were asked to complete multiple-choice questions about the ads in order to measure recognition. Lastly, participants were asked to fill out online questionnaires that included evaluation criteria for the website, its ad, and its PSA, as well as demographic information.

Index Construction and Preparation for Data Analysis

An exploratory factor analysis was conducted upon the thirteen items relating to attitude toward the website, yielding three factors accounting for 87 percent of the variance. Upon varimax rotation, six items (entertaining, appealing, interesting, stimulating, likeable, attractive) loaded under the first factor labeled "attitude toward the website" (A_w). This item exhibited a high degree of internal consistency (Cronbach's $\alpha = .97$). Three items (trustworthy, honest, believable) loaded under the second factor labeled "cognitive perception of the website" (C_w) (Cronbach's $\alpha = .92$), and the other three items (bookmark, revisit, recommend) loaded under the third factor labeled "revisit intention of the website" (R_w) (Cronbach's α = .95). The last item (intelligent) cross-loaded across factors and was dropped from all further analysis.

For attitudes toward the ad, twelve items yielded two factors, accounting for 77 percent of the variance. After rotating, eight items (stimulating, appealing, interesting, attractive, relevant, believable, persuasive, bad/good) loaded under the first factor labeled "attitude toward the ad" (A_a) (Cronbach's α = .95). The other two items (degree of anxiousness and uncomfortable) were labeled "ad-provoked worry about hair" (W_a) (Pearson's r = .71, $p < .05$). Two items (informative and important) were dropped due to cross-loading.

The fifteen items relating to attitudes toward the PSA yielded three factors, accounting for 81 percent of the variance. After rotating, ten items loaded under the first factor labeled "attitudes toward the PSA" (A_p) (Cronbach's α = .96). Three items loaded under the second factor labeled "perceived risk of skin cancer" (S_p) (Cronbach's α = .93), and the last two items (degree of being anxious and uncomfortable) were labeled "PSA-provoked worry about skin cancer" (W_p) (Pearson's r = .80, $p < .05$).

The scales for perceived novelty, perceived involvement, perceived interactivity, and sense of agency indexes exhibited high levels of internal consistency (Cronbach's α = .91, .85, .84, and .90, respectively).

RESULTS

One-way, between-participants analyses of variance (ANOVAs) were employed to test the effect of avatar presence and customization upon users' concerns about body-related health (H_1) and their attitudes toward the website, its ad, and its PSA (H_2 and H_3). For the mediating effect (RQ_1), a multiple regression was performed, followed by analyses of covariance (ANCOVAs).

For H_1, three separate ANOVAs were performed on W_a (ad-provoked worry about hair), W_p (PSA-provoked worry about skin cancer), and S_p (perceived risk on skin cancer), which are all health-related outcome measures. The results showed that only perceived risk of skin cancer was significantly affected by avatar presence. We combined the S_p scores for both avatar conditions and compared it to the S_p mean of those in the control condition. The difference was significant in the expected direction, t (71) = 2.15, $p < .05$. Therefore, H_1 was partly supported (see Table 9.1 for group means and F-values).

To test H_2 about the effect of avatar presence on attitudes toward a website, its ad, and its PSA, ANOVAs were employed, but none of the dependent variables (DVs) was significant. Therefore, H_2 was not supported.

For H_3, three more ANOVAs for the effect of customizing avatars also revealed that only the attitude toward the PSA was significant, $F(2, 69) = 3.49$, $p < .05$. However, the results' direction was opposite to what this study hypothesized: the avatar customization group showed the lowest favorability toward the PSA

Table 9.1

The Means (with Standard Deviations in Parentheses) and *F*-values for Perceived Risk of Skin Cancer as a Function of Avatar Presence

	Avatar presence		
Dependent variable	Avatar	No avatar	F
Perceived risk of skin cancer	6.36[a] (2.27)	5.05[b] (2.88)	4.62**

Note: Higher scores indicate more positive attitudes. Comparisons between means are specified by lowercase superscripts, and cell means that do not share a letter in their superscripts differ at $p < .05$ (**).

Table 9.2

The Means (with Standard Deviations in Parentheses) and *F*-values for Attitude toward PSAs as a Function of Avatar Presence and Avatar Customization

	Avatar customization			
Dependent variable	Customizing avatar	Noncustomizing avatar (selecting avatar)	No avatar	F
Attitude toward PSA	4.34[b] (2.32)	5.62[ab] (2.13)	5.83[b] (1.73)	3.49**

Note: Higher scores indicate more positive attitudes. Comparisons between means are specified by lowercase superscripts, and cell means that do not share a letter in their superscripts differ at $p < .05$ (**) according to Tukey-Kramer HSD test.

compared to avatar noncustomization group and no-avatar group. Therefore, H₃ was not supported. Post hoc analysis using Tukey-Kramer HSD was conducted to compare the group means of the attitude toward the PSA, which showed significant difference among avatar groups (see Table 9.2 for group means and *F*-values). Attitudes toward PSA were most positive in the non-avatar condition, intermediate in the noncustomized avatar condition, and lowest in the customized avatar condition.

For answering RQ₁, if we were to follow Baron and Kenny's (1986) causal-steps approach for estimating mediated effects, the absence of a direct effect of customization upon the DVs would preclude further analysis. As an alternative, this study attempted to find indirect effects, which are used when there is not an initial significant total effect of X on Y because X could influence Y through M (Holbert and Stephenson 2003; MacKinnon et al. 2002; Preacher and Hayes 2004). However, unfortunately, none of the possible mediators—perceived involvement, perceived interactivity, perceived novelty, and perceived sense of agency—showed significance.

DISCUSSION

This study explored the effects of the presence of avatars on users' cognitive and psychological responses from the various perspectives. More specifically, the study attempted to answer to the following questions: First, what do avatars mean to avatar users? Given that the avatar plays the role of representing the user's self, affording users a third-person view of themselves, are avatars able to increase self-awareness and self-preservation in terms of physical health? Do avatars influence avatar users' attitudes toward the website in which the avatars appear while browsing and toward online banner ads that are embedded in the site? Lastly, if avatars do influence users' attitudes, then what are the psychological mechanisms for doing so?

Based on Biocca's (1997) theoretical argument that avatars induce a feeling of presence by allowing users to observe their self-identified embodiments, this study expected that the presence of avatars would increase users' concerns about their physical body. This hypothesis was supported by data. The results showed that avatar users perceived higher risks of skin cancer than non-avatar users. This means that avatars successfully increase self-awareness and highlight users' concepts of self-preservation when they encounter a message regarding a threat to their survival. However, for the questions regarding how much the shampoo ad or the skin cancer PSA provoked concern, there were no differences between the avatar and non-avatar groups. This difference in response to a commercial ad compared to a PSA suggests that while avatars promote self-preservation, they do not necessarily stimulate a need for self-enhancement.

Based on the idea of "implicit egotism," which states that human beings inherently "gravitate toward things that resemble the self" (Pelham et al. 2003, p. 800), this study also predicted that avatar users might have positive attitudes toward their "self-resembled creatures" (i.e., avatars), and in turn, the positive effect would be transferred to the evaluation of the website and its ads, but this was not supported. These findings tell us that although avatars may trigger implicit egotism, their presence does not translate into positive cognitive evaluation of the avatar-hosting site.

Kalyanaraman and Sundar (2006) found significant effects of customization on attitudes toward websites. Customization enables users to feel that they are "in control" and provides them a greater sense of agency, leading to a higher level of involvement and more favorable attitudes toward a website or its content (Sundar 2008). Based on this argument, this study predicted that the individuals who customized their avatars would show the most favorable attitudes compared to the noncustomizing group and non-avatar group. Contrary to prediction, this study found that the customizing avatar group showed the lowest favorability toward the website. And, interestingly, the noncustomizing avatar group showed the highest favorability. We believe that the reason behind these results is due to the frustration of avatar customizers, who may have performed a mental calculation of the costs and benefits of going to all the trouble of customizing their avatars. As we describe in the limitation section, avatar customizers might have expected that their avatars would play a "role" in the site; however, when they found that their avatars simply appeared in the corner while they browsed the site, they may have been disappointed, which could have adversely affected their evaluations of the website.

Another interesting finding of this study regards avatar creators' attitudes toward the PSA. Avatar creators showed the lowest favorability toward the PSA, but the non-avatar users showed the highest favorability. Considering this finding in light of the argument that avatars induce greater self-awareness and self-preservation in terms of physical health (supported by our study data), it is likely that avatar users employed a different evaluation frame than non-avatar users in this study, due perhaps to different levels of scrutiny given to the PSA. It appears that receiving the PSA via an avatar predisposes users to pay more attention to the content and production quality of the PSA.

LIMITATIONS

Being a pilot, this study has several limitations in its design. First of all, in the experiment, to grasp the attention of participants, this study designed highly interactive ads, resulting in a highly interactive experience for participants in all three conditions, thus undermining any unique effect that avatar customization might have had on real or perceived interactivity of the ad. Second, for an ecologically valid study and, at the same time, to reduce the confounding effect of familiarity, we used an existing Korean social networking website (SNW) that provides avatar service. However, it generated an ecological validity issue since most participants in our study were only familiar with avatars in virtual reality, games, and chat rooms, but not in SNWs. In addition, the disabling of the links may have made participants feel uncomfortable, leading to the lower favorability of attitudes regarding the website compared to attitudes toward the ad or the PSA.

The most significant pitfall of the current study was the limited role of the avatar in the SNW. In a chatting environment or a normal SNW, avatars appear next to users' writings. However, for the purpose of this study, we just briefly touched on the function of avatars in the introductory video clip. While browsing the website, participants merely saw their self-created avatar on the left side of the web page, which may have frustrated the avatar creators because their elaborate effort in carefully creating their online persona was not rewarded or utilized commensurately.

Despite the insignificant results, this study makes an important, even if empirically modest, connection between avatars in virtual spaces and welfare of oneself, especially under conditions of benevolent persuasion. In addition to the technological benefits of avatars, this study addresses the psychological function of an avatar as a virtual self, particularly on the social networking sites where people establish and maintain social contacts. The advance of new technology was initially blamed for deindividuating and unitizing people under the label of "mass." Given that, the avatar enables people to focus more on the self. If we say that the function of customization enables people to *feel* their existence through changing content or structures, the avatar enables people to *see* their existence through a self-resembling object. This has strong implications in health intervention. Most health messages are inherently self-focused and emphasize self-preservation. Given that the virtual population, including Internet users, has grown epidemically, this study will contribute to the development of more effective intervention programs as well as more effective advertising on websites and other virtual venues.

REFERENCES

Alpert, S.R., J. Karat, C.M. Karat, C. Brodie, and J.G. Vergo. 2003. "User Attitudes Regarding a User Adaptive eCommerce Web Site." *User Modeling and User-Adaptive Interaction* 13: 373–396.

Baron, R.M., and D.A. Kenny. 1986. "The Moderator-Mediator Variable Distinction in Social Psychological Research: Conceptual, Strategic, and Statistical Considerations." *Journal of Personality and Social Psychology* 51: 1173–1182.

Biocca, F. 1997. "The Cyborg's Dilemma: Progressive Embodiment in Virtual Environments." *Journal of Computer-Mediated Communication* 3 (2): 12–26.

Choi, Y.K., G.E. Miracle, and F. Biocca. 2001. "The Effects of Anthropomorphic Agents on Advertising Effectiveness and the Mediating Role of Presence." *Journal of Interactive Advertising* 2 (1): 3–21.

Eagly, A.H. 1987. *Sex Differences in Social Behavior: A Social-Role Interpretation.* Hillsdale, NJ: Lawrence Erlbaum Associates.

Holbert, R.L., and M.T. Stephenson. 2003. "The Importance of Indirect Effects in Media Effects Research: Testing for Mediation in Structural Equation Modeling." *Journal of Broadcasting and Electronic Media* 47: 556–572.

Kalyanaraman, S., and S.S. Sundar. 2006. "The Psychological Appeal of Personalized Content in Web Portals: Does Customization Affect Attitudes and Behavior?" *Journal of Communication* 56: 110–132.

MacKinnon, D.P., C.M., Lockwood, J.M., Hoffman, S.G., West, and V. Sheets. 2002. "A Comparison of Methods to Test Mediation and Other Intervening Variable Effects." *Psychological methods,* 7 (1): 83–104.

Nan, X., G. Anghelcev, J. Myers, S. Sar, and R.J. Faber. 2005. "The Influence of Anthropomorphic Agents on Attitudes toward the Website: A Test of Two Mediating Routes." Paper presented at the annual meeting of the International Communication Association, New York, NY.

Nowak, K. 2000. "The Influence of Anthropomorphism on Mental Models of Agents and Avatars in Social Virtual Environments." Department of Telecommunications, Michigan State University.

Pelham, B.W., M. Carvallo, T. DeHart, and J.T. Jones. 2003. "Assessing the Validity of Implicit Egotism: A Reply to Gallucci." *Journal of Personality and Social Psychology* 85 (5): 789–799.

Petty, R.E., J. Barden, and S.C. Wheeler. 2002. "The Elaboration Likelihood Model of Persuasion: Health Promotions That Yield Sustained Behavioral Change." In *Emerging Theories in Health Promotion Practice and Research,* ed. R.J. DiClemente, R.A. Crosby, & M. Kegler, 71–99. San Francisco: Jossey-Bass.

Preacher, K.J., and A.F. Hayes. 2004. "SPSS and SAS Procedures for Estimating Indirect Effects in Simple Mediation Models." *Behavior Research Methods, Instruments, and Computers* 36: 717–731.

Skalski, P., and R. Tamborini. 2007. "The Role of Social Presence in Interactive Agent-based Persuasion." *Media Psychology* 10: 385–413.

Suler, J. 1999. *The Psychology of Cyberspace.* Online book, Rider University. Available at http://www-usr.rider.edu/~suler/psycyber/psycyber.html.

Sundar, S.S. 2008. "Self as Source: Agency and Customization in Interactive Media." In *Mediated Interpersonal Communication,* ed. S.U.E. Konijn, M. Tanis, and S. Barnes. Mahwah, NJ: Lawrence Erlbaum Associates.

Sundar, S.S., and S. Kalyanaraman. 2004. "Arousal, Memory, and Impression-Formation Effects of Animation Speed in Web Advertising." *Journal of Advertising* 33: 7–17.

Sundar, S.S., and J. Kim. 2005. "Interactivity and Persuasion: Influencing Attitudes with Information and Involvement." *Journal of Interactive Advertising* 5 (2): 6–29.

Sundar, S.S., and S. Marathe. 2006. "Is It Tailoring or Is It Agency? Unpacking the Psychological Appeal of Customized News." Paper presented at the Communication Theory and Methodology Division of the Association for Education in Journalism and Mass Communication (AEJMC) 89th Annual Convention, San Francisco.

Witte, K. 1998. *Theory-based Interventions and Evaluation of Outreach Efforts.* Seattle, WA: National Network of Libraries of Medicine.

Zillmann, D. 1991. "Empathy: Affect from Bearing Witness to Emotions of Others." In *Responding to the Screen: Reception and Reaction Processes,* ed. J. Bryant and D. Zillmann, 135–167. Hillsdale, NJ: Lawrence Erlbaum Associates.

Zimmerman, M.A. 1990. "Taking Aim at Empowerment Research: On the Distinction Between Individual and Psychological Conceptions." *American Journal of Community Psychology* 18: 169–177.

PART IV

PERSON PERCEPTIONS IN VIRTUAL WORLDS

CHAPTER 10

Effects of Ethnic Identity and Ethnic Ambiguous Agents on Consumer Response to Websites

OSEI APPIAH AND TROY ELIAS

The concomitant effects of the emergence of new media tools and communication technology include an almost infinite supply of information sources for consumers at almost zero cost (Tharp 2001). Computer-mediated technologies afford consumers greatly enhanced informational and interactive access (Papacharissi and Rubin 2000). In light of this, and given the amount of advertising and mediated messages that consumers are subjected to on a daily basis, it has become exceedingly challenging for any one advertiser's message to resonate (Rosen 2000). Naturally, a severe implication of all the clutter and noise in both the online market and the traditional brick and mortar marketplace is that customers are hardly able to differentiate one company's offerings from another's. As a result, corporations are continuously looking for new and innovative ways to capture their audiences' attention and to do so in ways that still manage to invoke feelings of credibility, trust, and overall goodwill. Holzwarth, Janiszewski, and Neumann (2006) contend that an additional hurdle to online sales is the impersonal nature of web-based shopping. They maintain that one way to increase the entertainment value and customer satisfaction of consumers' online shopping experiences is to use computer-generated characters, or "avatars."

AVATARS AND ANTHROPOMORPHIC AGENTS

Derived from the ancient Indian Sanskrit language, *avatar* initially meant the embodiment of a deity on earth (Holzwarth, Janiszewski, and Neumann 2006); historically, the word avatar described the incarnation of the Hindu god Vishnu (Hemp 2006). Today, however, the word has a different connotation, and is more likely to conjure up images of computer-generated anthropomorphic characters. Computer-generated anthropomorphic characters are computer agents or avatars that possess human traits or qualities; most specifically, computer-generated faces (Gong and Nass 2007). In addition to faces, these characters are also frequently imbued with the ability to speak through either computer-generated speech or prerecorded natural speech (Gong and Nass 2007). Computer-generated anthropomorphic characters are usually classified either as agents, which are computer-controlled characters, or avatars, which are user-controlled (see Nowak 2004; Eastin, Appiah, and Cicchirillo forthcoming; Gong and Nass, 2007). The value of research on avatars and anthropomorphic agents cannot be understated as computer-generated characters are being used as digital communicators on websites as well as in computer games and applications with increasing frequency (Gong and Nass 2007).

The use of computer-generated anthropomorphic characters by advertisers and marketers is becoming more and more commonplace. For instance, IKEA offers an "Ask Anna" interactive agent feature on its website. "Anna," an agent, engages website visitors in conversation and helps them locate products while addressing any customer service issues that they might have. Companies such as Accuweather, L'Oréal, Global Gillette, and DaimlerChrysler AG are using agents to handle consumer questions online (Ahrens 2006), while other companies are using agents to provide entertainment gratification for their online visitors. ESPN, for instance, provides an avatar-based program entitled "Voice of the Fan" on their website that allows their fans to record their own analyses, synopses, and opinions of various aspects of different sports or sports figures. The fans then choose an avatar, complete with a personalized recorded voice, to represent themselves online (Ahrens 2006). Other companies use computer-generated anthropomorphic characters as part of their marketing strategy; marketers have even begun using avatars and anthropomorphic agents for content they distribute virally. An example is Oddcast, which created a pass-along avatar for the online job website CareerBuilder.com. Users choose a monkey avatar made popular by the CareerBuilder television commercials, they then dress him and then have him recite a brief message that the user creates by typing text or dialing a phone number and recording it (Ahrens 2006).

So how effective have these campaigns been? According to Ahrens (2006), the monkeys have had over 44 million hits, from one computer to another, since they came online. Ahrens maintains that research by New York–based Oddcast Inc. indicates that the consumer-created avatars sent to friends get opened about 70 percent of the time as opposed to a more traditional e-mailed marketing pitch from a company that shows up in consumers' inboxes, which has about a 15 percent chance of being opened.

Furthering the work of Cassell et al. (2000), Gong and Nass (2007) argue that the ability of many computer-generated anthropomorphic characters to talk is a result of computer-generated speech or prerecorded natural speech using lip synchronization and facial animation technology. This study looks at the effect of pairing intelligent animated agents with human voices that are either congruent or incongruent with the ethnicity of the agent. To date, very few studies have examined the impact of computer-generated anthropomorphic agents in a consumer-related setting while looking at the effect of consumers' strength of ethnic identity, the ethnicity of the agents, and the congruency of features of the agents, such as their voices, on consumer attitudes.

ETHNICALLY AMBIGUOUS CHARACTERS

The latest cultural trend among U.S. marketers is to use ethnically ambiguous models in advertising to appeal to ethnic specific consumer segments (Arlidge 2004). Given that nearly seven million Americans identified themselves as members of more than one race in the 2000 census, there appears to be an emerging trend in advertising and marketing to use ethnically neutral, diverse, or ambiguous characters to reach consumers (La Ferla 2003). A number of marketing experts perceive that character ambiguity in an advertisement is effective because there is a current fascination, particularly among young consumers, with racial-hybrid-looking models (Arlidge 2004). This attraction by young consumers may be due in part to census data that indicate audiences 25 and under are twice as likely as older adults to identify themselves as multiracial (La Ferla 2003). For young blacks ages 18–29, 44 percent of them no longer believe it is appropriate to consider black people as one race (Williams 2007).

This apparent trend has led some marketers to assume that it may be time to dismiss the use of a specific race as a consumer segmentation indicator (Arlidge, 2004). Some critics argue that the infrequent use of ethnic-specific models in lieu of ethnically ambiguous models is not a recent phenomenon. Sengupta (2002) contends that mixed-raced models have long been cast in advertisements that would generally call for the presence of black models, and have frequently been used by advertisers as the prototype of ethnic beauty.

This seeming increase in the use of ethnically ambiguous models in consumer advertising suggests an implicit assumption within the advertising industry that ethnically ambiguous models are more effective than black models in persuading black consumers (Sengupta 2002). Out of this concern, and the prevailing evidence that avatars and anthropomorphic characters by marketers are becoming more commonplace on commercial websites, it seems reasonable to examine the effect that black, white, and ethnically ambiguous computer-generated agents on a commercial website may have on black consumers' evaluations of brand sites.

DISTINCTIVENESS PRINCIPLE AS A THEORETICAL FRAMEWORK

The available research on audiences' responses to ethnically ambiguous characters seems inconclusive. Some research suggests that people perceive racially ambiguous characters as neither a member of one's in-group nor of one's out-group, while other research suggests there is more of a tendency for audiences to categorize ethnically ambiguous characters as members of an out-group (Willadsen-Jensen and Ito 2006).

The distinctiveness principle should provide a better understanding of how audiences process information from both ethnically ambiguous and unambiguous sources. The distinctiveness principle (Breakwell 1986; Brewer 1991) postulates that individuals have a natural motivation to establish a sense of differentiation from others (Brewer 1991) and to see themselves as unique (Snyder and Fromkin 1980). The process of establishing a positive group distinction from other groups leads to enhanced self-esteem and identity (Breakwell 1986). Some scholars also argue that distinctiveness is important because it maintains or enhances one's self-esteem through social comparison (Festinger 1954).

Individuals from certain cultures are particularly motivated to distinguish themselves from others and are likely to do so when their distinctiveness or identity is threatened, challenged, or salient (Vignoles, Chryssochoou, and Breakwell 2000), which is particularly true for blacks. Given their history of discrimination and their negative depictions in the media, blacks may sense competition from whites that may threaten their identity and lead to in-group favoritism (Mastro 2003). Current representation of blacks in the media may lead blacks to seek positive media messages and characters that can support or enhance their need for a positive social identity and positive distinctiveness. Therefore, it is reasonable to suspect that seeing a positive black spokesperson (human or computer-generated) in an advertisement for a leading brand may enhance their identity. This may lead blacks to identify with and develop more positive attitudes toward the black spokesperson (in-group member) featured in the advertisement than they would a white spokesperson (out-group member) featured in the advertisement.

Salience and Accessibility

It should be noted that the availability, accessibility, and value of a specific identity (e.g., ethnic identity) or distinctive trait (e.g., being black) varies based on an individual's culture and the specific context. According to the distinctiveness principle, the salience of a distinctive trait determines its accessibility and meaningfulness for group members (Vignoles, Chryssochoou, and Breakwell 2000). Oakes, Haslam, and Turner (1994) imply that the distinctiveness principle posits that people categorize themselves in terms of a salient group membership, which will in turn lead to the level of meaningfulness they attach to a particular social identity. For numeric minority members, the characteristic that makes them distinctive (e.g., being black) from numeric majority members (e.g., whites) is highly salient among their numeric minority group (McGuire 1984; McGuire et al. 1978). Therefore, race will be more salient for people whose racial group is part of a numeric minority than it will be for members of a racial majority in a particular social environment. A distinctive characteristic that sets a numeric minority apart from the majority is highly salient for members of that numeric minority group (McGuire 1984). Blacks, being a racial minority, are found to have more salient awareness of their race compared to whites (McGuire et al. 1978), and as a result, a greater sense of belonging to their numerically distinctive group.

This sense of belonging and identification is generally strengthened by a group's unique size in a particular community (Appiah 2007; Brewer 1991; Vignoles, Chryssochoou, and Breakwell 2000). The smaller the group's size the more likely they are to distinguish themselves from other groups (Brewer 1991). Research has shown that numeric minorities express more in-group bias than those members who are apart of a numeric majority (see Appiah 2002, 2003). This leads to the first hypothesis:

H_1: Black participants will respond more positively toward the black agent than they will toward either the white or the ethnically ambiguous agent.

Influence of Ethnic Identity on Consumers

Research based on the distinctiveness theoretical framework implies that when blacks encounter a black computer-generated agent on a commercial website they should respond more positively than they would to a computer-generated out-group member such as a white agent or an ethnically ambiguous agent. However, these expectations should be qualified based on the ethnic identity of the black audience.

Ethnic identity is a subjective orientation that captures one's attitudes toward his/her ethnic membership. Phinney (2005) defined ethnic identity as "a self-constructed understanding of oneself in terms of one's cultural and ethnic background and the attitudes and feelings associated with that background" (p. 189). A positive ethnic identity entails affirmation of one's ethnic membership and an occurrence of positive attitudes such as pride and happiness.

Among blacks who maintain strong racial identities, their awareness of and preference for black media characters vis-à-vis white media characters should be heightened. Blacks with strong ethnic identities—because of their greater connection to their ethnicity and expression of traditional black values—should exhibit a greater sense of awareness of and appreciation for black characters, leading them to respond more favorably to in-group characters (e.g., blacks) than they would to out-group characters (e.g., whites, multiracial members).

In contrast, weak black ethnic identifiers may possess attitudes and behaviors that are not strongly tied to black culture and may even see the world in ways that reflect dominant mainstream culture (see Appiah 2004). This may lead them to demonstrate a weaker understanding of and appreciation for black media characters than their strong ethnic identifier counterparts. Weak black identifiers may be less aware of their ethnicity and minority status and may, therefore, feel less distinctive. Among weak identifiers, "blackness" may not be a particularly salient or meaningful characteristic (Appiah 2004), which should lead them to respond no differently to in-group or out-group members. This is supported by empirical work that demonstrates blacks with strong ethnic identification perceive themselves more similar to and identify more strongly with black media and characters (Appiah 2001), and express greater liking for black media and characters (Appiah 2004) than do those blacks with weak ethnic identities. Research also shows that blacks with weak ethnic identities typically respond either indifferently to or more favorably toward white media and models vis-à-vis black media and models (Appiah 2004).

Hence, ethnic identity appears to be a key factor that elicits in-group preference among ethnic minorities, particularly blacks. In this study, in-group favoritism is most likely to occur among strong black ethnic identifiers. This discussion leads to the following hypotheses:

H_{2A}: Blacks with strong ethnic identities will respond more positively to a black computer-generated agent on a commercial website than they will to a computer-generated agent from a different ethnic background.

H_{2B}: In contrast, blacks with weak ethnic identities will show no difference in their responses to a computer-generated agent on a commercial website based on whether the agent is black, white, or ethnically ambiguous. This same pattern of results is expected for each of the five dependent variables.

STUDY 1 METHOD

Participants and Design

One hundred twenty-one black undergraduate students from a large midwestern university participated in the study. Participants were recruited from courses in the School of Communication, Black Cultural Center, and the Office of Minority Affairs. Participants in the study received $10. The study utilized an experimental method to examine the effects of using black, white, and ethnically ambiguous agents on participants' evaluations of a commercial website. The experiment used a 3 (computer-generated agent: black, white, or ethnically ambiguous) × 2 (ethnic identity: strong or weak) between-subjects design. The study examined the extent to which the race of an agent affected users' evaluations of the brand displayed on the website. The five dependent variables include: (1) perceived similarity to agent; (2) identification with the agent; (3) attitude toward the agent; (4) attitude toward the brand; and (5) recall of product information.

Stimuli

A version of the Acura car web page was re-created by a professional web designer. An automobile site was used because cars tend to represent a product class of general interest and usage among a broad cross-section of the student collegiate population. Three versions of one of its commercial pages were created, each with identical images and accompanying text related to Acura cars. For each condition a talking, female, computer-animated product spokesperson was used. The computer spokespersons used were SitePal generated characters. SitePal is a relatively new Internet-based subscription service that allows users to create animated speaking characters that can be incorporated onto a website. One basic female character design was used for all three conditions in the study; however, the character's race was modified across the three experimental conditions. That is, the only difference among the three web pages was the ethnicity of the agent (i.e., black, white, or ethnically ambiguous).

The first condition was the talking, black animated female agent condition. For this condition a 210×315 pixel animated black female agent with black eyes was placed on the left-hand side of the screen. This computer-generated anthropomorphic agent used a prerecorded, ethnically ambiguous natural voice, which was synchronized to the lip and facial movements of the character. The second condition was exactly the same as the first condition except that the agent used was a white female with blue eyes. The same ethnically ambiguous, prerecorded natural voice from condition one was used for condition two. The third condition followed the same format, except that the computer-generated character used in this condition was an ethnically ambiguous female with black eyes. The voice used for this character was the same used in the previous experimental conditions. Both the ethnically ambiguous voice and the ethnically ambiguous character were selected based on a majority of pretest participants identifying the voice and the character as either "biracial/multiracial" or "can't tell/don't know" (see manipulation check).

The computer-generated female agents were used as spokespeople on the Acura website. Each agent greeted the user and provided instructions concerning how to browse the Acura web page. For example, the character greeted the participants with the following: "Hello. Welcome to Acura Right Ride! My name is Angie, and I'll be your personal guide today. Based on your responses to just a few questions, we'll help you find a car that best suits your lifestyle." In order to create interaction between the participant and the spokesperson, the agent engaged the user in a number of questions—which were not recorded—to which the user responded. Each response by the user activated the agent, leading the agent to provide another statement or ask another question. Each agent asked the user eight questions. Viewers responded to each question by clicking one of five options available for each question. The spokesperson was positioned on the left side of the page, and on the right side of the page were the same questions asked by the female agents (in word format) along with five mutually exclusive answer options. It should be noted that the questions asked by the agents were merely used to get the participants to interact with the agents in a commercial environment. No data were saved from these questions. Once participants selected an answer, the agent would respond in a reassuring way. For example, one question that the agent asked was, "You like clothes that are . . . ?" The response options were: trendy, vintage, sporty, classic, or wacky. When participants selected their answer the agent's verbal reply was always, "I don't know about you but I like to mix it up a little." Another question asked by the agent was, "What is your favorite form of entertainment?" The response options were: movies, comedy, theatre, sports, or music. After selecting a response option, the agent would always reply with, "Those all sound like fun." After each question the user would then click on the "next" button to take them to the next question.

After responding to the eight questions, the agent generated a picture of three cars (Acura RSX, Acura TSX, and Acura MDX) that were supposed to represent cars that fit the lifestyle and personality of the participants based on their responses to the eight questions. The same three cars always appeared at the end of the session for each condition. The agent concluded the session by stating: "Based on your answers to our 8 questions, we feel that any of these 3 cars would be an ideal match for your personality and lifestyle. Thanks for stopping by, and good luck! We know you'll make the right choice!"

Procedure

Participants were randomly assigned to browse through only one of the three experimental conditions. Prior to navigating the web page, participants were told that the purpose of the Internet study was for researchers to test some changes to Acura's website. They were told that their feedback would enable researchers to improve the look, style, and content of the site. All participants navigated through the eight questions on the website, after which they then answered a questionnaire. Once they completed the questionnaire, participants were debriefed and asked not to tell anyone about what they had seen in the study.

Measurement Instrument

The measurement instrument collected information for the five dependent variables: (1) perceived similarity to the agent; (2) identification with the agent; (3) attitude toward the agent; (4) attitude toward the brand; and (5) recall of product information.

Perceived Similarity

Participants rated their degree of similarity to the agent in terms of overall lifestyle, cultural background, dress, appearance, and basic values (Whittler 1989). A similarity scale was created by averaging the mean scores from each of the five scales. For this scale a coefficient alpha was computed ($\alpha = .86$).

Identification with the Agent

Participants were asked to indicate how strongly they identified with the agent (Aaker, Brumbaugh, and Grier 2000) on the Acura website on a seven-point Likert scale ranging from "not at all" (one) to "very strongly" (seven).

Attitude Toward the Agent

Participants were asked to provide their attitude toward the agent. An index was created by averaging the mean scores of eleven 7-point semantic differential scales: boring/interesting, bad/good, negative/positive, useless/useful, worthless/valuable, poor/outstanding, not for me/for me, weak/strong, not appealing/appealing, not attractive/attractive, and not likable/likable. Although these scales have been used successfully in other studies and have shown strong evidence of reliability (e.g., Appiah 2001), a reliability analysis was conducted for all scales to assess the degree to which the items measured a single variable or dimension. For the attitude toward the agent scale, the coefficient alpha was computed ($\alpha = .93$).

Attitude Toward the Brand

Participants were asked to provide their attitude toward Acura the brand. An index was again created by averaging the mean scores of eleven 7-point semantic differential scales: boring/interesting, bad/good, negative/positive, useless/useful, worthless/valuable, poor/outstanding, not for me/for me, weak/strong, not appealing/appealing, not attractive/attractive, and not likable/likable. For the attitude toward the brand scale, the coefficient alpha was computed ($\alpha = .96$).

Recall

The questionnaire assessed aided recall of specific visual and verbal aspects from the Acura website and the spokesperson. The recall procedure used in this study was modeled after that used by Appiah (2002) and Gunter, Furnham, and Frost (1994). This procedure cued participants with verbal and nonverbal aspects of the stimuli to probe recall of media content. There were eight questions in total that assessed aided recall. These questions included: "Name the models of the 3 Acura cars shown at the end of your session on the website." "Where on the site was the following logo located?" "What was the name of the animated female character?" "What color were the 3 Acura cars shown at the end of your session on the website?" "The slogan located above the animated character read: The Unsurpassed Standard of _____." Participants were given one point for a correct reply, and zero points for an incorrect answer. Thus, a total score of eight points could be achieved.

Race of Participants

Participants were given a list of racial and ethnic groups from which to choose. Only subjects who indicated their identification with black/African American were included in the analysis.

Ethnic Identity

Ethnic identity was measured with the widely used Multigroup Ethnic Identity Measure by Phinney (1992). The Affirmation and Belonging subscale, which assesses the affective and identification core of ethnic identity, was used to capture participants' ethnic identity, consistent with Appiah (2004). This subscale included five statements measured on 7-point Likert scales. Two sample items are "I have a lot of pride in my ethnic group and its accomplishments" and "I have a strong sense of belonging to my own ethnic group." The scale had high reliability, $\alpha =$ .88. Reponses to the five items were averaged. Higher scores indicate strong black ethnic identity. In experimental studies using ethnic identity as a moderator, it is common to do a median split to create two groups representing relatively strong and relatively weak ethnic identity (e.g., Appiah 2004). A split was done by the median value of 6.2. Values lower than 6.2 constituted the relatively weak ethnic identity group (n = 55); values higher than 6.2 constituted the relatively strong ethnic identity group (n = 63).

STUDY 1 RESULTS

Manipulation Check

A pretest was conducted whereby twenty black undergraduates were exposed to fifteen female computer-generated characters with varying skin complexions. Among the fifteen characters were the three experimental characters, which were randomly mixed in with the group. Each participant was asked to indicate the race/ethnicity of the female character from a list of racial/ethnic groups (e.g., Asian/Asian American, black/African American, white/Caucasian, Hispanic, etc.). Among this list, participants also had the option of selecting "biracial/multiracial" or "can't tell/don't know." One hundred percent of the participants identified the black character as "black/African American," 100 percent identified the white character as "white/Caucasian," and 75 percent (15) of the participants identified the ethnically ambiguous character as either "biracial/multiracial" or "can't tell/don't know."

A pretest was also conducted on the prerecorded human voice to ascertain participants' perception of the ethnicity of the character speaking. Fifteen black undergraduates listened to the human voice and were asked to indicate the speaker's race/ethnicity—eight (53 percent) participants indicated they "can't tell/

Table 10.1

Means for Black Participants' Responses to Race-Specific Computer-Generated Female Agents

	Black Internet Browsers		
	Black Female Agent	White Female Agent	Ethnically Ambiguous Agent
Similarity to agent	4.40[a]	2.66[c]	3.58[b]
Identification with agent	4.25[a]	2.62[b]	3.96[a]
Attitude toward agent	4.91[a]	4.19[b]	4.67
Attitude toward brand	5.72	5.37	5.48
Recall of product information	5.78[a]	4.79[b]	5.59

Note: Means with different superscripts differ significantly from each other at $p < .05$.
$N = 121$.

don't know," four (27 percent) indicated "white/Caucasian," and 3 (20 percent) indicated "black/African American."

Hypotheses Testing

A series of two-way analyses of variance were conducted to test the hypotheses. Follow-up analyses were conducted to examine significant findings. The same analyses were conducted for all five dependent variables.

Perception of Similarity

It was hypothesized that blacks would perceive themselves more similar to the black agents than they would to either the white or ethnically ambiguous agents. Moreover, it was predicted that blacks with strong ethnic identities would perceive themselves more similar to the black computer agent than they would the white or the ethnically ambiguous agent, whereas blacks with weak ethnic identities would show no difference in perceptions of similarity based on the race of the agent.

No significant interaction was found based on ethnic identity and agent's race. However, a main effect for agent's race was found ($F[2, 114] = 15.08, p < .001$). Further examination of the means using pairwise comparisons (see Table 10.1) showed that blacks overall perceived themselves as more similar to the black agent (M = 4.40, SD = 1.05) than they did the white agent (M = 2.66, SD = 1.27, $p < .001$) and the ethnically ambiguous agent (M = 3.58, SD = 1.32, $p < .01$). Moreover, blacks perceived themselves more similar to the ethnically ambiguous agent (M = 3.58, SD = 1.32) than they did the white agent (M = 2.66, SD = 1.05, $p < .001$).

Identification

It was hypothesized that blacks would identify more with the black agent than with either the white or the ethnically ambiguous agents. Moreover, it was expected that blacks with strong ethnic identities would identify more with the black agent than they would either the white or the ethnically ambiguous agent. Although no significant interaction between ethnic identity and agent's race was found, a significant main effect was found for agent's race ($F[2, 114] = 10.00, p < .001$) was found. Further examination of the means using pairwise comparison indicated that blacks identified more strongly with the black agent (M = 4.25, SD = 1.70) than they did with the white agent (M = 2.62, SD = 1.48, $p < .001$). Moreover, blacks identified more with the ethnically ambiguous agent (M = 3.96, SD = 1.44) than they did with the white agent (M = 2.62, SD = 1.48, $p < .001$).

Attitude Toward the Agents

No significant interaction was found between ethnic identity and agent's race. However, a significant main effect was found for agent's race ($F([2, 107] = 4.45, p < .01$). Closer examination of the means using pairwise comparisons indicated blacks have more positive attitudes toward the black agent (M = 4.91, SD = 1.34) than they did toward the white agent (M = 4.19, SD = 1.04, $p < .01$). Moreover, blacks had more positive attitudes toward the ethnically ambiguous agent (M = 4.67, SD = 1.36) than they did toward the white agent (M = 4.19, SD = 1.04), but this was only marginally significant ($p = .09$).

Attitude Toward the Brand

No significant interaction or main effects were detected for ethnic identity and agent's race.

Recall

No significant interaction was found, but a significant main effect was found for agent's race ($F[2, 104] = 2.87, p < .05$). As shown in Table 10.1, the examination of the means indicated blacks recalled more information from the black agent (M = 5.78, SD = 1.83) than they did from the white agent (M = 4.79, SD = 1.83, $p < .05$). Moreover, blacks recalled more information from the ethnically ambiguous agent (M = 5.59, SD = 2.03) than they from the white spokesperson (M = 4.79, SD = 1.83), but this was only marginally significant ($p = .07$).

Study 1 Discussion

The findings from Study 1 partially support the hypotheses. The results demonstrate that blacks overall perceived themselves more similar to, identified more strongly with, had more positive attitudes toward, and recalled more information from the black agent than the white agent. Black participants also perceived themselves more similar to, identified more strongly with, had more positive attitudes toward, and recalled more information from the ethnically ambiguous agent than they did the white agent. Surprisingly, black participants demonstrated no significant response difference between the black and the ethnically ambiguous agents, with the exception of similarity. The findings from Study 1 do not support the hypotheses that blacks with strong ethnic identities will respond differently than blacks with weak ethnic identities. Ethnic identity may need to be primed among black participants by using black agents that are embedded with more race-specific cultural cues other than their skin color in order to truly elicit responses that will vary based on ethnic identity.

Study 2 replicates and extends Study 1 by incorporating an important race cue within each computer-generated agent—race-specific speech. Enhancing the agents with natural human voices that are specific to the race of the agent may provide the agents with a bit more racial authenticity, which is expected to make those blacks who strongly identify with their culture more mindful of their ethnicity and in turn respond differently to agents than blacks who are weak identifiers.

STUDY 2 INTRODUCTION

Voice Identification and Congruency

In 2004, Thomas and Reaser conducted a review of speech identification studies examining the abilities of listeners to distinguish black from white American voices and found that Americans can recognize black voices with a high degree of accuracy, even in the absence of stereotypical morphosyntactic and lexical features. Respondents, however, had more difficulty identifying blacks who exhibited less typical speech patterns. Thomas and Reaser argue that there are characteristics of voices that typify one or more ethnic groups, and for blacks there are certain prototypical "characteristics beyond salient morphosyntactic and lexical items that listeners strongly associate with African American speech" (2004, p. 55). Therefore, although not all black voices contain all the necessarily prototypical characteristics, both black and white American listeners are able to access and categorize these voices "according to their particular ethno-taxonomic inventory" (p. 55). The crux of the argument made by Thomas and Reaser is that if whites can identify black voices it creates opportunities for discrimination. An additional implication that they fail to mention, however, is that this ability to distinguish black voices from white by not only whites but also by ethnic minorities creates opportunities for ethnic minorities to make more in-group/out-group comparisons in mediated situations based on these culturally embedded cues.

The findings from Study 1 suggest that simply using a black computer-generated agent on a commercial site may not be sufficient to adequately prime black audiences' sense of ethnic identity. In order to most effectively appeal to black consumers, particularly those with strong ethnic identity, marketers may be required to incorporate more culturally relevant cues that are salient and valued among their target audience that go beyond just skin color.

In research conducted by Appiah (2001) and Forehand and Deshpande (2001) the respective authors proposed the idea of adding more rich cultural cues in marketing messages aimed at ethnic minorities. They argued that culturally embedded messages or ethnic primes in ads are visual or verbal cues that draw attention to ethnicity, which should increase ethnic minority consumers' awareness of their own ethnicity, and lead consumers to respond more favorably to same-ethnicity characters and advertising targeting their ethnicity. In their study, Forehand and Deshpande (2001) found that Asian participants exposed to same-ethnicity ethnic primes increased the rate at which they spontaneously mentioned their ethnicity, and the exposure to Asian ethnic primes led them to respond more favorably to same-ethnicity spokespeople and advertising targeting their ethnicity.

One cultural cue that is particularly important to black consumers is the speech patterns of a source. Speech characteristics allow audiences to make assumptions about a source's ethnicity, age, and social class, which in turn can influence other reactions to the source (Arphan 2002). The persuasiveness of a source has been shown to be enhanced based on the extent to which the source used or was perceived to use the language or speech pattern that is consistent with the audience (Holland and Gentry 1997). Studies indicate that ethnic minorities who indicate they strongly identify with their own ethnic group have been found to prefer communication delivered by a same-race source. Some researchers contend that ethnic minority audiences with strong ethnic identities vis-à-vis weak ethnic identities may be more likely to classify a speaker without a similar speech pattern to their own as a member of an out-group (Phinney 1992).

Thus, strong ethnic identifiers should be more likely than weak identifiers to react positively to a computer-generated agent with the same race and speech pattern of their own. Similarly, strong ethnic identifiers should respond less positively than weak identifiers to a different race computer-generated agent with a different speech pattern from their own. Modifying the voice of the agent such that each agent has a voice that is specific to their race should lead to the following:

H_1:   Blacks with strong ethnic identities will respond more positively to a black computer-generated agent with a race-specific voice on a commercial website than will blacks with weak ethnic identity.

H_2:   Blacks with weak ethnic identities will respond more favorably to a white computer-generated agent with a race-specific voice on a commercial website than will blacks with strong ethnic identity.

RQ_1: Will there be any differences in blacks' responses to an ethnically ambiguous computer-generated agent based on the strength of their ethnic identity?

STUDY 2 METHOD

Participants, Procedure, Design, and Stimuli

Using the same recruitment strategy and incentives as Study 1, Study 2 had 60 black participants (38 percent males and 62 percent females) with a mean age of 21. The experimental procedure and design was identical with that used in Study 1, with the exception that the racially ambiguous natural voice that was used for the characters in Study 1 was replaced with a voice that was specific to the race of each computer-generated character.

The same Acura website and the same three computer-generated female characters were used for Study 2. The only difference in this study is that for the black female spokesperson, the voice of a young black female was used; for the white female spokesperson the voice of a young white female was used; and for the ethnically ambiguous character, the voice of a young multiracial female was used. A pretest was conducted on 8 different voices (3 black voices, 2 white voices, and 3 mixed-raced voices) that were from people representing black, white, and mixed-race ethnic groups. Sixteen black undergraduates individually listened to each of the human voices. After each voice they were asked to indicate the speaker's race/ethnicity. The voice that was identified as most closely representing each race was chosen for the study. The black voice that was selected was identified by all 16 participants as a black voice. The white voice that was selected was identified by all 16 participants as a white voice. The ethnically ambiguous voice that was selected was identified as either "biracial/multiracial" or "can't tell/don't know" by 10 (63 percent) of the participants, while 4 (25 percent) participants identified the person as white and 2 (13 percent) participants identified the person as black.

Measurement Instrument

The measurement instrument was the same used in Study 1. The perceived similarity scale coefficient alpha was .88, the attitude toward the agent scale coefficient alpha was .91, and the attitude toward the brand alpha was .94. There were also items that measured recall and participant's race. Only subjects who indicated their identification with black/African American were included in the analysis. Ethnic identity was measured using the same Affirmation and Belonging subscale (Phinney 1992) used in Study 1. A median split was done by the median value of 6.2. Values lower than 6.2 constituted the relatively weak ethnic identity group ($n = 28$); values higher than 6.2 constituted the relatively strong ethnic identity group ($n = 30$). An ethnic identity scale was created by averaging the mean scores from each of the 5 items, which yielded a coefficient alpha = .90. The median black ethnic identity score was 34.

Results

The results of the experiment are presented and discussed according to the hypotheses presented earlier. A series of two-way analyses of variance (ANOVAs) for all hypotheses are provided below with follow-up analyses conducted to examine significant findings. The same analyses were conducted for all five dependent variables.

Similarity to Agent

It was predicted that blacks with strong ethnic identities would perceive themselves more similar to the black computer-generated female agent with a race-specific voice than would blacks with weak ethnic identities. It was also predicted that blacks with weak ethnic identities would perceive themselves more similar to the white agent than would blacks with strong ethnic identities. A significant main effect for agent race ($F[2, 53] = 26.08$, $p < .001$) demonstrated that black participants in general perceived themselves more similar to the black female agent ($M = 5.02$) than they did either the white female agent ($M = 2.39$; $p < .001$) or the ethnically ambiguous female agent ($M = 4.39$; $p < .05$). Also, the black participants perceived themselves more similar to the ethnically ambiguous female agent ($M = 4.39$; $p < .05$) than they did the white female agent ($M = 2.39$; $p < .01$). However, the main effect was qualified by a significant interaction between agent race and ethnic identity ($F[2, 53] = 4.08$; $p < .05$). Further examination of the means using one-way ANOVA (see Table 10.2) showed that blacks with strong ethnic identities perceived themselves more similar to the black female agent ($M = 5.60$, $SD = .76$) than did blacks with weak ethnic identities ($M = 4.44$, $SD = 1.58$, $p < .05$). This supports Hypothesis 1. The analysis also showed that blacks with weak ethnic identities perceived themselves more similar to the white female agent ($M = 2.83$, $SD = .76$) than did blacks with strong ethnic identities ($M = 1.95$, $SD = .82$; $p < .05$). This supports Hypothesis 2. No significant response difference based on ethnic identity was found for the ethnically ambiguous female agent.

Identification with Agent

It was predicted that blacks with strong ethnic identities would identify more with the black female agent than would blacks with weak ethnic identities. It was also predicted that blacks with weak identities would identify more with a white female agent than would blacks with strong identities. A significant main effect for agent race ($F[2, 53] = 11.25$, $p < .001$) demonstrated that black participants in general identified more with the black female agent ($M = 4.55$) than they did the white female agent ($M = 2.25$, $p < .01$). They also identified more with the ethnically ambiguous agent ($M = 4.35$) than they did the white agent ($M = 2.25$; $p < .01$). However, the main effect was qualified by a marginally significant

Table 10.2

Means for Black Participants' Responses to Race-Specific Computer-Generated Female Agents with Race-Specific Voice

	Black Female Agent		White Female Agent		Ethnically Ambiguous Agent	
	Black Strong Identity	Black Weak Identity	Black Strong Identity	Black Weak Identity	Black Strong Identity	Black Weak Identity
Similarity to agent	5.60[a]	4.44[b]	1.95[b]	2.83[a]	4.18	4.60
Identification with agent	5.11[a]	4.00[b]	1.67[b]	2.83[a]	4.50	4.20
Attitude toward agent	5.24[a]	4.34[b]	3.07[b]	4.15[a]	5.13[a]	4.13[b]
Attitude toward brand	5.48	4.31	5.46	4.49	5.51	5.56
Recall of product information	9.00	10.00	5.00	7.00	7.00	6.00

Note: Means with different superscripts within the same agents' race column differ significantly from each other at $p < .05$. $N = 60$.

interaction between agent race and ethnic identity ($F[2, 53] = 2.38; p = .10$). Further examination of the means using one-way ANOVA showed that blacks with strong ethnic identities were more likely to identify with the black female agent ($M = 5.11$, SD = 1.45) than blacks with weak ethnic identities ($M = 4.00$, SD = 2.00, $p < .05$). This supports Hypothesis 1. Also, blacks with weak ethnic identities were more likely to identify with the white female agent ($M = 2.83$, SD = 1.17) than blacks with strong ethnic identities ($M = 1.67$, SD = 1.15; $p < .05$). This supports Hypothesis 2. No significant response difference based on ethnic identity was found for the ethnically ambiguous female agent.

Attitude Toward the Agent

A significant main effect for agent race ($F[2, 53] = 4.28, p < .05$) demonstrated that black participants in general identified more with the black female agent ($M = 4.79$) than they did the white female agent ($M = 3.61, p < .05$). They also identified more with the ethnically ambiguous agent ($M = 4.63$) than they did the white agent ($M = 3.61; p < .01$). However, the main effect was qualified by a significant interaction between agent race and ethnic identity ($F([, 53] = 3.54; p < .05$). Further examination of the means demonstrated that blacks with strong ethnic identities had a more positive attitude toward the black female agent ($M = 5.24$, SD = 1.23) than did blacks with weak ethnic identities ($M = 4.34$, SD = 1.50, $p < .05$). This supports Hypothesis 1. An examination of the means also showed that blacks with weak ethnic identities had a more positive attitude toward the white female agent ($M = 4.15$, SD = .61) than did blacks with strong ethnic identities ($M = 3.07$, SD = 1.49). This supports Hypothesis 2. An examination of the means also showed that blacks with strong ethnic identities had a more positive attitude toward the ethnically ambiguous female agent ($M = 5.13$, SD = 1.01) than did blacks with weak ethnic identities ($M = 4.13$, SD = 1.00; $p < .05$).

Attitude Toward the Brand

A main effect for ethnic identity was found ($F[1, 50] = 3.60, p < .05$). This indicated that blacks with strong ethnic identities had a more positive attitude toward the Acura brand ($M = 5.49$) than blacks with weak ethnic identity ($M = 4.79; p < .05$). No significant interactions were found. This does not support Hypothesis 1 or Hypothesis 2.

Recall of Product Information

A significant main effect for agent race ($F[2, 53] = 4.28, p < .05$) demonstrated that black participants in general recalled more with the black female agent ($M = 9.50$) than they did the white female agent ($M = 5.00; p < .05$). They also recalled more with the black female agent (M = 9.50) than they did the ethnically ambiguous agent (M = 4.63). The results did not support Hypothesis 1 or Hypothesis 2.

Study 2 Discussion

The findings from Study 2 provide support for the notion that ethnic identity influences blacks' responses to race-specific computer-generated agents with race-specific voices. In general, the results suggest that blacks with strong ethnic identities perceive themselves as being more similar to a black female agent with a voice they identify as sounding black, identify more with a black female agent that sounds black, and have more positive attitudes toward a black female agent that sounds black than do blacks with weak ethnic identities. In fact, blacks with weak ethnic identities were more likely to perceive themselves similar to the white female agent, identify more with the white female agent, and have more positive attitudes toward the white female agent than did blacks with strong ethnic identities. Also noteworthy is that blacks' strength of ethnic identity does not influence their responses to an ethnically ambiguous computer-generated character. The results show that in-group favoritism demonstrated by black participants with strong ethnic identity is consistent with findings of previous research (e.g., Appiah 2004). Responses of blacks with weak ethnic identity were also consistent with previous research (e.g., Appiah 2004), further suggesting that weak ethnic identifiers do not demonstrate racial in-group favoritism.

GENERAL CONCLUSION

Avatars and anthropomorphic characters have become commonplace on commercial websites but few studies have examined their impact on black consumers. Moreover, a recent trend among marketers has been to use ethnically ambiguous characters—racially neutral characters or characters whose race or ethnicity are unidentifiable—in advertisements to appeal to a broader consumer segment. This study contributes to the literature by examining the combined effects of web-based avatars and ethnically ambiguous characters on black web browsers' psychological responses. Given that much of the previous work in advertising and communication tends to treat members of the black race as responding uniformly to advertising stimuli, it was particularly important to examine how the ethnic identity of blacks may influence their responses to race-specific avatars. The few studies that exist on identity and acculturation of ethnic minorities have documented substantial individual variation in strength of ethnic identification among ethnic minorities (Phinney 1992). Our findings demonstrate that ethnic identity is a key variable that predicts blacks' responses to race-specific messages on the web. Certainly, the results and implications of this research are preliminary because both studies might be firsts in directly comparing race-based effects of ethnic identity between web-based avatars. The results, however, are powerful as they provide constructive refinements and advances for theories and open up a promising and valuable venue for pushing our knowledge about established social processes further.

There are a few limitations of the study. First, the artificial viewing environment that forced participants to follow the commands of the computer agent may be a bit uncommon on most commercial websites. Moreover, the racially neutral context of the automobile website may have led to more conservative findings than what might be expected from websites where race of the agent is more salient or relevant, such as a site that features music, apparel, sneakers, or hair care products. These product contexts may be a type of ethnic prime that, according to Forehand and Deshpande (2001), should increase ethnic consumers' awareness of their own ethnicity, and lead these consumers to respond more favorably to same-ethnicity characters. Overall, the results of the study seem to indicate that for products that are not race-specific, the race of the agent still has a very powerful effect on consumer attitudes. Future studies should evaluate the impact of racially relevant products versus products that are racially irrelevant on consumer attitudes.

REFERENCES

Aaker, J., A. Brumbaugh, and S. Grier. 2000. "Non-Target Market Effects and Viewer Distinctiveness: The Impact of Target Marketing on Attitudes." *Journal of Consumer Psychology* 9 (3): 127–140.

Ahrens, F. 2006. "The Nearly Personal Touch: Marketers Use Avatars to Put an Animated Face with the Name." *Washington Post,* July 15, D1. Available at www.washingtonpost.com/wp-dyn/content/article/2006/07/14/AR2006071401587.html (accessed December 7, 2007).

Appiah, O. 2001. "The Effects of Ethnic Identification on Black and White Adolescents' Evaluation of Ads." *Journal of Advertising Research* 41 (5): 1–16.

———. 2002. "Black and White Viewers' Perception and Recall of Occupational Characters on Television." *Journal of Communication* 52 (4): 776–793.

———. 2003. "Americans Online: Differences in Surfing and Evaluating Race-Targeted Web Sites by Black and White Users." *Journal of Broadcasting and Electronic Media* 47 (4): 534–552.

———. 2004. "Effects of Ethnic Identification on Web Browsers' Attitudes Toward, and Navigational Patterns on, Race-Targeted Sites." *Communication Research,* 31 (3): 312–337.

———. 2007. "The Effectiveness of 'Typical-User' Testimonial Ads on Black and White Browsers' Evaluations of Products on Commercial Web Sites: Do They Really Work?" *Journal of Advertising Research* 47 (1): 14–27.

Arlidge, J. 2004. "The New Melting Pot: Forget Black, Forget White. The Future Is Generation EA." *The Observer,* January 4, 19.

Arphan, L.M. 2002. "When in Rome? The Effects of Spokesperson Ethnicity on Audience Evaluation of Crisis Communication." *Journal of Business Communication* 39 (3): 314–339.

Breakwell, G.M. 1986. *Coping with Threatened Identities.* London: Methuen.

Brewer, M.B. 1991. "The Social Self: On Being the Same and Different at the Same Time." *Personality and Social Psychology Bulletin* 17: 475–482.

Cassell, J., J. Sullivan, S. Prevost, and E. Churchill. 2000. *Embodied Conversational Agents.* Cambridge, MA: MIT Press.

Eastin, M., O. Appiah, and V. Cicchirillo. Forthcoming. Identification and the Influence of Cultural Stereotyping on Post Game Play Hostility, *Human Communication Research,* in press.

Festinger, L. 1954. "A Theory of Social Comparison Process." *Human Relations* 7: 117–140.

Forehand, M.R., and R. Deshpande. 2001. "What We See Makes Us Who We Are: Priming Ethnic Self-Awareness and Advertising Response." *Journal of Marketing Research* 38: 336–348.

Gong, L., and C. Nass. 2007. "When a Talking-Face Computer Agent Is Half-Human and Half-Humanoid: Human Identity and Consistency Preference." *Human and Communication Research* 33: 163–193.

Gunter, B., A. Furnham, and C. Frost. 1994. "Recall by Young People of Television Advertisements as a Function of Programme Type and Audience Evaluation." *Psychological Reports* 75: 1107–1120.

Hemp, P. 2006. "Avatar-Based Marketing." *Harvard Business Review* (June): 48–57.

Holland, J., and J. Gentry. 1997. "The Impact of Cultural Symbols on Advertising Effectiveness: A Theory of Intercultural Accommodation." *Advances in Consumer Research* 24: 483–489.

Holzwarth, M., C. Janiszewski, and M.M. Neumann. 2006. "The Influence of Avatars on Online Consumer Shopping Behavior." *Journal of Marketing* 70: 19–36.

La Ferla, R. 2003. "Generation E.A.: Ethnically Ambiguous." *New York Times,* December 28. Available at www.nytimes.com/2003/12/28/fashion/28ETHN.html (accessed December 28, 2003).

Lee, K.M., and C. Nass. 2005. "Social-Psychological Origins of Feelings of Presence: Creating Social Presence with Machine-Generated Voices." *Media Psychology* 7: 31–45.

Mastro, D. 2003. "Social Identity Approach to Understanding the Impact of Television Messages." *Communication Monographs* 70 (2): 98–113.

McGuire, W. 1984. "Search for the Self: Going Beyond Self-Esteem and the Reactive Self." In *Personality and the Prediction of Behavior,* ed. R.A. Zucker, J. Aronoff, and A.I. Rabin, 73–120. New York: Academic Press.

McGuire, W., V. McGuire, P. Child, and T. Fujioka. 1978. "Salience of Ethnicity in the Spontaneous Self-Concept as a Function of One's Ethnic Distinctiveness in the Social Environment." *Journal of Personality and Social Psychology* 36 (5): 511–520.

Nowak, K.L. 2004. "The Influence of Anthropomorphism and Agency on Social Judgment in Virtual Environments." *Journal of Computer Mediated Communication* 9 (2).

Oakes, P.J., S.A. Haslam, and J.C. Turner. 1994. *Stereotyping and Social Reality.* Oxford, UK: Blackwell.

Papacharissi, Z., and A.M. Rubin. 2000. "Predictors of Internet Use." *Journal of Broadcasting and Electronic Media* 44 (2): 175–196.

Phinney, J.S. 1992. "The Multigroup Ethnic Identity Measure: A New Scale for Use with Diverse Groups." *Journal of Adolescent Research,* 7 (2): 156–176.

———. 2005. "Ethnic Identity in Late Modern Times: A Response to Rattansi and Phoenix." *Identity* 5 (2): 187–194.

Rosen, E. 2000. *The Anatomy of Buzz: How to Create Word-of-Mouth Marketing.* New York: Doubleday Currency.

Sengupta, S. 2002. "In the Eyes of the Beholder: The Relevance of Skin Tone and Facial Features of African American Female Models to Advertising Effectiveness." *Communication Reports* 16 (2): 210–220.

Snyder, C.R., and H.L. Fromkin. 1980. *Uniqueness: The Human Pursuit of Difference.* New York: Plenum.

Tharp, M.C. 2001. *Marketing and Consumer Identity in Multicultural America.* Thousand Oaks, CA: Sage.

Thomas, E.R., and J. Reaser. 2004. "Delimiting Perceptual Cues Used for the Ethnic Labeling of African American and European American Voices." *Journal of Sociolinguistics* 8 (1): 54–87.

Vignoles, V., X. Chryssochoou, and G.M. Breakwell. 2000. "The Distinctiveness Principle: Identity, Meaning, and Bounds of Cultural Relativity." *Personality and Social Psychology Review* 4 (4): 337–354.

Whittler, T.E. 1989. "Viewers' Processing of Actor's Race and Message Claims in Advertising Stimuli." *Psychology of Marketing* 6: 287–309.

Willadsen-Jensen, Eve C., and T.A. Ito. 2006. "Ambiguity and the Timecourse of Racial Perception." *Social Cognition,* 24 (5): 580–606.

Williams, J. 2007. "Redefining What It Means to Be Black in America." Available at www.npr.org/templates/story/story.php?storyId=16266326 (accessed December 15, 2007).

CHAPTER 11

Ethnic Matching

An Examination of Ethnic Morphing in Advertising

YULIYA LUTCHYN, BRITTANY R.L. DUFF, RONALD J. FABER, SOYOEN CHO, AND JISU HUH

In the modern media environment, mass marketing is becoming an increasingly obsolete idea. In order to persuade the consumer, marketers are trying to narrow-target, or even personalize, their messages. Research shows that the perception of being targeted by an advertisement is an important mediator of a consumer's response to advertising (Aaker, Brumbaugh, and Grier 2000). To create such perception, communicators must be especially sensitive to the range of ways in which people define themselves, and must be able to create a strong match between a consumer and an endorser. The positive effect of such perceived similarity is well known, and lies at the heart of target marketing.

In the realm of advertising, the effect of perceived similarity is usually created via demographic matching. Ideological similarity has also been shown to be effective (Park and Schaller 2005), but demographic matching has tended to receive the greatest attention because it is the easiest to quickly communicate. For example, age, gender, and ethnicity are some of the basic and visible characteristics that serve people as a fundamental frame of reference for evaluating similarity. Such evaluations are often automatic and subconscious. Advertisers have always tried to appeal to the consumers by creating a demographic match—using endorsers that are similar in appearance to the target. Research suggests strong empirical support for the effectiveness of this approach. Demographically similar sources are viewed as more attractive, credible, persuasive, and trustworthy (Appiah 2001; DeShields and Kara 2000; DeBruine 2002).

Ethnicity is one of the primary demographic dimensions of self-concept used in advertising. Ethnically matched models were shown to be more compatible with self-schema, thus facilitating self-referencing. Increased self-referencing, in turn, facilitates attention, ad processing, and recall (Burnkrant and Unnava

1995; Meyers-Levy and Peracchio 1996). Models that appear ethnically similar to the typical consumer were also found to be perceived as more likable, and led to more positive brand and ad attitudes (Deshpande and Stayman 1994; Whittler 1991). Overall, the persuasive effect of a message is usually enhanced to the degree that the demographic—and specifically, ethnic—characteristics of the ad endorser match those of the consumer.

It has never been easier or less expensive to develop globalized campaigns with promotional messages that can reach consumers all around the world. Yet there are many situations in which localized advertising or segmentation is a much more effective way to influence consumers. Some of these benefit from a sense of ethnic identity. Thus, even globalized campaigns often produce separate advertising executions where the race of the models in an ad is changed to better match with that of the target market being exposed to the campaign. This strategy may work reasonably well when people are geographically separate and likely to encounter only the ad execution designed for them. However, the Internet makes any version of the ad only a few keystrokes away and thus the ability to appropriately segment ethnic groups may not be as accessible as it once was. Perhaps even more critical, the meaning of ethnicity is changing with a growing number of multiethnic consumers. A possible solution for advertising comes from new technological developments. An alternative approach to providing the sense of credibility and similarity found in ethnically matched spokesperson could be possible in advertising thanks to a new form of technology called digital morphing.

DIGITAL MORPHING

While not yet common, this new technology has created the ability to utilize visual similarity on a level that is not consciously detectable. This can be done by digitally morphing the facial features of an advertising model with those of other models, and even consumers themselves.

Digital morphing is a new technique that potentially allows an advertiser to create a sense of similarity on an implicit level. Morphing software merges a digital image of two or more faces to form a composite image. A computer program delineates corresponding points located at several facial landmarks, such as the corner of the eyes and the mouth, of two photos and generates a new face based on a weighted average of the landmark characteristics of the source faces. Pixel values are averaged to represent information regarding both shape and color. The resulting face appears realistic and normal to the viewers (DeBruine 2002). Depending on the relative proportion of each face that is used to create the morphed picture, the resulting alteration is undetectable by viewers (see Figure 11.1).

Morphing has already been utilized in an advertising context. General Mills used it to update the image of their spokes-character Betty Crocker for their seventy-fifth anniversary. They invited consumers to submit their own photos. The new Betty Crocker was a morphed composite of seventy-five different con-

Figure 11.1 **Digital Morphing**

Subject   Model   Morph (40:60)

sumers selected from this promotion. The result was a far more heterogeneous spokesperson that embodied characteristics of a number of different racial and ethnic groups.

Some scholars have recently begun to examine the opportunities to use morphing in strategic communication domains. Initial studies primarily focus on attitudinal and behavioral effects of morphing a participant's own face with that of a model or known source (Bailenson et al. 2006; DeBruine 2002, 2005). For example, DeBruine (2002) found that people exhibited greater trust in an online partner when the partner's photo was morphed with the subject's own face. In another study, she found that people exhibited greater altruistic behavior when the photo of the person they thought they were helping was a self-morphed photo (DeBruine 2005). Vote preference has also been found to be influenced by seeing photos of candidates that have been morphed with photos of the respondents (Bailenson et al. 2006; Bailenson, Iyengar, and Yee 2005). Other studies found evidence that in an advertising context, consumers who see an ad with a self-morphed model may project some of their own traits to the brand, and that self-morphed models can significantly affect attitude toward the ad and the brand (Faber, Duff, and Lutchyn 2006). This study also compared the effects of self-morphs with morphs of a model with another ordinary consumer. The other-morphs also caused significant changes in viewers' perceptions of the brand. However, while self-morphs led to a perception of a positive relationship between one's own and the brand image (assimilation effect), seeing a model morphed with another person led people to contrast the brand with the self and resulted in a negative relation between self traits and brand traits. Overall, findings from this study suggest that evaluating similarity is a complex process that involves both assimilation and contrast effects with perceived brand personality.

The initial morphing studies were based on the idea of phenotype matching, where the predicted effect is due to the ability to recognize oneself or one's genetic relatives in a morph and distinguish them from the others. Effect of self-morph images exploits the case of the strongest form of similarity—when one has a kinship or genetic relationship with another. A similar effect could be produced by interracial morphing. Although ethnic matching represents a less extreme example of visual similarity than self-morph, implicit resemblance of the model to the self could still produce a significant effect on individuals' evaluation of the messages. While morphing technology can easily be used, no prior research has examined the impact of ethnic morphing in advertising. The current study served to examine the relative impact of ethnically matched, ethnically mismatched, and ethnically morphed models in an ad.

EFFECT OF ETHNIC MORPH

Prior research on morphing suggests that it may be a potentially influential technique in the future. Studies on self morphing and ethnicity effects in advertising show that individuals have preferences for models that appear similar to them (Faber, Duff, and Lutchyn 2006; Deshpande and Stayman 1994). In the present chapter we suggest that the use of ethnically matched morphs in an ad may help to generate an implicit sense of similarity between the viewer and a resulting morphed model. However, the exact mechanism through which ethnic morphing may influence consumers' attitudes toward the model and the ad is still unknown.

An intuitive prediction is that an ad with an ethnically matched (vs. mismatched) morph will create a greater sense of similarity and will increase persuasiveness of the message. However, as previous studies show, evaluating similarity involves both assimilation and contrast processes (e.g., Herr 1986; Pelham and Wachsmuth 1995). While increasing similarity may lead to greater assimilation, it is also possible that the greater explicit similarity of the matched morph may prompt closer comparison and ultimately lead to greater contrasting with the model (Mussweiler 2003). It is known that initial comparison sets a reference point for subsequent evaluation. If another person is initially perceived as quite different, the likelihood of comparison decreases, which leads to lower standards for comparison and reduced contrast. In this case, even a small resemblance in those who appear very different (e.g., people of another race) can make us focus on common features and lead to perception of relative similarity. Alternatively, if initial evaluation signals similarity, standards for comparison get higher. In this case, even small dissimilarities of those who are similar (e.g., people of our own race) may be perceived as more significant and may encourage contrasting.

In a case of digital morphing, similarity assessment will likely occur on both an explicit and implicit level, and may be affected by both faces in the morph. How exactly morphs affect viewers' perceived similarity is difficult to predict. To examine these issues, an exploratory study was conducted to further understand the potential impact of interracial morphing in advertising. More specifically, it was designed to test the following competing hypotheses:

H_{1A}: Greater similarity of the ethnically matched model morph will result in assimilation, leading people to respond more favorably to ads that contain ethnically matched versus mismatched model morphs.

H_{1B}: Greater similarity of the ethnically matched model morph will encourage contrasting, thus leading people to respond less favorably to ads that contain ethnically matched versus mismatched model morphs.

METHOD

To explore effects of interracial morphing on attitudes toward the model and the ad, our study used a 2 (viewer's ethnicity: Caucasian and Asian) × 4 (ethnically matched and mismatched model morphs, ethnically matched and mismatched unmorphed models) experimental design. Two separate experimental administrations were conducted, first using U.S. student subjects and then replicated with Korean students as subjects.

Participants

Participants in the U.S. study were recruited from classes in a large midwestern university. Participants in the Korean study were also students, recruited at a major Korean University. A total of 189 subjects (112 American and 77 Korean) signed up for and completed the study. Data from 6 American participants who self-identified as Asians were dropped.

Procedure

Procedure and stimulus materials were identical in both parts of the study. The study was initially designed in English, and then a native Korean speaker translated instructions, stimuli materials, and the questionnaire into Korean. A second bilingual researcher then reviewed content to ensure equivalency of both versions. All participants were told that they would be assessing advertisements. Then they were invited to sit in front of a computer screen, and were randomly assigned to see one of the four target ads and a filler ad. The order of the target and the filler ads was rotated between subjects. Participants were instructed to look at the ad like they would a normal ad in a magazine. Following each ad exposure, participants filled out a questionnaire. First, they were asked to list all the thoughts they had when viewing the ad. This open-ended question was included in order to determine if any of the subjects recognize anything unusual in the picture of the model. After this, participants answered questions assessing perception of model similarity and model evaluation, as well as ad and brand attitude.

Stimulus Ad

The product chosen for the experimental manipulation was a camera. This product was something that could be used by both males and females, in the United States and in Korea. To make the ad both neutral and as realistic as possible, a

Figure 11.2 **Advertisements with Morphed Models**

real European brand was used. The target ad featured a Philips camera with a shoulders-up shot of a model (see Figure 11.2).

The model shown in the ad was either Caucasian, 60 percent Caucasian–40 percent Asian morph, Asian, or a 60 percent Asian–40 percent Caucasian morph. Morphing was done using MorphX freeware. The 60:40 ratios were used since previous research has found this to be an optimal level to avoid detection of morphing at a conscious level and still produce implicit effects (Bailenson, Iyengar, and Yee 2005). Pictures of both Caucasian and Asian models were pretested to ensure equal likability.

Measures

After viewing each ad, subjects were asked to list all the thoughts they had when viewing the ad. This open-ended measure was used to check whether participants recognized when and if interracial morphing has taken place in ads. Attitude toward the ad was measured by asking subjects to indicate on a 7-point scale how they felt the ad rated on each of 11 attributes such as *believable, informative, clear, likeable, persuasive,* and so forth. Scores on these items were then summed and averaged to indicate overall attitude toward the ad. Attitude toward the brand was assessed using similar 6-item instrument. On a scale ranging from 1 to 7, subjects were asked to rate the brand on attributes such as quality, appeal, desirability, and usefulness.

To assess perception of model similarity, participants were explicitly asked to indicate how similar they felt the model was to them on each of 7 attributes such as *lifestyles, values, background, tastes, intelligence,* and so on. They also indicated their overall attitude toward the model. This was assessed using a

4-item scale measuring model's *likeability, trustworthiness, attractiveness,* and *appropriateness for the ad.*

RESULTS

Open-ended responses to the thought-listing question were reviewed to determine if any of the subjects recognized anything unusual in the picture of the model or if their comments about the ads differed across conditions. None of the students commented on quality of the picture, or gave any indication that they recognized that morphing (or any picture alteration) had taken place. Therefore, interracial morphing at the 60:40 ratio appears undetectable at the explicit level.

To examine the possible effect of the ethnic morph on the endorser's evaluation, a series of ANOVAs was run. Although Caucasian and Korean models were pretested for equal likability among American subjects, initial analysis of data from the main experiment revealed that evaluations of the two unmorphed models had great variance in responses from both American and Korean participants. Since the Asian and Caucasian models were perceived as too different for direct comparison, only ads with the two morphed models were further analyzed.

The central finding of the study appears to be an interaction effect of participant race and the morphed models. Overall, participants seemed to prefer morphs where the base (explicitly recognizable) picture was a model of the other rather than their own race.

Surprisingly, both American and Korean students consistently evaluated the model in the "60 percent other–40 percent own race" morph condition as more similar to themselves than the model in the "60 percent own–40 percent other race." Korean students perceived the Caucasian-Asian morphed model (M = 3.4, SD = .8) as more similar to themselves than the Asian-Caucasian model (M = 2.9, SD = 1.2). American students, on the other hand, saw the Asian-Caucasian morph as more similar to themselves (M = 4.4, SD = .7) than the Caucasian-Asian morph (M = 3.9, SD = 1.3). This difference was significant ($F[1, 90] = 4,7, p < .05$). Interestingly, a main effect of race also emerged. Students in the American sample perceived both models as more similar than did Korean students ($F[1, 90] = 21.9, p < .05$).

The effect of the morphs on the perception of model similarity was also reflected in evaluation. Korean students rated the Asian-Caucasian morph model as less likable (M = 3.1, SD = 1.7) than the Caucasian-Asian morphed model (M = 4.1, SD = 1.5). American students had the opposite evaluation: they rated the Asian-Caucasian morph (M = 5.5, SD = 1.30) as more likable than the Caucasian-Asian morph (M = 4.9, SD = 1.2). This interaction effect was significant ($F[1, 91] = 6.8, p < .05$).

The same pattern also emerged for other dimensions of model evaluation. While Koreans saw the Caucasian-Asian model as more trustworthy (M = 3.6, SD = 1.5) than the Asian-Caucasian one (M = 3.2, SD = 1.8), Americans revealed an exactly opposite pattern: the Caucasian-Asian model (M = 4.0, SD = 1.1) rated lower on this dimension than the Asian-Caucasian morph (M = 5.0, SD = 1.2). Both the race × condition interaction effect ($F[1, 91] = 7.2, p < .01$), and the main effect of the race were significant ($F[1, 91] = 19.4, p < .01$).

Consistent with other results, the reverse pattern of preferences emerged for evaluation of the model's attractiveness. Here again, Korean students felt like the Caucasian-Asian morph (M = 4.0, SD = 1.6) was more attractive than the Asian-Caucasian model (M = 3.0, SD = 1.6), and American students felt the opposite (M = 5.1, SD = 1.2 and M = 5.4, SD = 1.1, respectively). The difference between all conditions was significant ($F[1, 91] = 5.6, p < .05$).

Overall, American students assigned the Caucasian-Asian morph model (M = 4.7, SD = 1.0) a significantly lower rating than Asian-Caucasian (M = 5.3, SD = 1.0). Korean students had an opposite pattern of preferences: the Asian-Caucasian morph (M = 3.2, SD = 1.3) was given a lower rating than the Caucasian-Asian morph (M = 3.9, SD = 1.2).

Overall, the interaction effect of the viewer's ethnicity and the morphs was significant and consistent across different model evaluation measures. However, these effects did not extend to evaluation of the ads and the brand. While the same patterns emerged, Caucasian participants rated ads with Caucasian-Asian (M = 4.4, SD = 1.3) and Asian-Caucasian morphs (M = 4.6, SD = .9) equally. Korean participants also saw both versions of the ad as quite similar (with the Caucasian-Asian morph M = 3.6, SD = 0.9 and the Asian-Caucasian morph M = 3.3, SD = 1.2). Overall, Caucasian participants had a more positive evaluation of both ads than Korean participants ($F[1, 91] = 18.4, p < .001$). However, the interaction between the viewer's race and morph version was not significant.

The pattern of the effects on brand attitude was also consistent with that of the model evaluation. Specifically, American students rated the brand higher when the model was an Asian-Caucasian morph (M = 4.5, SD = 1.1) than when she was Caucasian-Asian morph (M = 4.2, SD = 1.2). The opposite was true for Korean students: the brand received higher evaluations when endorsed by the Caucasian-Asian morph model (M = 3.9, SD = 1.0), than by the Asian-Caucasian (M = 3.4, SD = 1.4). Although it went in the expected direction, the interaction effect of the participant's race and the morph did not reach significance. Once again, American participants gave brands in both conditions higher ratings than did Korean students ($F[1, 91] = 8.4, p < .01$).

DISCUSSION

Recent years have seen a dramatic increase in efforts to personalize messages to consumers. This study was an initial effort to explore a potential next step in this area, where an advertising image is modified in appearance in order to attempt to maximize influence. Results indicate that interracial morphing may create a significant effect on perception of the ad endorser, but the underlying mechanism of such perceptions and preferences is quite complex.

First, our results revealed the main effect of the viewer's race. Americans seemed to consistently evaluate both morphed models higher than did Korean students. This may be due to the fact that American students live in a more heterogeneous society and are more "attuned" to similarities. With so many people of different ethnic backgrounds, their latitude of similarity acceptance may be broader. Korean students, on the other hand, live in a homogenous society and may be more sensitive to differences. Thus even small changes in appearance may result in lowered perception of similarity. This effect of the consumer's ethnic environment on effectiveness of the morphs is a novel finding and might deserve further exploration.

Another interesting finding concerns the effect of the interracial morph itself. Across different dimensions, participants invariably rated the model that was actually less similar to them as more trustworthy, attractive, likable, and even more similar to themselves. These results contradict previous work that found that degree of similarity is strongly and positively correlated with positive perceptions of the endorser. However, while initially counterintuitive, the results of this study are consistent with research on social comparison. Specifically, our findings suggest that interracial morphing may trigger a complex assimilation-contrast reaction. It appears that the dominant element in the morph acts as a cue for whether to compare or contrast oneself to the model. When similarities are dominant (as in the "own-other" morph condition) people seem to be motivated to contrast themselves to the model and notice ways in which that model is different and thus inappropriate. On the other hand, when viewers encounter an image morphed with another race, differences appear dominant and viewers are motivated to compare themselves to the model. As a result, similarities are implicitly perceived as diagnostic, which increases perception of similarity and favorable attitude toward the model.

Contrary to expectations, morphing and its interaction with the viewer's ethnicity did not affect ad and brand attitudes. Although consistently in the predicted directions, findings did not reach significance. This may be explained by some limitations of the study design. First, a well-known brand was used. In such cases, information in the ad—including characteristics of the endorser—may not be very diagnostic and, thus, have a weak effect on ad and brand attitudes. Second, it is likely that one-time exposure to the ad was not sufficient to drastically alter previous brand perceptions. It is possible, however, that morphed models might significantly influence ad and brand attitudes if used in long-term campaigns and/ or for the new brands.

Despite these limitations, the current study suggests that morphed images may influence consumers' perceptions of models in an ad. This has important practical implications for development of strategic communications online. For instance, the findings indicate that demographically matched avatars—a traditional choice of marketers—may not be the most effective virtual agents. Instead, interracial morphed avatars may be perceived by consumers as more similar, trustworthy, likable, attractive, and, therefore, more persuasive overall. This may be especially true for multiethnic markets such as the United States (vs. ethnically homogenous markets such as Korea, for example). Using digital morphing, marketers can quickly and easily create ethnic morphs to modify the appearance of their avatars (virtual agents, sales representatives, ad endorsers) to make them most appealing to each group or to individuals in the diverse web audience. Digital morphing has already been successfully used in traditional forms of media, but using it in the virtual world seems especially promising.

Morphing suggests many possible avenues for future research. For example, it would be interesting to retest the hypotheses employing a longitudinal design in order to account for any possible cumulative effect of the morphs. It would be also helpful to replicate the current study with different target stimuli (e.g., unfamiliar brands) to establish whether effect of the morphs on perceived endorser similarity can translate into brand attitude and purchase intent.

REFERENCES

Aaker, Jennifer L., Anne M. Brumbaugh, and Sonya A. Grier. 2000. "Nontarget Markets and Viewer Distinctiveness: The Impact of Target Marketing on Advertising." *Journal of Consumer Psychology* 9: 127–140.

Appiah, Osei. 2001. "Ethnic Identification and Adolescents' Evaluation of Advertisements." *Journal of Advertising Research* 41: 7–22.

Bailenson, Jeremy N., Phillip Garland, Shanto Iyengar, and Nick Yee. 2006. "Transformed Facial Similarity as a Political Cue: A Preliminary Investigation." *Political Psychology* 27: 373–385.

Bailenson, Jeremy N., Shanto Iyengar, and Nick Yee. 2005. "Facial Identity Capture and Candidate Preference in the 2004 Presidential Election." Draft manuscript, College of Communication, Stanford University, Stanford, California.

Burnkrant, Robert E., and H. Rao Unnava. 1995. "Effects of Self-Referencing on Persuasion." *Journal of Consumer Research* 22: 17–26.

DeBruine, Lisa M. 2002. "Facial Resemblance Enhances Trust." *Proceedings of the Royal Society of London, Series B* 269: 1307–1312.

———. 2005. "Trustworthy But Not Lust-Worthy: Context-Specific Effects of Facial Resemblance." *Proceedings of the Royal Society of London, Series B* 272: 919–922.

DeShields, Oscar W., and Ali Kara. 2000. "The Persuasive Effects of Spokesperson Similarity Moderated by Source Credibility." *American Marketing Association Education Proceedings* 11: 132–143.

Deshpande, Rohit, and Douglas M. Stayman. 1994. "A Tale of Two Cities: Distinctiveness Theory and Advertising Effectiveness." *Journal of Marketing Research* 31: 57–64.

Faber, Ronald J., Brittany R.L. Duff, and Yulia Lutchyn. 2006. "Can You See Yourself in the Brand: An Experimental Examination of Facial Morphing in Advertising." Paper presented at the New Media Research at UMN Conference, Minneapolis.

Herr, Paul M. 1986. "Consequences of Priming: Judgment and Behavior." *Journal of Personality and Social Psychology* 51 (6): 1106–1115.

Meyers-Levy, Joan, and Laura A. Peracchio. 1996. "Moderators of the Impact of Self-Reference on Persuasion." *Journal of Consumer Research* 22 (March): 408–423.

Mussweiler, Thomas. 2003. "Comparison Processes in Social Judgment: Mechanisms and Consequences." *Psychological Review* 110 (3): 472–489.

Park, Justin H., and Mark Schaller. 2005. "Does Attitude Serve as a Heuristic Cue for Kinship? Evidence of an Implicit Cognitive Association." *Evolution and Human Behavior* 26: 158–170.

Pelham, Brett W., and Jeff Orson Wachsmuth. 1995. "The Waxing and Waning of the Social Self: Assimilation and Contrast in Social Comparison." *Journal of Personality and Social Psychology* 69 (5): 825–838.

Whittler, Tommy E. 1991. "The Effects of Actors' Race in Commercial Advertising: Review and Extension." *Journal of Advertising* 20: 54–60.

CHAPTER 12

Mirror, Mirror on the Web

Understanding Thin-Slice Judgments of Avatars

MELISSA G. BUBLITZ, CRAIG C. CLAYBAUGH, AND LAURA A. PERACCHIO

People who know Sarah describe her as a demure, shy, thoughtful young woman with a very placid nature and a pretty smile. Roxxy is an athletic-looking female avatar with heavy black eye makeup, purple spiked hair, and a reputation for aggressive tactics in the virtual gaming world she frequents. Most would be surprised to learn that Roxxy is Sarah's avatar. In the virtual world, people have the opportunity to reinvent themselves; they can be anyone they want to be online. The question is, will people choose to be themselves, idealized versions of themselves, or someone completely different online?

The Internet provides a unique environment for people to create a new identity in an anonymous fashion, and it also "enables people the opportunity to take on various personas, even a different gender, and to express facets of themselves without fear of disapproval" (Bargh, McKenna, and Fitzsimons 2002, p. 34). However, one stream of research suggests that despite this opportunity to reinvent themselves, people tend to present their true selves online (Bargh et al. 2002). If people present their true selves online, then what do others infer about them based on the avatars they create to represent themselves in the virtual world? In face-to-face interactions, people automatically and unintentionally communicate information through nonverbal gestures and mannerisms that may be more accessible to the observer than to the sender and quite difficult for the sender to suppress (DePaulo 1992). Does this same phenomenon occur in the virtual world? This chapter explores how we make judgments about avatars in a virtual world and introduces consumer psychology implications of these judgments.

Why study avatars? Businesses and consumers are flocking to virtual worlds. *Second Life,* with more than sixteen million users, is a user-generated virtual world where people connect, conduct business, and engage in a wide variety of social interactions. In *Second Life,* consumers are represented by an avatar, which is their persona in the virtual world. The founders of *Second Life* state that "*Second Life* is about personal expression and your avatar is the most personal expression of all" (Second Life 2007). As online social communities continue to grow, the world of communication is also changing. Personal forms of communication are evolving in the online world and many forms of social interaction have moved online. Online communication has moved beyond the initial media of e-mail and instant messaging to become a way for individuals to interact with each other and with organizations. But the question remains, how much does the behavior of avatars in the virtual world emulate consumer behavior in the real world? Marketers are working to understand avatars and are investing millions in advertising within virtual worlds (Lowry 2008). In the offline world, a significant body of research informs us about how individuals quickly and automatically form judgments. Applying research on judgment formation to avatars in the virtual world provides a framework for understanding online consumer psychology.

An understanding of the evaluations consumers make about avatars may be gained from examining the literature on *thin-slice judgments.* Thin-slice judgments are based on brief excerpts of expressive behavior, for example, a five-second exposure to a salesperson talking about a product. What theoretical or substantive contribution might the examination of thin-slice judgments offer to knowledge about avatars? As Bargh and Ferguson (2000) described, automatic judgments occur when cues from the environment interact with categorical knowledge stored in our memory. People often use their prior knowledge and experiences to automatically and quickly form judgments. As an example, Ambady, Krabbenhoft, and Hogan (2006, p. 4) demonstrate how relationships often "hinge on first impressions" in their thin-slice analysis of consumer perceptions of salespeople. Similarly, thin-slice judgments of avatars are likely formed automatically during an initial online encounter. This chapter highlights how research on thin-slice judgments may augment our understanding of avatars.

Our commentary begins by introducing research on thin-slice judgments in the context of information processing theory. Then we focus on how thin-slice judgments are influenced by interactions and verbal communication with avatars in the virtual world. Finally, we describe several potential applications of thin-slice judgments of avatars relevant to understanding consumer psychology and marketing in the virtual world. The goal of this approach is to illustrate how the study of thin-slice judgments may offer insight into avatars as well as how judgments of avatars influence marketing in the virtual world.

THIN-SLICE JUDGMENT FORMATION: JUDGING AVATARS

Over the last decade researchers have begun to explore how consumers use automatic and nonconscious processes to form judgments (Johar, Maheswaran, and Peracchio 2006). Research shows that people form accurate judgments about

others by observing thin-slices (thirty seconds or less) of expressive human behavior (Ambady, Bernieri, and Richeson 2000). One example demonstrating the
accuracy of thin-slice judgments is found in Ambady and Rosenthal's (1993) study
of teacher assessments. Students who had no previous experience with an instructor viewed short segments (6 to 30 seconds) of a videotaped teaching session and
then rated the instructor's teaching performance. These thin-slice judgments of
performance based on brief video segments were quite accurate when compared
to evaluations by students who had spent an entire semester with the same instructor (Ambady and Rosenthal 1993). Thin-slice judgments of others have been
shown to be highly accurate in a wide variety of settings, including evaluations
of employees in the workplace (Ambady et al. 1993), physicians (Ambady et al.
2002), and salespeople (Ambady, Krabbenhoft, and Hogan 2006). Building on
thin-slice research, we posit that avatars interacting in a virtual world may offer
insights into the person behind the computerized image, and these insights may
be assessed in a thin-slice judgment.

   In the next sections, we explore the formation of thin-slice judgments of avatars.
We focus on the role of nonverbal communication, expertise, and environmental
context in forming accurate thin-slice judgments. We also explore how thin-slice
judgments can be updated. Our theorizing is presented with examples of how
these concepts might be applied to judgments of avatars.

The Role of Nonverbal Communication in Thin-Slice Judgments

Peracchio and Luna (2006, p. 26) suggest that "Successful decoding of nonverbal
information is essential to accurate thin-slice assessments." The importance of
nonverbal communication to judgment accuracy likely explains why thin-slice
judgments based on video accompanied by audio are more accurate than those
based on video alone (Ambady, Bernieri, and Richeson 2000). Visual and auditory
stimuli together convey nonverbal cues. A person's mannerisms, tone, and facial
expression add meaning to the words spoken during an exchange between two
people. Written communication lacks these nonverbal cues as well as the intonation
and emphasis that help us to interpret verbal communication. Avatars add imagery
and visual stimuli to enhance personal communication online. Personalization
of an avatar may also convey information used as the basis of judgment formation. Clothing choice, background, body shape, and facial expression contribute
nonverbal cues that influence judgments. The image the avatar presents may
provide clues to help marketers understand the avatar as a consumer and how
to best advertise or promote products to that avatar and their creator. Aspects of
image may trigger thin-slice judgments of both the avatar and its creator. In this
way, avatars bring nonverbal elements of communication to online interactions
that may allow us to form accurate thin-slice judgments of those we encounter
in the virtual world.

   One point of difference between judgments based on avatars and judgments based on traditional forms of interpersonal interaction is that avatars are a product of a creator. This implies that aspects of image used as a basis of judgment formation are controlled with the intent of conveying the image desired by the avatar's creator. By contrast, many of the nonverbal cues shown to facilitate accurate thin-slice judgments are derived from expressive human behavior not under conscious control (DePaulo 1992). However, we propose that an avatar's image is not unlike our attempts at impression management in everyday social interactions, which DePaulo and colleagues (1996, p. 980) describe as a "deliberate fostering of a false impression" to produce "psychic rewards such as self-esteem, affection, and respect." In this way, controllable aspects of an avatar's image, much like our attempts at impression management, may not completely disguise the creator's underlying qualities and desire for esteem. Future research should investigate the role of the controlled imagery of avatars in terms of our ability to form accurate thin-slice judgments of both the avatar and its creator.

As technology advances, avatars are increasingly able to convey lifelike forms of nonverbal communication such as gestures, body language, and eye contact. In addition, as more virtual worlds incorporate voice communication rather than text-based chat, the intonation and emphasis of the human voice behind the avatar also sends nonverbal cues. Research in virtual worlds increasingly replicates research on social interaction, finding that computer-mediated environments are quite capable of simulated human interaction. As you interact with another person in a face-to-face setting, mimicking the body movements and gestures of the other person increases how much that person likes you (Chartrand and Bargh 1999). Bailenson and Yee (2005) found a similar effect in the virtual world. Specifically, those avatars who mimic head movements of their interaction partner in a virtual environment were more liked and more persuasive than those who did not mimic their interaction partner (Bailenson and Yee 2005). In some ways technology may actually enhance our ability to mimic. In the virtual world, a computer can be programmed to integrate a blend of mimicked movements with random movements, making mimicry less detectable. Bailensen and Yee (2005) were able to record and replay with a short time delay the movements of the interaction partner. The integration of natural body movements by avatars into virtual worlds should enhance our ability to use nonverbal forms of communication to facilitate accurate thin-slice judgments.

Ambady and Rosenthal (1992, p. 267) describe how nonverbal cues make certain attributes such as "anger, fear, or dominance . . . quickly and easily recognizable because they are more essential for survival" and necessary for successful navigation of the environment. By furrowing their brow and pursing their lips to show anger, avatars convey mood or emotion that adds layers of meaning in an interaction. Active emotions such as cheerfulness, happiness, and optimism (Ambady, Bernieri, and Richeson 2000) as well as anger and surprise (Apple and Hecht 1982) are more accurately assessed from thin slices of expressive behavior. DePaulo, Lanier, and Davis (1983) demonstrate the accuracy of deceptive behavior by showing how people accurately detect when a person is trying to deceive them by observing nonverbal cues unintentionally sent by the liar. Accurate assessment of avatar mood, affect, or intent may play a critical role to survival in extreme gaming environments online such as *World of Warcraft*. Thin-slice judgments of avatars in *World of Warcraft* may be based on the characteristics of the avatar itself or behavioral displays by the avatar. Formal reputation (e.g., Honored, Friendly, Neutral, Hostile, or Hated), race (e.g., Dwarves, Gnomes, Humans, Night Elves), class (e.g., Druid, Hunter, Priest, Rogue), profession, or talent of the character may reveal potential alliances or signal weaknesses that could be exploited. Quickly reading avatar traits gives an advantage to a player during combat situations. Additionally, an avatar's name may imply it belongs to a specific clan or community. For example, including KOA in your call name affiliates your avatar with the Knights of the Alliance community. Using nonverbal cues may help players in *World of Warcraft* form accurate judgments of characters they encounter and aid their advancement in this virtual world.

Nonverbal cues provide critical information that may be used as the basis for thin-slice judgment formation. Following Pham et al. (2001), informational cues sent by an avatar may stimulate an affective response that initiates a thin-slice judgment. As they suggest, "The remarkable ability of feelings to predict spontaneous thoughts helps explain why immediate judgments based on very brief exposure to other individuals' nonverbal cues can be highly predictive of judgments based on much more extensive information about these individuals" (2001, p. 185). Ambady and colleagues (2000) describe how general affect or mood influences both impression judgment formation and judgment accuracy. They provide evidence that positive affective states generally result in more positive but less accurate judgments, and negative affect leads to more negative but more accurate thin-slice judgments (Ambady, Bernieri, and Richeson 2000). Future research should investigate the role of affect in thin-slice judgment formation of avatars as well as judgment accuracy.

The Influence of Expertise in the Formation of Thin-Slice Judgments

Thin-slice judgments are formed automatically to help us process information efficiently and conserve our cognitive energy (Peracchio and Luna 2006). One strategy consumers use to process information efficiently is to categorize new information based on their own prior knowledge (Sujan 1985). Research shows how "experts" possess "enriched knowledge structures" using technical and descriptive information in their decision making and judgment formation (Maheswaran and Sternthal 1990). By contrast, "novices" rely on more general or abstract information to form judgments. Research investigating thin-slice judgments of avatars may reveal differences between how experts or avid users of avatars differ from novices or those new to avatar interaction online. Experts likely draw from their past experiences with avatars in virtual worlds when forming judgments, while novices may be more likely to rely on stereotypes when forming automatic judgments of avatars. Each experience online adds to our working knowledge of avatars and an "elaborate knowledge structure . . . affords complex inferential processing" that may increase judgment accuracy (Peracchio and Tybout 1996, 178). We automatically compare the incoming stimuli sent by an avatar to our knowledge and past experiences with avatars. Such depth of knowledge may also prompt strong affective responses, further influencing the thin-slice judgments of avatars (Peracchio and Tybout 1996). Investigation into thin-slice judgments of avatars by experts and novices in the virtual world may reveal differences in judgment accuracy and aid our understanding of thin-slice judgment formation in the virtual world.

Experts, in particular, may also automatically assess the verbal communication between avatars and use this information diagnostically in forming thin-slice judgments. Peracchio and Luna (2006) assert that language choice and language use prompt thin-slice judgments by activating different schemas. Compared to novices online, experts may also exhibit a unique online vernacular that not only facilitates inferences about the user but also enables experts to detect subtle verbal cues sent in online communication between avatars. Zinkhan et al. (2003) describe how "Virtual communities develop unique, group-specific consumption vocabularies that influence members' social norms and cognitive processes." In the virtual world, sophistication of a user's online vernacular may signal experience that differentiates "expert" from "novice" users and provides insights that can be used to form thin-slice judgments about an avatar's creator.

The Contribution of Environmental Context to Thin-Slice Judgments

Ambady and Rosenthal (1992) suggest that context may increase the accuracy of thin-slice judgments by contributing environmental cues that aid in judgment formation. Context effects of the virtual world in which an avatar exists likely influence thin-slice judgments of that avatar. Avatars may exhibit different images and behaviors depending on the virtual environment they inhabit, much in the same way we project different images in our different roles in life. Expectations for avatars on a dating website likely differ substantially from expectations of avatars on a gaming or social networking website. People may construct multiple avatars that reflect the different roles they play in the real world or even roles they desire but do not currently perform. Connecting aspects of the avatar's image to the context of the website in which the avatar is engaged may also influence the extent to which an avatar represents aspects of self.

Research on the social identity of children in the virtual world suggests that as children and teens progress through the stages of social development, so do their avatars and online representations in the virtual world (Bryant and Akerman

2008). Bryant and Akerman (2008) explore how children change their avatars as they progress through the stages of self-development. Children often begin with concrete avatars then adapt their avatars during the identity-development stage, finally as they enter the identity-projection stage teens begin to create avatars they feel convey their true identity (Bryant and Akerman 2008). The context in which an avatar is encountered and the different roles an avatar portrays are likely to facilitate very different thin-slice judgments of avatars and their creators. Future research should explore how avatars in different types of virtual worlds facilitate accurate thin-slice judgments of not only the avatar but also the creator behind the computerized image.

Updating a Thin-Slice Judgment

Thin-slice judgments may provide a starting point for a judgment that is later confirmed or revised through more conscious and controlled deliberative processing (Peracchio and Luna 2006). Consumer research provides empirical evidence that many consumer psychological processes have both automatic and conscious components (Raghubir and Krishna 1996; Raghubir and Srivastava 2002; Yorkston and Menon 2004). For example, Yorkston and Menon (2004) show how consumers form automatic judgments based on the sound symbolism associated with a brand name. This thin-slice judgment based on sound is later updated as the consumer systematically processes more diagnostic information about the brand. In this way, screen names may trigger thin-slice judgments of the avatar. A screen name registers in our memory and may be shaped by the person perceptions we have stored related to that name or similar names. The process of updating this initial thin-slice judgment follows the two-stage or dual-processing model of cognition that describes how judgments are formed automatically and subsequently updated based on additional information that may come from interaction or prolonged exposure to an avatar in a virtual world (Chaiken and Trope 1999). Marketers also may continuously update their judgments of avatars as they interact and obtain more information that reveals the preferences of the avatar as a consumer. Research on thin-slice judgments of avatars should investigate both the initial judgments formed as well as how those judgments evolve as extended avatar interactions reveal more information over time.

As Ambady and colleagues report, thin-slice judgment accuracy is not diminished by cognitive load, that is, processing and thinking about a difficult problem (Ambady, Bernieri, and Richeson 2000). This provides evidence for the automatic nature of such processing. However, because updating a judgment relies on deliberative cognitive processing, cognitive load may play a role in the active decision to revise an initial judgment. This may mean that updating and changing an initial evaluation only occurs in certain situations, such as when users are highly involved with the avatar they encounter in a virtual world. Future research on thin-slice judgments of avatars should investigate not only the initial judgment formation but also the influences and effect of follow-up processing on the subsequent judgment of an avatar.

SUMMARY

This overview of the research on how thin-slice judgments are formed provides a theoretical basis for judgments of avatars in the virtual world and suggests potential research opportunities for investigating thin-slice judgments of avatars. In the next section, we explore how thin-slice judgments of avatars influence online consumer psychology. We also consider the broader implications of research on thin-slice judgments of avatars for marketing in the virtual world.

Thin-Slice Judgments of Avatars: Consumer Psychology and Marketing Implications

In this section, we explore the potential application and extension of thin-slice judgments of avatars to consumer psychology and marketing. Our purpose is not to be inclusive of every application of thin-slice judgments in the virtual world, but rather to illustrate how research based on thin-slice judgments can offer theoretical and substantive progress to our understanding of avatars. To this end, we consider the application of thin-slice judgments to marketing in virtual worlds, relationship marketing, customer service, and marketing ethics.

Marketing in Virtual Worlds: Consumer Applications

Perhaps the most relevant and intriguing aspect of thin-slice judgments of avatars is how these judgments are currently used in a consumer setting within the virtual world and how they will be used in the future as this medium continues to evolve. Peracchio and Luna (2006, p. 26) infer from the research on thin-slice judgments that "Many of our day-to-day consumer judgments, at an aggregate level, may be more accurate than we previously expected." Ambady, Krabbenhoft, and Hogan (2006) demonstrate how our thin-slice judgment of a salesperson is a good predictor of sales performance. Holzwarth, Janiszewski, and Neumann (2006) extend these judgments of salespeople into the virtual world by providing empirical evidence of how avatars as sales agents influence a consumer's online shopping behavior. Changing the characteristics of an avatar sales agent—altering attractiveness or expertise—can "increase the customer's satisfaction with the retailer, attitude toward a product, and purchase intention" (Holzwarth et al. 2006, 32). Thin-slice judgments may facilitate online consumer decision-making processes, influencing what, when, and whom consumers purchase from.

Other aspects of the virtual shopping environment may influence avatars as consumers. Technology is advancing our ability to replicate the social aspects of shopping online. Most people enter virtual worlds such as *Second Life* not for the convenience associated with e-commerce but rather to engage in social interaction online. As more commercial enterprises invest in storefronts within virtual communities, the social aspects of shopping may also influence what and how much avatars buy. Recent research on the presence of avatars in both a salesperson role as well as a peer shopper role demonstrated that the presence of another avatar within a store in a virtual shopping environment in *Second Life* increases the amount avatar consumers spend in that store (Moon, Sung, and Choi 2008). Research investigating online consumer behavior should explore how avatars and the shopping environment they inhabit influence judgment formation and purchase decision-making processes.

Relationship Marketing: Thin-Slice Judgments Facilitate Relationship Marketing

Marketers can utilize the advantages of the online medium to engage in more targeted one-to-one relationship marketing. Much in the same way consumers form thin-slice judgments of products and services online, marketers may form thin-slice judgments of consumers based on their avatar. As marketers gain experience in the virtual world, they may be able to use these judgments to determine which avatars represent superior targets for their marketing efforts. Online, marketers may segment consumers using thin slices of avatar behavior. Because of the one-to-one nature of the online environment, targeting much smaller, more homogeneous segments may be more feasible and cost effective compared to offline targeted marketing efforts. The virtual world presents the opportunity for a marketer to interact with an avatar, assess the avatar's consumer needs, and customize their promotional pitch to best fulfill those needs. Marketers may combine thin-slice judgments of avatars with online profile information such as their number of log-ins, recent activity, number of posts, recommendations, or buddy lists, which also contribute to understanding the avatar as a prospective customer. The World Wide Web represents an important tool marketers can use to interact directly with customers (Peracchio and Luna 2006).

As Crosby, Evans, and Cowles (1990) point out, salespeople often perform the role of relationship manager when buyers and sellers interact. Trust forms the foundation of relationship marketing and this trust is initially created by interaction with the salesperson. Nicholson, Compeau, and Sethi (2001) identified the importance of "liking" the salesperson in trust formation. In the virtual world, companies are able to create unique avatar salespeople to target prospective buyers, building relationships based on the dimensions most likely to engage and persuade an individual consumer. If an initial contact by an avatar sales representative fails, companies may have the opportunity make multiple attempts to find an effective avatar salesperson within the virtual world. Peracchio and Luna (2006) identify several research questions about the impact of thin-slice judgments on relationship marketing that also apply to the virtual world. These include assessing the impact of initial thin-slice judgments on longer-term relationships and the long-term impact of thin-slice assessments throughout the marketing relationship (Peracchio and Luna 2006).

Consider the relationship marketing example of Webkinz, a virtual world where children and their adopted furry friends (which are purchased either online or offline) play. By playing games online with their adopted pet as their avatar, children earn activity points they can use to buy clothes, rooms, and furnishings for their virtual pet. Buying new Webkinz pets, clothing, and other accessories at traditional retailers is also part of the Webkinz experience. If a child doesn't visit the Webkinz site regularly, their virtual pet lacks exercise and starts feeling sick, which may lead to a trip to the virtual clinic. Webkinz customizes some of its interactions with children by recognizing their virtual pet's birthday and encouraging children to visit unexplored places in this virtual world. Using relationship marketing techniques, Webkinz has created a loyal following that has generated a substantial offline revenue stream. Research should investigate the implications and benefits of pursuing relationship marketing in virtual environments with avatars as compared to the pursuit of offline relationship marketing.

Thin-Slice Judgments and Customer Service

Research in marketing has acknowledged the importance of customer service and service quality to the consumer's experience of and associations with a brand (Iacobucci 2001). Researchers studying service quality have emphasized the importance of the service provider in delivering excellent customer service and presenting a face for an organization—in essence, personifying the brand (Barker and Hartel 2004). Online, an avatar representing the company may give the customer service representative a tangible face. Companies may perpetuate multiple avatar service providers that match the visual demographics of the customer's avatar to some degree. As in the offline world, avatar customers may feel they relate better to an avatar service provider that is somewhat like themselves. Customers' thin-slice judgments of the quality of service delivered by an avatar customer service representative, and thus the company, may influence future behaviors, such as loyalty and price sensitivity (Doucet 2004).

Marketing Ethics: Public Policy Implications of Marketers Moving into Virtual Environments?

As these virtual environments grow in importance to marketers, consumer psychologists should also consider the public policy implications of thin-slice judgments of avatars. In the virtual world, marketers, salespeople, and advertisers have an even greater ability to manipulate their online persona and message. Research by Holzwarth, Janiszewski, and Neumann (2006) clearly illustrates how manipulating an avatar characteristic, such as attractiveness, may influence purchasing intentions. While the attraction effect may be similar to more traditional, offline forms of advertising, online ads may be more susceptible to extremes since they do not face the same regulatory scrutiny as television, radio or print media. In 2008 and 2009, advertisements deemed too risqué to air during the Super Bowl received extremely large viewing audiences as millions flocked to the Internet to view the banned ads (Mullman 2009). Thus, it would seem that thin-slice judgments may be susceptible to predatory marketing practices. From a public policy perspective, this ability to manipulate marketing tactics and personification online may require more vigilant efforts to monitor and promote ethical marketing practices.

The use of virtual environments as marketing media may leave vulnerable populations such as children, the elderly, and low-income consumers exposed to marketers and the negative consequences of consumerism. At the same time, avatars present new communication opportunities with populations already online and could also be used in the nonprofit and public policy sectors as a cost-effective marketing tool. Peracchio and Luna (2006, p. 29) suggest that "dynamic interaction between the users and a website may allow the formation of a thin-slice judgment even without interpersonal interaction." As an example of this type of interactive website, the Centers for Disease Control recently launched a new public health campaign to encourage tweens, children ages nine to twelve, to become more physically active. The campaign, entitled *VERB: It's What You Do,* consists of television commercials, print ads, and an online component where users can create an avatar character, or a *Virt,* which learns new dance moves every time the user logs their physical activity online. Tweens can also develop a picture blog to share physical activity ideas and photos with their friends. Harnessing the power of thin-slice judgments in the virtual world could have important and actionable public policy implications for marketers. Research on thin-slice judgments of avatars and websites may benefit the creation of public policy that will moderate new and existing virtual environments.

CONCLUSION

This chapter examines avatars through the conceptual lens of thin-slice judgments. The primary purpose was to describe how research on thin-slice judgments could enhance our understanding of avatars in the virtual world. As marketers expand their presence online, understanding thin-slice judgments of avatars may also inform us about consumer psychology in the virtual world. Calder and Tybout (1987) suggested that consumer research should advance theoretical knowledge about the consumer. Our examination of thin-slice judgments of avatars reveals opportunities for researchers to make theoretical and substantive contributions to consumer psychology and the field of marketing. Suggestions for research to advance our understanding of thin-slice judgments of avatars as put forth in this chapter are summarized in Appendix 12.1.

Studying the similarities and differences between thin-slice judgments online and offline may advance our understanding of consumers in the virtual world. John Vail, director of interactive marketing at Pepsi-Cola North America, states that, "If [consumers] are engaged with us in the virtual world, we know they will be engaged with our products in the real world" (Lowry 2008, p. 52). Studying the consequences and applications of thin-slice judgments of avatars offers many opportunities for theoretical as well as managerial and public policy advances within marketing. Research investigating thin-slice judgments of avatars presents an opportunity to make substantive contributions to our discipline.

APPENDIX 12.1. PROPOSED FUTURE RESEARCH TO INVESTIGATE THIN-SLICE JUDGMENTS OF AVATARS

1. The role of avatar image in thin-slice judgment formation:
   - Hair, clothing, body shape, and facial expressions
   - Accuracy of controlled image factors as the basis of thin-slice judgment formation
2. How nonverbal cues influence thin-slice judgments of avatars:
   - Eye contact, head movements, mimicry, facial expressions, and outward signs of mood or affect
   - Avatar affiliations or associations in virtual worlds
3. Experts vs. novices in virtual worlds:
   - Differences between the thin-slice judgments formed by experienced and novice users
   - How language may signal experience and influence thin-slice judgments of others
4. The role of website context in thin-slice judgments of avatars:
   - How website context contributes to expectations and thin-slice judgments of online behavior
   - Influences of context on thin-slice judgment accuracy of avatars and their creators
5. When and how do avatars provide insight into the avatar's creator:
   - Which aspects of self are revealed by avatars
   - When do thin-slice judgments of avatars yield accurate assessments of the person behind the computerized image
6. Evolving judgments of avatars:
   - The role of extended interactions, how initial thin-slice judgments are updated over time

7. The influence of thin-slice avatar judgments on consumer decision making:
   - The role of virtual sales representatives in online consumer decision making
   - How avatars in commercial settings represent visual presence and influence consumer perceptions of customer service, satisfaction, and loyalty in the virtual world
   - The role of avatars in relationship marketing efforts

REFERENCES

Ambady, Nalini, Frank J. Bernieri, and Jennifer A. Richeson. 2000. "Towards a Histology of Social Behavior: Judgmental Accuracy from Thin-Slices of Behavior." In *Advances in Experimental Social Psychology,* ed. M.P. Zanna, 201–272. Stanford, CA: Academic Press.

Ambady, Nalini, Daniel B. Hogan, L.M. Spencer, and Robert Rosenthal. 1993. "Ratings of Thin-Slices of Behavior Predict Organizational Performance." Poster presented at the 5th Annual Convention of the American Psychological Society, Chicago.

Ambady, Nalini, Mary Anne Krabbenhoft, and Daniel B. Hogan. 2006. "The 30-Second Sale: Using Thin-Slice Judgments to Evaluate Sales Effectiveness." *Journal of Consumer Psychology* 16 (1): 4–13.

Ambady, Nalini, Debi LaPlante, T. Nguyen, Robert Rosenthal, N. Chaumeton, and W. Levinson. 2002. "Surgeon's Tone of Voice: A Clue to Malpractice History." *Surgery* 132 (July): 5–9.

Ambady, Nalini, and Robert Rosenthal. 1992. "Thin Slices of Expressive Behavior as Predictors of Interpersonal Consequences: A Meta-Analysis." *Psychological Bulletin* 111 (March): 256–274.

———. 1993. "Half a Minute: Predicting Teacher Evaluations from Thin Slices of Nonverbal Behavior and Physical Attractiveness." *Journal of Personality and Social Psychology* 64 (March): 431–441.

Apple, William, and Kenneth Hecht. 1982. "Speaking Emotionally: The Relation Between Verbal and Vocal Communication of Affect." *Journal of Personality and Social Psychology* 42 (May): 864–875.

Bailenson, Jeremy N., and Nick Yee. 2005. "Digital Chameleons: Automatic Assimilation of Nonverbal Gestures in Immersive Virtual Environments." *Psychological Science* 16 (October): 814–819.

Bargh, John A., and Melissa J. Ferguson. 2000. "Beyond Behaviorism: On the Automaticity of Higher Mental Processes." *Psychological Bulletin* 126 (November): 925–945.

Bargh, John A., Katelyn Y.A. McKenna, and Grainne M. Fitzsimons. 2002. "Can You See the Real Me? Activation and Expression of the 'True Self' on the Internet." *Journal of Social Issues* 58 (Spring): 33–48.

Barker, Sunita, and Charmine E.J. Hartel. 2004. "Intercultural Service Encounters: An Exploratory Study of Customer Experiences." *Cross Cultural Management* 11 (1): 3–14.

Bryant, J. Alison, and Anna Akerman. 2008. "Finding Mii: Virtual Social Identity and the Young Consumer." Paper presented at the Advertising and Consumer Psychology Conference on Virtual Social Identity and Consumer Behavior, May 1–2, Philadelphia.

Calder, Bobby J., and Alice M. Tybout. 1987. "What Consumer Research Is . . ." *Journal of Consumer Research* 14 (June): 136–140.

Chaiken, Shelly, and Yaacov Trope. 1999. *Dual Process Theories in Social Psychology.* New York: Guilford.

Chartrand, Tanya L., and John A. Bargh. 1999. "The Chameleon Effect: The Perception-Behavior Link and Social Interaction." *Journal of Personality and Social Psychology* 85 (June): 1170–1179.

Crosby, Lawrence A., Kenneth R. Evans, and Deborah Cowles. 1990. "Relationship Quality in Services Selling: An Interpersonal Influence Perspective." *Journal of Marketing* 54 (July): 68–81.

DePaulo, Bella M. 1992. "Nonverbal Behavior and Self-Presentation." *Psychological Bulletin* 111 (March): 203–243.

DePaulo, Bella M., Deborah A. Kashy, Susan E. Kirkendol, Melissa M. Wyer, and Jennifer A. Epstein. 1996. "Lying in Everyday Life." *Journal of Personality and Social Psychology* 70 (May): 979–995.

DePaulo, Bella M., Keith Lanier, and Tracy Davis. 1983. "Detecting the Deceit of the Motivated Liar." *Journal of Personality and Social Psychology* 45 (November): 1096–1103.

Doucet, Loma. 2004. "Service Provider Hostility and Service Quality." *Academy of Management Journal* 47 (October): 761–771.

Holzwarth, Martin, Chris Janiszewski, and Marcus M. Neumann. 2006. "The Influence of Avatars on Online Consumer Shopping Behavior." *Journal of Marketing* 70 (October): 19–36.

Iacobucci, Dawn. 2001. "Services Marketing and Customer Service." In *Kellogg on Marketing,* ed. Dawn Iacobucci, 320–329. New York: Wiley.

Johar, Gita V., Durairaj Maheswaran, and Laura A. Peracchio. 2006. "*MAP*ping the Frontiers: Theoretical Advances in Consumer Research on *M*emory, *A*ffect, and *P*ersuasion." *Journal of Consumer Research* 33 (June): 139–149.

Lowry, Tom. 2008. "The Game's the Thing at MTV Networks." *BusinessWeek,* February 18, 51–52.

Maheswaran, Durairaj, and Brian Sternthal. 1990. "The Effects of Knowledge, Motivation, and Type of Message on Ad Processing and Product Judgments." *Journal of Consumer Research* 17 (June): 66–73.

Moon, Jang H., Yongjun Sung, and Sejung M. Choi. 2008. "Understanding Shopping Experience in Virtual Environments: The Role of Salesperson and Peer Consumer Avatars." Poster session presented at the Advertising and Consumer Psychology Conference on Virtual Social Identity and Consumer Behavior, May 1–2, Philadelphia.

Mullman, Jeremy. 2009. "Yes, the Super Bowl Is Well Worth $3M a Spot." *Advertising Age,* January 26, 1.

Nicholson, Carolyn Y., Larry D. Compeau, and Rajesh Sethi. 2001. "The Role of Interpersonal Liking in Building Trust in Long-Term Channel Relationships." *Journal of the Academy of Marketing Science* 29 (Winter): 3–15.

Peracchio, Laura A., and David Luna. 2006. "The Role of Thin-Slice Judgments in Consumer Psychology." *Journal of Consumer Psychology* 16 (1): 25–32.

Peracchio, Laura A., and Alice M. Tybout. 1996. "The Moderating Role of Prior Knowledge in Schema-based Product Evaluation." *Journal of Consumer Research* 23 (December): 177–192.

Pham, Michael T., Joel B. Cohen, John W. Pracejus, and G. David Hughes. 2001. "Affect Monitoring and the Primacy of Feelings in Judgment." *Journal of Consumer Research* 28 (September): 167–188.

Raghubir, Priya, and Aradhna Krishna. 1996. "As the Crow Flies: Bias in Consumers' Map-based Distance Judgments." *Journal of Consumer Research* 23 (June): 26–39.

Raghubir, Priya, and Joydeep Srivastava. 2002. "Effect of Face Value on Product Valuation in Foreign Currencies." *Journal of Consumer Research* 29 (December): 335–347.

Second Life. 2007. Available at http://secondlife.com/whatis/ (accessed November 19, 2007).

Sujan, Mita. 1985. "Consumer Knowledge: Effects on Evaluation Strategies Mediating Consumer Judgments." *Journal of Consumer Research* 12 (June): 31–46.

Yorkston, Eric, and Geeta Menon. 2004. "A Sound Idea: Phonetic Effects of Brand Names on Consumer Judgments." *Journal of Consumer Research* 31 (June): 43–51.

Zinkhan, George M., Hyokjin Kwak, Michelle Morrison, and Cara O. Peters. 2003. "Web-based Chatting: Consumer Communication in Cyberspace." *Journal of Consumer Psychology* 13 (1–2): 17–27.

Name Index

Subject Index

About the Editors and Contributors

Anna Akerman is an assistant professor of communications at Adelphi University. She received her PhD in social psychology from New York University, where she concentrated in developmental psychology and is presently a visiting scholar. Dr. Akerman is also a freelance research consultant with Nickelodeon's Kids & Family Group. Her research interests include investigating the role of media in children's development.

Osei Appiah (PhD, Stanford University) is an associate professor in the School of Communication at Ohio State University. His research interests are in advertising effects on ethnic minorities, and the impact of ethnic identity on audiences' responses to media. His research has been published in leading journals such as the *Journal of Advertising Research, Journal of Current Issues & Research in Advertising, Journal of Communication, Journal of Broadcasting & Electronic Media, Media Psychology, Communication Research,* and *Human Communication Research*. His professional experience includes working in marketing and advertising at such companies as Apple Computer, Nike, and Ogilvy & Mather.

Nicolas Arsenault holds a master's of science from HEC Montréal. He teaches electronic marketing at the University of Quebec at Montreal.

Gary Bamossy is professor of marketing at the McDonough School of Business, Georgetown University, Washington, D.C. His research focuses on materialism, the global diffusion of consumer culture, and sustainable consumption.

Peter H. Bloch is professor of marketing and Pinkney C. Walker Teaching Excellence Fellow at the Trulaske College of Business at the University of Missouri. He studied at the University of Texas at Austin and has published over thirty articles dealing with various aspects of consumer behavior. His current research interests include product design effects on consumers, the origins of product-related hobbies, and the modern culture of celebrity. Bloch teaches consumer behavior at the undergraduate and graduate levels and is a leader in the use of classroom technology.

James E. Brown is a graduate of Virginia Commonwealth University and president of Emulsion Marketing in Richmond, Virginia. His research interests include international business, foreign language barriers, virtual worlds, and the impact of the Internet on business practices. When not working, he enjoys collecting wine, reading modern American literature, and traveling overseas.

J. Alison Bryant is senior research director for the Nickelodeon/MTV Networks Kids & Family Group. She leads Nickelodeon's efforts to understand the digital lives of kids and families. Her PhD is from the Annenberg School of Communication at the University of Southern California, and before joining Nickelodeon she was an assistant professor of telecommunications at Indiana University. She has published and presented extensively on media, kids and families, including two edited books: *The Children's Television Community* and *Television and the American Family* (2nd ed.), and she is associate editor for the *Journal of Children & Media*.

Melissa G. Bublitz is a doctoral student at the University of Wisconsin–Milwaukee. She received her BS in marketing and her MBA from the University of Wisconsin–Oshkosh. Her research interests are focused on consumer judgment and buyer behavior in the areas of food and nutrition, health decision making, philanthropy, public policy, marketing to children, and online consumer behavior. She is a member of the Society for Consumer Psychology and the Association for Consumer Research.

Soyoen Cho is a doctoral candidate in the School of Journalism and Mass Communication at the University of Minnesota–Twin Cities. Her research focuses on strategic communication in the online environment, including viral marketing and electronic word-of-mouth.

Craig C. Claybaugh is a doctoral student at the University of Wisconsin–Milwaukee. He received his BS in sociology from the University of Wisconsin–Madison and his MBA and MSIS from the University of Wisconsin–Oshkosh. His research interests include information technology vendor client relationships, Internet abuse, avatar marketing, and social networking. Claybaugh is a member of the Association for Information Systems.

David Crete is currently a PhD candidate at HEC Montréal. He is also member of the RBC Financial Group Chair of e-Commerce. Prior to joining the PhD program, Crete worked for twelve years in the media industry. He now works as a marketing director for a major television network. His research interests focus on online advertising, retailing, and consumer behavior.

Antonella de Angeli is an associate professor at Manchester Business School. With a PhD in experimental psychology, her research explores what humans need from technology, how they exploit it and are affected by it. Before joining the Manchester faculty, Dr. de Angeli was senior HCI researcher at NCR. She also researched at the University of Trieste, Italy; University of Amsterdam; Oregon Graduate Institute, Portland; Loria in Nancy France; and IRST, Trento, Italy. Her work has been published in a range of journals, including *Interacting with Computers, International Journal of Human-Computer Studies*, and *Social Science Computer Review.*

Brittany R.L. Duff is a doctoral candidate at the University of Minnesota. Her research interests include affective responses to advertising, negative effects of advertising avoidance, use of new technologies, and how neuropsychology can inform message effectiveness. She is also part of an ongoing grant project examining the neuroanatomical basis of drug message processing in adolescents.

Troy Elias is a doctoral candidate in the School of Communication at the Ohio State University. His concentration is in strategic communication, with an emphasis in race/ethnicity, communication technology, and Internet advertising. His research explores the impact of social identity, psychological distinctiveness, and word-of-mouth advertising on consumer attitudes in online commercial environments. He has taught courses in communication technology, visual communication, persuasion, and news reporting and writing. He earned his master of arts in communication at Ohio State, and in 2008, was awarded the Lionel Barrow Minority Doctoral Scholarship from the AEJMC's Communication Theory and Methodology Division.

Leila El Kamel is a PhD candidate and an auxiliary teacher at the marketing department of the Faculty of Business Administration at Université Laval. Her main research interests are marketing and postmodernism; self-concept and social interactions in virtual worlds; and online research methods. She also has a great deal of experience in advertising and marketing consultancy. Very active in the academic community, she organized several seminars and has held many positions in the executive level of student associations of the Université Laval in Quebec. She has also contributed to improving the doctoral program at the Faculty of Business Administration.

Ronald J. Faber is professor of advertising and mass communications in the School of Journalism and Mass Communication at the University of Minnesota.

He is a Fellow of the American Academy of Advertising, former editor of the *Journal of Advertising*, and serves on the editorial and policy boards of several leading journals. His current research interests focus on compulsive and impulsive behaviors, advertising using new media formats and techniques (e.g., advergames, blogs, advitars, and morphing), advertising and neuroscience; and advertising effectiveness. He co-edited the book *Advertising, Promotion and the New Media*. His research has appeared in numerous journals, including the *Journal of Advertising*, *Journal of Advertising Research*, *Journal of Consumer Research*, *Journal of Marketing*, and *Communication Research*, and has been cited in articles in the *New York Times*, *Washington Post*, *Wall Street Journal*, *Forbes*, and *Psychology Today*.

Christian Hinsch is a PhD student at the Robert J. Trulaske Sr. College of Business at the University of Missouri. He received his MBA and undergraduate degrees in business administration and management information systems from the University of Missouri–St. Louis. His research interests revolve around advertising effectiveness and consumer information processing as well as the consumption of products and services that facilitate social interaction. Prior to his academic career he spent ten years in the printing industry in marketing and marketing management.

Jisu Huh (PhD, University of Georgia) is assistant professor at the School of Journalism and Mass Communication, University of Minnesota. Her research centers on advertising effects and consumer behavior. Her work has been published in the *Journal of Advertising*, *Journal of Current Issues & Research in Advertising*, *Journal of Consumer Affairs*, *International Journal of Advertising*, *Communication Research*, and the *Journal of Health Communication*. She is a member of the American Academy of Advertising, the Association for Education in Journalism and Mass Communication, and the International Communication Association.

Richard Kedzior is a doctoral student at Hanken-Swedish School of Economics and Business Administration in Helsinki, Finland. His netnographic thesis project takes him daily into *Second Life* where, embodied in an avatar, he tries to find answers to questions pertaining to the nature of virtual consumption and digital materiality.

Debbie Keeling is a research associate within the Marketing Group at Manchester Business School, the University of Manchester. Her expertise is based in applied psychology and she has worked on a range of British and European projects with interests that span service innovation, social support and networks, virtual communities, motivation, technology acceptance, learning, and innovation. She is particularly interested in enhancing consumer experiences and service engagement through technology. She is a founding member of the Centre for Service Research and the Consumer, Retail and Services Group within MBS.

Kathy Keeling is an associate professor of marketing research and statistics at Manchester Business School in the United Kingdom. As deputy director of the Manchester Retail Research Forum, she has worked closely and gained research support from major airlines, retail, banking, media, and computer software organizations. With a background in applied psychology, her cross-disciplinary interests are reflected in work at the intersection of consumer behavior and technology, and in publications across the fields of retailing, marketing, e-commerce, human-computer interaction, and universal access to IT.

Youjeong Kim is a doctoral student in the College of Communications at the Pennsylvania State University. Her research investigates the effects of new media technology, including video games and virtual reality in health and marketing communications, with particular emphasis on the role of avatars in audiences' and consumers' psychological and behavioral responses. Prior to entering the doctoral program, Kim worked for Korea Broadcasting System for two years as a TV producer. She received her MA from the A.Q. Miller School of Journalism and Mass Communications at Kansas State University. Her teaching experience and interests center around communication technologies, video production, and research methods.

Robert V. Kozinets is a global authority on online communities and Internet ethnography. He has extensive consulting and speaking experience with corporations around the world, including American Express, Campbell's Soup, Merck, and eBay. His research interests include online communities, word-of-mouth marketing, branding, technology and media, retailing, subcultures, and communities. He has written and published over fifty articles and chapters. He has published several books, including *Consumer Tribes*, co-authored with Avi Shankar and Bernard Cova (2007). He is based at York University's Schulich School of Business in Toronto, Canada.

Yuliya Lutchyn is a doctoral candidate in the School of Journalism and Mass Communication at the University of Minnesota. Lutchyn's research interests focus on implicit information processing, habitual consumer behaviors, and temporal effects on decision making, especially in the domains of advertising and health communication. Before entering academics, Lutchyn worked as a public relations specialist in the Ukraine.

Peter McGoldrick is the Tesco Professor of Retailing at Manchester Business School within the University of Manchester. He is chair of the Consumer, Retail and Services Group at MBS and director of the Retail Research Forum. Professor

McGoldrick has published over 150 books and papers, mainly within the fields of retailing and consumer behavior. His textbook, *Retail Marketing*, is in its second edition and is also available in Chinese. He has co-authored books on international retailing, the retailing of financial services, and shopping centers. He serves on editorial review boards for the *Journal of Business Research, Journal of Marketing Management, Journal of Marketing Communications*, and *European Retail Research*, and is a member of the AMS board of governors.

Aurelie Merle is professor of marketing at Grenoble Ecole de Management, France. She is also associate researcher at the Research Center in Management (CERGAM), Paul Cezanne Aix Marseille University. Her research focuses mainly on mass customization and personalization from the consumer viewpoint. She is currently working on several research projects and has written book chapters and articles in academic journals on these topics.

Jacques Nantel has been acting as secretary general at HEC Montréal since April 2007. He has served for more than twenty-five years as professor of marketing at the same institution. Prior to his nomination he was the founder and the director of the RBC Financial Group Chair of e-Commerce. Dr. Nantel is author or co-author of four marketing textbooks. He has also published several articles in journals such as the *Journal of Retailing, Journal of Interactive Marketing, International Journal of e-Commerce, Journal of Business Research, European Journal of Marketing, Journal of Social Behavior and Personality*, and *Journal of Business Ethics*. Professor Nantel's work focuses on the impact of new technologies on the behavior of consumers and on the marketing strategies of organizations.

Laura A. Peracchio is professor of marketing at the University of Wisconsin–Milwaukee. She received her PhD from Northwestern University and a dual BA and BSE from the Wharton School and the College of Arts and Sciences at the University of Pennsylvania. Professor Peracchio's areas of research interest are focused on consumer information processing, including visual persuasion, language and culture, and food and nutrition issues. Her work has appeared in the *Journal of Consumer Research, Journal of Marketing Research, Journal of Consumer Psychology, Journal of Public Policy and Marketing*, and *Journal of Advertising*. She is an associate editor of the *Journal of Consumer Psychology* and past president of the Society for Consumer Psychology.

Michael R. Solomon is professor of marketing and director of the Center for Consumer Research in the Haub School of Business at Saint Joseph's University in Philadelphia. He has been recognized as one of the ten most productive scholars in the field of advertising and marketing communications. He is the author of several leading business textbooks, including the widely used *Consumer Behavior: Buying, Having and Being*, 8th edition.

Anik St-Onge is an assistant professor of marketing at University of Quebec at Montreal and a PhD candidate at HEC Montréal. She is also an associate researcher at the RBC Financial Group Chair of e-Commerce at HEC Montréal. Her research focuses mainly on electronic word-of-mouth and personalization from the consumer viewpoint.

S. Shyam Sundar is professor and founding director of the Media Effects Research Laboratory at Penn State University's College of Communications. His research investigates social and psychological effects of technological elements unique to Web-based mass communication. Sundar was among the first to publish refereed research on the effects of new media in leading communication journals, and has been identified as the most published author of Internet-related research in the field during the medium's first decade. A frequently cited source on technology, Sundar has testified before the U.S. Congress as an expert witness and delivered talks at universities in several countries. He serves on the editorial boards of *Communication Research, Human Communication Research, Journal of Communication, Media Psychology, Journalism & Mass Communication Quarterly, Journal of Broadcasting & Electronic Media*, and *Communication Methods & Measures*, among others. He is chair of the Communication and Technology division of the International Communication Association.

Tracy L. Tuten is the author of *Advertising 2.0: Social Media Marketing in a Web 2.0 World*. Frequently quoted in the press, including in *New York Times, Brandweek, International Herald Tribune*, and the *Washington Post*, she is a leading contributor to industry views on how marketers can leverage the Internet to meet corporate objectives. She serves often in the roles of speaker, trainer, and consultant to organizations including Royall & Company, Samsung Electronics, the NFL Coaches Association, and the Interactive Marketing Institute, among others. An award-winning teacher and scholar, she is an associate professor of marketing with East Carolina University. Her next book series, now in progress, is entitled *Enterprise 2.0: How E-Commerce, Technology, and Web 2.0 Are Changing Business Virtually*.

Jeff Wang (PhD, University of Arizona) is an assistant professor in the marketing department, City University of Hong Kong. His main research area is consumer behavior with a specific interest in consumer culture theory. He is currently studying some fascinating consumption phenomena in China such as online gaming, team purchase, feng shui, and Chinese medicine. By using qualitative methods, he aims to understand the sociocultural aspects of these phenomena and their deep meanings to consumers.

Natalie T. Wood is assistant professor of marketing, and assistant director of the Center for Consumer Research in the Haub School of Business at Saint Joseph's

University in Philadelphia. Her research on avatars and virtual worlds has been published in journals such as *Marketing Education Review, International Journal of Internet Marketing and Advertising, Journal of Website Promotion,* and *Journal of Advertising Education.* She is also an advisory editor for the *Journal of Virtual Worlds Research.*

Xin Zhao is assistant professor of marketing at the Shidler College of Business, University of Hawaii at Manoa. He received his PhD in marketing from the David Eccles School of Business at the University of Utah. Professor Zhao is interested in sociocultural aspects of advertising, consumer culture theory, globalization, and virtual consumption in China.